REFUGEES AND MIGRA
THE MIDDLE EAST

Edited by Dawn Chatty, Stacy D. Fahrenthold, and Annika Rabo

This series explores new research on refugees and migrants within the Middle East and North Africa to present some of the most innovative work on displacement and mobility coming out of Middle Eastern studies. It engages with the legacies of migration on the region and aims to reclaim refugees' agency through examinations of, among other topics, livelihoods, advocacy, cultural production, social movements, resilience, and resistance.

SYRIA, REVOLT AND WAR IN THE DIGITAL AGE

**EDITED BY CÉCILE BOËX
AND AGNÈS DEVICTOR**

**TRANSLATED BY
JANE KUNTZ**

The American University in Cairo Press

Cairo   New York

First published in 2025 by
The American University in Cairo Press
113 Sharia Kasr el Aini, Cairo, Egypt
420 Lexington Avenue, Suite 1644, New York, NY 10170
www.aucpress.com

This book will be made open access within three years of publication thanks to
Path to Open, a program developed in partnership between JSTOR, the American
Council of Learned Societies (ACLS), University of Michigan Press, and The
University of North Carolina Press to bring about equitable access and impact
for the entire scholarly community, including authors, researchers, libraries,
and university presses around the world. Learn more at https://about.jstor.org/
path-to-open/

ISBN 978 1 649 03423 6

Library of Congress Cataloging-in-Publication Data

Names: Boëx, Cécile, editor. | Devictor, Agnès, editor. | Kuntz, Jane, translator.
Title: Syria, revolt and war in the digital age / edited by Cécile Boëx and Agnès
    Devictor ; translated by Jane Kuntz.
Other titles: Syrie, une nouvelle ère des images. English.
Identifiers: LCCN 2024049028 | ISBN 9781649034236 (hardback) | ISBN
    9781649034243 (epub) | ISBN 9781649034250 (adobe pdf)
Subjects: LCSH: Information warfare--Syria. | Syria--History--Civil War, 2011---
    Mass media and the war.
Classification: LCC DS98.6 .S974513 2025 | DDC 956.9104/23--dc23/
    eng/20241213

1 2 3 4 5   29 28 27 26 25

Designed by Trinity Designs

CONTENTS

PREFACE

Since this book was first published in French in 2021, the conflict evolved and ended on 8 December 2025 with the flight of Bashar al-Assad to Russia, following the armed offensive led by Hay'at Tahrir al-Sham (HTS) on 27 November 2024. Between 2021 and 2024, the northwestern province of Idlib, controlled by the opposition, was being bombed by Syrian–Russian air strikes targeting civilian infrastructure. The Turkish army, which deployed troops in northern Syria, regularly carried out strikes against Kurdish-controlled areas in the northeast. Israeli strikes, most numerous since the war on Gaza, targeted Hezbollah, Iranian-led militia leaders, and ammunition depots in Damascus, Homs, Aleppo, and Qunaytra. On a daily basis, Syrians suffered from a disastrous economic situation. According to the United Nations, in 2023, over 90% of the population was living below the poverty line. The devastating earthquake that hit Turkey and northern and western Syria on 6 February 2023 has worsened an already dire situation.

Syrian security forces and militias associated with the regime continued to arbitrarily detain, disappear, and torture people across the country. The authorities also continued to illegally confiscate property and restrict access to their regions of origin for Syrians who had returned home. At the end of August 2023, spurred initially by deteriorating economic conditions, anti-government protests spread to the Druze-majority province of Suwayda, and to a lesser extent to the neighboring province of Daraa, formerly controlled by the opposition. These were the largest protests to be held in government-controlled Syria since 2011. This period was also marked by a double logic of normalization of Syria's relations on the Arab scene, with its reintegration into the Arab League in May 2023 and the first trials in Europe against members of the Syrian regime for crimes against humanity and war crimes, as in Koblenz (2021) and Paris (2024). Many others are to come. In these trials, images—and in particular the Caesar files, which contain 45,000 leaked photos of the dead bodies of detainees held in various branches of the Damascus governorate—as well as the testimony of survivors play an essential role. Syria is now once again accessible for judicial inquiries, and we can also hope that members of the al-Assad clan and the senior officials will soon be brought to trial in Damascus.

During the offensive conducted by HTS at the end of 2024, many videos filmed by fighters circulated. The most stunning were those of the release of prisoners in Aleppo, Hama, Homs, and Saidnaya. Men, women, and children, looking haggard, not really understanding what was happening, not knowing where to go, were coming out of the inferno. On the night of 7 to 8 December, in the well-off neighborhood of Malki in Damascus, someone filmed the flight of guards from the aviation directorate. A little later, still in the capital, a woman filmed the street from the window of her flat. A man can be heard shouting: "God is great! He has fallen! Freedom is for everyone!" The woman can be heard sobbing as other voices join the man in singing and applauding. In 2011, a video showing a similar scene on Avenue Bourguiba in Tunis after Ben Ali fled was widely circulated. The fall of the regime came quickly and unexpectedly. Millions of Syrians were overjoyed—a sentiment which was expressed in Syria and in the major cities of the places of exile. But this joy was tinged with pain and rage. While the prisons have been emptied, the fate of over 110,000 missing persons is still unknown. Syria is a devastated country. The political, economic, and justice stakes are immense.

However, what's striking is the speed with which a variety of citizens' initiatives are emerging and getting organized in Syria and abroad. This shows the extent to which the culture and memory of the revolution has remained alive, despite the years, and how it is being reactivated and reconfigured today. The images discussed in this book record part of the history and memory of this revolution. Since 2021, a number of YouTube links have disappeared, which we have reported. Documenting this loss shows just how fragile are the images we worked on, taken in the midst of a conflict by those directly involved. Over the years, this book has also become an archive of these evanescent images. Furthermore, as real-time video documentation by ordinary people, activists, or fighters becomes a crucial issue in contemporary conflicts, as seen in Ukraine and Palestine, the multiple uses of the camera and the varied trajectories of the images studied here provide a few reference points in this visual profusion.

CONTRIBUTORS

Emma Aubin-Boltanski is an anthropologist and research director at the CNRS. Her research areas include the anthropology of religious mechanisms (worship of the Blessed Virgin, devotion to saints in Lebanon, Syria, and Palestine), as well as the intersection of religion and politics. Her most recent work explores the issue of women and counter-behavior in the Middle East, as well as fractured masculinities. She is the author of *Le corps de la Passion. Expériences religieuses et politiques d'une mystique au Liban*, published in 2018 by EHESS Éditions. In addition to this, she wrote and directed the film *Catherine ou le Corps de la Passion* (Joun Films/CNRS Images, 2012).

Cécile Boëx is a senior lecturer, *maître de conférences*, at the *École des Hautes Études en Sciences sociales* (EHESS) in France. Her research deals with the linkage of images and politics in the Middle East, particularly in Syria. Since the 2011 revolt, she has been studying the practices and uses of video by ordinary protestors, activists, and armed groups. At the intersection of political science and audiovisual anthropology, she has explored the different grammars of these videos as the conflict evolved, notably the emergence of novel forms of protest, commemoration, and practices of image-making in warfare within a context of extreme violence.

Erminia Chiara Calabrese is an associate researcher at the *Centre d'études en sciences sociales du religieux* (CéSor) at the *École des hautes études en sciences sociales* (EHESS). She researches the sociology of war, armed partisan engagement, and various shades of political Shiism. She is the author notably of *Militer au Hezbollah. Ethnographie d'un engagement dans la banlieue sud de Beyrouth* (Ifpo/Karthala, 2016). She co-directed with Robin Beaumont the issue "Chiismes politiques. Pouvoirs, engagements, imaginaires politiques chiites au XXIe siècle" (*REMMM*, 2019) and, with Marie-Noëlle Abi-Yaghi, "Liban–Syrie. Circulations et réactivations de réseaux militants en guerre (2011–2018)" (*Revue Internationale de Politique Comparée*, 2018).

Agnès Devictor is a senior lecturer, *maître de conférences* HDR, at the University of Paris 1 Panthéon-Sorbonne and member of the working group Cultural and Social History of Art. Her main research interest involves Iranian cinema and war films shot during wars in Iran and Afghanistan, and how these are being archived. She co-authored, along with J.-M. Frodon, *Abbas Kiarostami, l'œuvre ouverte* (Gallimard, 2020), and with G. Chahverdi Kharmohra, *l'Afghanistan au risque de l'art* (MUCEM-Actes Sud, 2019). She is also author of *L'Iran mis en scène* (Espace&Signe, 2017); *Images,* *combattants et martyrs. La guerre Iran-Irak vue par le cinéma iranien* (Karthala, IISMM, IFRI, 2015); *Politique du cinéma iranien, de l'âyatollâh Khomeyni au président Khâtami* (CNRS Éditions, 2004).

F. was studying at the University of Damascus. At the start of the revolution, he left Damascus for his hometown Homs. He was part of a coordinating committee and filmed demonstrations in his neighborhood. He also got involved with the Red Crescent [Muslim Red Cross], helping to relieve displaced families or civilians caught in besieged zones or in bombing campaigns. Arrested in 2012, he was forced to leave Syria in 2015, initially making it to Turkey, and eventually to France in 2016. Today, he is employed by an organization that cares for people with disabilities.

Giulia Galluccio holds a degree in Eastern Languages and Civilizations (*Università di Roma La Sapienza*). She earned an international master's degree in Euro-Mediterranean Relations (*Universitat Rovira i Virgili*/Paris 8), and now works at the CNRS-IISMM as head of European projects. Recently, she has been analyzing the audiovisual productions of jihadist-Salafist groups emerging from the Syrian conflict, particularly those of the Nusra Front and the Islamic State. She has taught classes and led workshops and seminars for different audiences and at a variety of institutions on the propaganda of these two jihadist-Salafist groups fighting in Syria, and the evolution of their communication strategies.

H. was one of the founders of the coordinating committee of Kafr Sousa in Damascus, where he was active from March 2011 to August 2012 whilst also supervising their media bureau. Prior to the revolution, he was studying business and economics at the University of Damascus. Arrested and conscripted into the army, he deserted and had to flee Syria. Since 2013 he has been living in Sweden where, after working a number of odd jobs, he is currently pursuing a degree in prosthetics and orthotics.

Lucile Irigoyen holds an associate technical degree (BTS) specializing in audiovisual editing and post-production, and is preparing a doctorate at the *École des hautes études en sciences sociales* (EHESS). Her second master's thesis studied the creation of the Rojava Film Commune [Komîna Fîlm a Rojava]—a model film production institution underway since 2015—in Rojava, which she was able to observe doing fieldwork in Kobanê, Sêrêkaniyê, Amûde, Derbesiyê, and Qamishli. Her dissertation project proposes to comprehend the transformations undergone by Kurdish society in northern Syria since 2011 through the prism of this region's film production.

Shahriar Khonsari holds a doctorate from the Center for Research in the Arts, Tehran. His dissertation, "Analysis of the Critical Discourse of Non-Professional Photographs from the Iran-Iraq War," was defended in 2020. For several years, Shahriar Khonsari has been teaching photography and art history at different Iranian universities. A photographer, he has taken part in a dozen exhibitions in Iran and abroad. His photographs, with social overtones, have been widely published in both Iranian and foreign media. He also does social work with several NGOs with links to the United Nations High Commission for Refugees (UNHCR).

Cédric Labrousse is a certified teacher of history and geography. He is working toward a doctorate at the *École des hautes études en sciences sociales* (EHESS) on relations, especially conflictual ones, between the various actors in the Syrian region of Al-Jazira between 2004 and 2017. He has been interested in the Arab world since 2008 and more so in 2010 with the outbreak of the Arab Spring in various countries. He has been publishing regularly over the years in a *Chronique des printemps arabes* on several social media, with a consistent focus on Syria. He is narrowing down his research and analysis work, creating the Syrian Rebellion Observatory, devoted to the study, investigation, and archiving of the history of the Syrian insurrection in all its dimensions.

Anna Poujeau is an anthropologist and researcher at the CNRS. She has been studying the Christians of Syria since the early 2000s. After working on monasticism, sainthood, and how Syrian Christians relate to the regime in power, she examined the oral funerary poetry of Christians in southern Syria, and the interfaith relations in that region. Her most recent work focuses on religious, social, and political recompositions based on the study of collective abductions of members of religious minorities during the conflict.

Chamsy Sarkis, a biologist by training, defended a doctoral dissertation in 2001 on human genetics at the University of Paris 6. Specialized in biotechnologies, he then began working at the CNRS. He is currently president of the Pax Syriana Foundation as well as the *Association franco-syrienne de soutien aux médias libres* (ASML) [Franco-Syrian Association for the Support of Free Media], created in late 2011 to foster the work of media activists in Syria. He is also co-founder of SMART, the Syrian Media Action Revolution Team.

ACKNOWLEDGMENTS

This work is collective in several respects. We are deeply grateful to the authors who so graciously undertook the analysis of videos from within their fields of research, even when it meant deploying new tools, and who were always open to fresh directions we would suggest. We also heartily thank F. and H. for their warm welcome and for the time they spent with us to share bits of their experience: You are part of the memory of the revolution, and you keep it alive from where you are today.

Much of the thinking we developed here first emerged during our seminars at the EHESS and at the Université Paris 1 Panthéon-Sorbonne, where students helped us hone our processes with their many questions and remarks, providing a constant source of stimulation and raising the bar of excellence—much gratitude to you, in the hope that this work will contribute to furthering and deepening our discussions. Thanks also to colleagues and friends who, through their own work or our interactions, accompanied the writing: Dounia al-Dahan, Nisrine al-Zahre, Ali Atassi, Emma Aubin Boltanski, Stéphane Audouin Rouzeau, Nibras Cheyahed, Véronique Ginouvès, Sylvie Lindeperg, Franck Mermier, Elizabeth Picard, Rania Stefan, Stefan Tarowski, and Sana Yazigi. Grateful thoughts go out as well to the "SHAKKers"; here's to our projects underway and those to come: Thierry Boissière, Alain Carou, Myriam Catusse, Rana Diab, Vanessa Guéno, Boris James, Jean-Christophe Peyssard, Thomas Pierret, and Paolo Pinto. We would like to specially thank our patient proofreaders Jean-Michel Frodon and Joséphine Morano.

We also extend thanks to the CNRS team at the Center for Research on the Iranian World, especially to Pollet Samvelian and Maria Szuppe. We should mention here that this work enjoyed support from the *Agence Nationale pour la Recherche* SHAKK program—From Revolt to War in Syria: Conflicts, Displacement, Uncertainty—which associates the *Centre d'Études en sciences sociales du religieux* (CéSor; CNRS/EHESS), the *Institut français du Proche Orient* in Beirut (Ifpo; CNRS/MAE), the audiovisual department of the French *Bibliothèque nationale* (BnF), and the *Institut de recherches et d'études sur les mondes arabes et musulmans* (IREMAM; CNRS/Aix Marseille University). We are grateful to Anne Routon and the American University of Cairo Press team who believed in this book. Also, a warm thanks to Jane Kutz and Elete Nelson-Fearon for their translation and proofreading.

INTRODUCTION
Cécile Boëx and Agnès Devictor

Since the start of the revolt in Syria on 15 March 2011, demonstrators, activists, and militant fighters have posted several million videos online. Their prime objective has been to work around the media blackout imposed by Bashar al-Assad's regime, and its questioning of the scope of the activism and repression on the ground, by filming the demonstrations, the repression, and the funerals. The use of video quickly diversified to include protest action, testimonies, military defections, creations of combat brigades, tributes to martyrs, and live combat. These videos document not only the events, but also the modes of showing, telling, and experiencing engagement and extreme violence. By 2012, the revolt was gradually turning into armed conflict, with the repression militarizing as other actors were coming onto the scene, be they jihadist groups, various Kurdish factions, or militias affiliated with Iraq or Iran. Based on their interpretation of the conflict and the role they assume in it, these groups have also set about massively producing images, whether centralized or individual, professional or amateur. Processing this vast amount of audiovisual material in chronological order has allowed us to grasp the revolt's many forms of expression and its pivot into war. This diachronic but also dialogical perspective sheds light on the political agendas and spheres of influence at the State or militant group level that exceed and splinter Syria's national framework. Whether shared online or saved to flash drives or SIM cards, posted from Syria or a place of exile, videos shot by the various protagonists of the revolt and subsequent war have helped us map out a vast territory of images and sounds. Their borders, trajectories, and formats have been in constant flux, producing an array of competing projections and imaginaries. The point is not to analyze them all as a single phenomenon, but rather to observe how and why people take up video.

This territory of images and sounds is a major vantage point for observing deep shifts in the production, use, and dissemination of images of revolt and war in the digital age. It is also a precious resource for better understanding this conflict—which ended on 8 December 2025 with the flight of Bashar al-Assad to Russia following the armed offensive led by Hay'at Tahrir al-Sham (HTS) on 27 November 2024. This introduction will provide a historical, theoretical, and methodological context to help gauge the magnitude of the issues as they relate to how images, politics, and the violence of war have intermeshed in Syria since 2011. This interdisciplinary approach explores videos in all their sensitive, material, formal, contextual, and political layers. The first part of this introduction, "A New Territory of Image and Sound," focuses first on the importance of video and what it meant during the revolt from the standpoint of contemporary Syrian history. Next, we narrow our field of research by referencing works on images and conflict, in Syria and elsewhere. We also point to the methodological difficulties inherent in the vast audiovisual and digital territory that we cover—a dispersed and particularly unstable space—while simultaneously highlighting the broad heuristic range and research paths that it enables. The second part, "Images in Conflicts: Flashbacks," revisits the mobilization of images historically as political, religious, and war-directed resources. Though hardly exhaustive, it recalls historical sequences—associated with certain technological advances—that tipped the production and spread of images accompanying revolts and significant conflicts. In the final part of the introduction, we present the two-part structure of this book.

A New Territory of Image and Sound
Why Image?
Since 2011, events in Syria have followed fast upon each other in consecutive or partially overlapping phases of protest, militarization, and conflict. These phases are deployed both locally, in an increasingly fragmented territory, and globally via the different regional and international actors involved in the repression, the regime's endurance, the armed rebellion, and the reactivation of jihad* (notions and names marked with an asterisk are explained in the glossary) in Syria and beyond. In 2000, the rise to power of Bashar al-Assad after his father's death and the release of hundreds of political prisoners had given cause for hope, albeit briefly. During the fleeting "Damascus Spring," there were calls, predominantly by intellectuals, for democratization in Syria—notably for multiparty politics, free and fair elections, and an end to the state of emergency in force since 1963. These calls were, however, quickly dismissed.[1] The decade that followed was marked by a return to authoritarianism alongside neo-liberal economic policies.[2] By the seventies and eighties, Hafez al-Assad had consolidated his clan's power through the partisan apparatus, the army, and a multi-branch security system by promoting high-ranking officers that were from the Alawite community. Relations with society were based entirely on allegiance—particularly within the public sector and the economic bourgeoisie linked to the military—or otherwise on submission through violence.[3] Once in power, Bashar al-Assad "updated" his predecessor's authoritarianism by reallocating certain activities previously assumed by the state to private actors loyal to the regime.[4] This change, to the external observer, could appear as modernization. In the late 2000s, the consumer patterns of the business class and wealthy urbanites close to the regime were entirely at odds with the general population that was subjected to rampant corruption.

From 2011, the regime's initial response to the revolt involved a combination of repressing the demonstrators whilst also offering traditional attempts at appeasement and cooptation, which included salary raises for civil servants, privileges granted to religious and tribal notables, and promises of new reforms.[5] Within a few months repression had intensified, recalling the terror strategy adopted in 1982 by Hafez al-Assad to suppress the insurrection in Hama:[6] mass arrests, torture, arbitrary executions, destruction of whole neighborhoods, and the forced displacement of populations. The Hama Massacre, which took place in a total news blackout (apart from a handful of photos taken by foreign journalists once the siege was lifted), gave way to a deafening silence.[7] In 2011, repression led to anger and mobilization: funerals turned into demonstrations against the regime. Everywhere in Syria, protestors were recording what was happening, to bear witness to the reality of the revolt but also in the hope of curbing the repressive violence, figuring that images could serve as a rampart against impunity. Many of those involved in this documentation, whether shooting videos or helping to broadcast them, mentioned the trauma of Hama and the need to reckon with this blind spot in the history of Syria. Indeed, the revolt brought back to the surface these suppressed memories, with video tributes to the martyrs posted on social media and included in the film *Hama* (2011)—an anonymous documentary smuggling 23 minutes of a revolution that weaves the memory of the 1982 massacre into the 2011 insurgency in Hama. But this belief in the power of images gradually wavered, especially after the chemical attack against civilians in east Damascus on 21 August 2013, which the Obama administration claimed was its "red line."[8] And yet, atrocities committed against the population have been continuously documented. When we interview the people behind these cameras about their perseverance, their answer is often the same: "We don't want to die for nothing, in silence."[9] The "image" is thus an existential issue in this struggle to the death with the regime.

For us as researchers, images help us to interface with a country which, since 2012, has become hard to access. Still, research on Syria has moved forward. There are those with extensive prior field experience who have pursued their research work from bases in neighboring countries (Turkey and Lebanon, notably) or at a greater distance (Germany, France, and Sweden), all default places of residence for numerous Syrians forced to leave their country. Online communication platforms such as Skype and WhatsApp have enabled outsiders to stay in touch with people "on the inside." Their work sheds light on the political, social, religious, economic, and geostrategic dimensions of the revolt and subsequent conflict.[10] A few rare researchers remained on the ground between 2012 and 2014 in the liberated areas (mainly around Aleppo and Hama) in order to study, for instance, the "micro-politics" of daily life.[11] Others, however, specializing in conflict situations and violence, ventured into these zones for the first time to observe civilian and military forms of revolutionary organization, to witness how armed groups[12] relate to the territory or how they mobilize for combat.[13] Elsewhere, Syrian intellectuals, young researchers, and writers living abroad (recently settled or longstanding residents) have produced a crucial body of knowledge on the multifaceted realities of the revolutionary process, the way it shifts into armed conflict, and the regime's repressive strategies. Analyses,[14] testimonies,[15] chronicles,[16] and essays also give evidence of new writing that is emerging with the revolution, strongly marked by lived experience.[17] Within this knowledge production based on remote ethnographies or on-the-ground observations over a given period, video takes on a particular interest in that it gives access to snippets of events but also to subjectivities, experiences, and imaginaries. The images and sounds communicate something about the events and those who take part in them.

Approaching the Revolt and the War Through the Senses: Video as Site and Object of Inquiry

Ever since Marc Ferro's pioneering work was published in 1977,[18] still photography and motion pictures have deepened our understanding of the major conflicts of the twentieth century. At the same time, they provide material for research and rich epistemological reflection: Hayden White, for example, presented the notion of "historiophoty,"[19] which places visual documents at the heart of the historiographic perspective. Sylvie Lindeperg highlights how conflicts of memory of World War II appear in cinema,[20] looking at how archival war images have been redeployed by cultural industries,[21] and the crucial role they played in trials involving genocide.[22] Christian Delage studies how film is used in historical storytelling, while questioning the role of film recordings in high-profile trials of war criminals and their status as evidence.[23] Laurent Véray tracks the advent of a visual culture of war[24] in the context of World War I, and shows how analysis of images allows for a better understanding of the imaginaries of those on the battlefront and behind the lines, and of the rise of violence during this conflict. Georges Didi-Huberman challenges historians who are confronted with "four bits of film snatched from hell"—footage taken by Jewish prisoners inside the camp—to imagine Auschwitz by reconstructing the conditions in which these pictures were taken in August 1944[25] and how they managed to escape destruction; his is a text that resonates with certain videos from Syria that have come to light. Our mode of operation owes much to these historians' approaches, of which we cite but a few of the major works. It involves the painstaking labor of exhuming videos, most of which are somewhere on the digital space or the cell phones of those who shot them. We also aim to reconstruct, if only partially, the actions and contexts that gave rise to these recordings. In this respect, our approach differs from the work on conflicts developed in the field of Visual Studies, such as that of Nicholas Mirzoeff[26] and William John Thomas Mitchell[27] who are more interested in the perception, concepts, and mechanisms that accompany the circulation of images than in their function of mediating the imaginaries and discourses of those who look at them.

We also approach our material from an anthropological perspective as we deal with the images in all their contextual density, as defined by those who created them, and by their image-making that is always anchored in time, place, and singular forms of engagement. Until now, a significant part of work done on audiovisual production in Syria since 2011 has been focused on testimonials and the emblematic figure of the activist. Developments in media studies in the 2000s[28] were "transplanted" into Syria under the label of "citizen journalism." They highlight the ways the new information actors are mobilizing the latest digital technologies and creating innovative forms of communication, and examine how their videos are disseminated within transnational networks[29] and later reappropriated by traditional media.[30] This approach is focused on how international audiences are reached, and how effective the audiovisual content is at informing, mobilizing, or providing evidence, thus giving rise to work that is more attentive to local practices and contexts of media activism.[31] The topic of audiovisual testimony recorded and made public by those in direct contact with the events is also invoked in analyses of how violent content circulates, how it is perceived, and what forms it assumes.[32] It has also generated discussion on the status of audiovisual material as evidence in a judicial[33] or archival setting.[34] In addition to this, significant research has shed light on the wealth of cinematographic production resulting from the Syrian revolt. [35]

This wealth of literature, of which we will provide but a glimpse, does nevertheless leave certain videos and practices outside its scope. In effect, the focus on activism or cinematographic practice has eroded the number of actors, forms, uses, and modes of circulation of video in Syria. Furthermore, this literature does not address how video works alongside armed struggle and active combat. It would appear that there is no presence of the audiovisual productions by the Free Syrian Army* (FSA) in academic circles, while those of the Islamic State* are analyzed extensively in a broad range of research fields, reflecting the asymmetrical treatment of the two warring factions, both in political terms and with regard to their visibility in the media. Lastly, the audiovisual productions of the revolt's various actors are always framed in isolation,[36] despite the fact that they interact within their self-created system through imitation, reappropriation, or confrontation.

Processing these videos raises a number of methodological and epistemological questions, the first of which is how to deal with such diverse, tenuous formats. Since digital space is the principal matrix for broadcasting these videos, specific challenges arise when it comes to collecting and saving them. Here, traditional notions of typology and bodies of work falter amidst the ever-evolving state of data sampled from a living "archive": on a daily basis, new videos are posted online while others disappear.[37] This instability is further intensified by seemingly arbitrary parameters of visibility and accessibility, ruled by impenetrable algorithms and constant updates. Furthermore, researchers are faced with the issue of huge gaps and missing material in a given document—how do we analyze videos that are often fragmented and anonymous? Such omissions do, however, constitute precious clues as to how these videos are produced. Contextualization becomes central, as both a method and an element of the analysis in its own right. Such examination is carried out in various ways. The first is by allowing the videos to resonate among themselves to form "complexes of images."[38] These complexes (videos of the same event, a YouTube channel, an unusual video practice, a particular fighter group . . .), help us grasp the intentions, timelines, situations, uses, and circulations. This interrelating of images stems from varied sets of collection and inquiry that shape each specific corpus. The audiovisual and digital ethnographies—prerequisites to the analyses in this book—are informed by lengthy field experience in Syria (Boëx, Aubin-Boltanski, Poujeau), in Iran (Devictor, Khonsari), in Lebanon (Calabrese, Galluccio), or shorter stays in Kurdistan (Irigoyen). The move back and forth between virtual spaces and on-the-ground locations precludes any "reification of electronic space,"[39] thereby ensuring continuity with the "real." Only Cédric Labrousse was never physically present in Syria; however, by tirelessly monitoring social media over the past decade or so as a means of analyzing the revolt, he was able to acquire, at a distance, a granular knowledge of Syria, to pick up some Arabic, and to forge bonds with activists and fighters "on the inside." While our analyses do attend to the videos' formal features, they always link back to the intentions of those who made them or who appear in them. The sensitive subject matter embedded in the images and sounds, permeated with emotion, surprise, and inevitable gaps, and the pervasive presence of life-and-death issues, also constitutes a portal to understanding the politics of the revolt and the war.

Images in Conflict: Flashbacks
Filming and Publicizing the Revolt, from the Television Era to the Digital Age

Revolts have always given rise to self-communication practices[40] that bypass the hegemony of traditional media. Until the advent of lightweight cameras, stills and films were taken by photographers, journalists, and professional film-makers, or by militants affiliated with partisan or union organizations.[41] The politically tumultuous 1960s in the United States and in Europe represent a pivotal moment that fuses moving images and protest: cameras documenting the action had become active players in their own right, opening the way for countless experiments in militant film such as Newsreel, founded amid mobilization against the Vietnam War.[42] In Paris, the profusion of audiovisual content during the civil unrest of May 1968 was also a fertile terrain for a considerable number of amateurs who filmed in 16mm, 8mm, and the recently invented Super 8 (1965). They would cover demonstrations, strikes, and speakers who addressed crowds at their workplace.[43] The 1970s gave way to the development of analog video as a militant tool, notably in the United States and Western Europe. During the 1980s in Poland, with secret police cameras monitoring the population's every move, the movement headed by the Solidarność union led to clashes between the cameras of state-run television denouncing "anarchy" and the dissident cameramen who took advantage of first-generation video cameras to shoot spontaneous street action, the underground press at work, or clandestine interviews.[44] During this same period in Chile, the Teleanálisis collective was filming the daily resistance against the Pinochet regime (demonstrations, trade union meetings, and eye-witness reports). Distribution of these images, however, took place underground and haphazardly, and was confined to militant circles. The revolution of December 1989 in Romania against Nicolae Ceauşescu briefly merged televisual space with the unfolding of a revolutionary event in real time. As he delivers an appeasement speech broadcast live before an assembly handpicked for the occasion, demonstrators can be seen in the background. The images flicker briefly, and after a few seconds of a blank screen, one of the cameramen comments on the angry crowd.[45] Television had become the epicenter of broadcasting, but very quickly it was also reframing this revolution and taking back control.[46]

Between 1960 and 1980, then, imagery of revolt was developing against official media. With the advent of the Internet, inexpensive computers, and open-source software came new means of documenting protests. By the 1990s, militant groups were utilizing these networks to trade and circulate information, and create online documentary databases.[47] They were also mobilizing video (mostly from camcorders) to raise their groups' profile, as did the Zapatistas in Chiapas and various anarchist collectives in the United States.[48]

Demonstrations against the World Trade Organization (WTO) in November 1999 in Seattle birthed the world-famous transnational alternative media network Indymedia, whose motto is: "Don't hate the media, become the media."[49] Indymedia consists of local centers that share news and audiovisual resources on their central website. In 2005, Indymedia included some 110 centers in 35 countries.[50] At the G8 summit in Genoa in 2001, images of violent clashes between demonstrators of the Italian anti-globalization movement and security forces were captured and posted to blogs, then immediately rebroadcast by the media. This event marked a "turning point for militant video content on the Internet."[51] Throughout the 1990s and into the early 2000s, the Internet became the favored venue for marginalized militant groups whose goal was to raise the profile of their struggles by circumventing mainstream media. With the ubiquity of cell phones and the launch of video sharing platform YouTube[52] in 2005, the role of video in protest situations continued to grow, expanding beyond the scope of militant organizations.

It was in June 2009 in Iran, during the Green Movement revolt against the reelection of then President Ahmadinejad, that the use of image and the Internet ushered in a new kind of protest. To faithfully report on the ground, as official media kept silent and the foreign press was denied access, the protesters filmed the demonstrations and subsequent violent acts of repression, as well as the methods used to evade and defy state intervention.[53] But disseminating these brief (under three minutes) recordings was complex: while some were uploaded directly to the web—and viewed thanks to VPNs, since YouTube is filtered in Iran—many were relayed abroad. Foreign satellite channels in Persian picked up (illegally) in Iran also got them into circulation. Cell phones, rarely connected to the Internet back then, would record, photograph, and disseminate via SMS news pertaining to how a demonstration was being organized. It was also used to convey the jokes that spread through the movement. With this new tool came a new set of gestures: the raised fist was replaced by a cell phone held up at arm's length. But the phone also proved to be a dauntingly effective informant for localizing opponents. The regime even claimed to possess facial recognition software, implying that videos posted on the Internet helped it locate and arrest demonstrators. In response, protesters painted their faces green or hid behind colorful surgical masks, thereby inventing an "aesthetic" of anonymization. When the state didn't suspend it altogether, the Internet also served as a space where conservatives and reformers would spar. Already very active on the web, these groups took to social networks and other online media to counteract the Green Movement by creating "fake reformist videos" as well as their own propaganda material.[54] Created in 2009 to maintain this "cultural front" (*jebeh farhangi*) on the web, three years later the Ammar Center would become one of the most active media players in the production of documentary films on Iran's intervention in Syria.

Starting in 2010 with the revolt in Tunisia that triggered other revolts in Arab countries, the widespread use of video and the Internet became even more pronounced. It was a powerful mobilizer, starting with Mohamed Bouazizi, the itinerant vendor who set himself on fire in front of the statehouse (*gouvernorat*) on 17 December. His act (which was not filmed) was amplified in the media, based on an amateur video of a demonstration led by his mother that was posted on Facebook and later picked up by Al Jazeera Live, establishing Bouazizi as a symbol of great injustice and the shared sense of humiliation and indignation.[55] Still, the overwhelming majority of videos coming out of Tunisia, then Egypt, Libya, Syria, Yemen, and Bahrain never went viral. Filmed by ordinary protesters or collectives born of the events they were covering, these videos were about reappropriating public space and voice, which had been confiscated for so long.[56] The Internet and social media did not cause the revolts: it's what was happening in the streets that mattered. Still, these uprisings were concurrent with the emergence of new forms of protest in particularly authoritarian political contexts where the Internet has also been a site of confrontation and surveillance.[57] The Syrian case remains paradigmatic in several respects. First and foremost, the issues of documentation and certification are crucial given the media embargo imposed by the regime. Secondly, considering how long these events have been going on, video techniques have grown more professional and diverse, generating an unprecedented mass of images now estimated at several million.

Images of War: More, and More Spectacular

World War I ushered in the mass production of images and a diversification of viewpoints with the advent of amateur photography. By 1914, soldiers in both camps were equipped with cameras rendered accessible by their price, size, and film stock that could be loaded even in daylight.[58] From foot soldiers to officers, they took photos to provide a representation of themselves at the front, capture moments of camaraderie, and relieve boredom. Amateur photography would remain a fixture of warfare. As for the movie camera (as yet without a generic name), relatively rare during World War II, its use became more widespread during the Algerian War. The conscripts' films show evidence of their exoticizing gaze upon the landscapes and the Algerian "Other," and an esprit de corps in what look more like vacation pictures, concealing the atrocities they were witnessing, or sometimes committing.[59] Occasionally, the violence enters surreptitiously at the edge of a frame or in the deep background of a shot (a body search, a torched village, a man wrestled to the ground). But such images did not circulate. The few photos taken covertly by professionals or French conscripts that were sent—to no avail—to the Commission for the Safeguard of Individual Rights and Freedoms, attempted to denounce the use of torture.[60] Since the Great War, the production of unofficial images was a concern for military authorities that would proscribe it, or seek, often unsuccessfully, to format its content through regulations. However, digital tools have made this kind of monitoring all but impossible. During the American invasion of Iraq in 2003, for instance, soldiers shot their own videos during combat, on patrol, or in their barracks then posted them to blogs and, by 2005, to YouTube.[61] Those considered compromising were censored by the American government, while others were repurposed, for example, to highlight the American soldiers' good will toward the civilian population. The army was thus attempting, mostly in vain, to control and then exploit which images were taken and how they were disseminated on the Internet.[62]

Since the early twentieth century, the increase in amateur photography in situations of warfare was further prompted by newspapers that sought to tell the "true story" from the front, far from the sanitized official images. By 1914, the weekly *Le Miroir* was purchasing pictures outside the official purview so that French readers might experience the dreadful realities of combat, even if it meant deviating from the facts. Other newspapers even organized contests, setting off a race for the most "unusual," like the photos taken under fire in 1915 in an attempt to capture the instant of a soldier's death.[63] Although the public's attraction to violent spectacle certainly predates World War I and the invention of photography and cinema, the techniques of picture taking emerged concurrently with an intensification of violence on the battlefield starting around 1916. Here arose the more specific issue of representing the death of one's own combatants. The authorities feared the demobilizing effects of such images and censored them; in the United States, the press declared them all but taboo.[64] The Department of War banned the publishing of any image of American soldiers killed at the front until September 1943, when *Life* released a photograph of the lifeless bodies of some Marines on a beach in New Guinea. It was only in March 1944 that the ban was lifted for documentary films. In fact, in 1942, Hollywood was solicited by the Office of War Information to show "the deadly reality of war" but without actually depicting death, trusting the American public to be able to picture it without necessarily witnessing it.[65] Chapters in this book demonstrate how the representation of "their" dead remained topical for certain combat groups in Syria while being completely inverted by others, revealing differing attitudes toward representations of war, mobilization, and the concept of martyrdom.

With the Vietnam War (1961–1975), where television had become the medium of choice, warfare entered American households via the six o'clock news. Once the war was over, blockbuster films like Francis Ford Coppola's *Apocalypse Now* (1979) aestheticized the violence, producing codes that filtered down to war films worldwide and affected the industry for decades to come. These codes have played an important role in stripping the world of hard reality, a shift that evolved into armed conflict being commonly represented in video games.[66] This blurring of the real world and its representation was reinforced by new photographic tools developed by the military during this conflict, notably the high-altitude bombing that altered the perception of combat and the enemy, resulting in a new way of imagining war, as analyzed very early on by Paul Virilio.[67] In 1991, the Gulf War, as reported live by the Western media, with "surgical strikes" filmed by cameras mounted on the bombers and commented on by experts, was de-realized and sanitized, to the point of erasing its trivial reality.[68] In contrast to these different forms of warfare visibility, there are strategies of scarcity, where image taking is made difficult for security reasons, as in the French Resistance. But even in this case, the image remained a crucial resource for gaining support, displaying military credibility, and writing the Resistance into the history books.[69] In Syria, this tension within the economy of visibility varies among fighting groups: some produce massive amounts of imagery intended for a world audience, while others choose to hide their involvement.

The New Economy of Warrior Islam Since the 1980s

The year 1979 marked a watershed for political upheavals in the Middle East, notably with the so-called "Islamic" Revolution in Iran and the Red Army's invasion of Afghanistan.[70] The decade that followed featured wars that redefined notions of jihad* and martyrdom, giving rise to the production of images on a massive scale aimed at mobilizing in the name of a political Islam and its many facets. This first took place in Iran, during the war against Iraq (1980–1988), when strongly codified martyr figures started appearing in cinema. Certain filmmakers drew on Hollywood for inspiration—a paradoxical choice, given revolutionary Iran's anti-American stance—to portray heroic representations of combatants martyred for the nation. Others sought to devise a genre that broke with Western codes by staging martyrdom in the religious sense, according to two perspectives: either that which adopts the Quranic meaning of the term, where the martyr's death is never shown onscreen and is replaced with images such as a close-up of a fighter, eyes open and smiling at the moment he is "chosen by God"; or, alternatively, that which is based on the martyr figure typical of the Shiite tradition with reference to the Battle of Karbala*. In the latter case, extreme violence is depicted onscreen, such as a dismembered or decapitated body, impossible to show on a movie screen in wartime until that point. But in this case the violent onscreen death, which recalls that of the companions of the third Shiite imam, Husayn ibn Ali, at Karbala, is read as a sign that the victims are among the chosen.[71] These martyr figures, elaborated on-screen in Iran in the 1980s, would go on to influence Sunni representations of global jihadism, even stoking the existing rivalry between these two major currents of Islam.[72]

During this same decade, other uses of images emerged within the context of Afghanistan's jihad against the Red Army (1979–1989) and the pro-Soviet government in Kabul. Among the Afghan warlords, Ahmad Shah Mas'ud made intensive, groundbreaking use of video: he would prepare his offensives by sending out a cameraman to shoot footage of future fields of operation, but also to monitor how his mujahidin were fighting and whether they were observing their Islamic duties. These images, which were not intended for circulation, would remain as a record.[73] At the same time in Afghanistan, another approach to jihad was developing—no longer national but addressed to all the Muslims of Arab countries—matched by yet another use of image. By 1984, under the aegis of Abdullah al-Azzam, the father of "modern jihad," recruitment of volunteers was organized by the Services Bureau (*maktab al-khadamat*), the starting point of jihadist networks that would give rise to al-Qaeda*. It features a media center, low-tech at first, confined to filming the arrival of volunteers and showing the training camps. With the creation of al-Qaeda in 1987, new uses of video were deployed, including filmed interviews with Bin Laden (sitting in a cave) and hagiographies of martyrs. In the series *Sacrifice and Conquest* filmed in 1989 and 1990, Azzam's notions of global jihad were illustrated through images. Certain features that would later characterize al-Qaeda's productions were already present: Bin Laden as a simple combatant, images of plundered military equipment, the reuse of images from Western television networks, and the depiction of the smiling martyred combatant as a portrait floating between earth and sky with *nashids** as soundtrack.[74] These videos are a matter of internal communication within the al-Qaeda network, but also address the world. They constitute the basis of an imagery at odds with Islamic tradition.[75]

This conception of jihadism stemming from Afghanistan was exported to the Bosnian War (1992–1995). There, audiovisual communication became more professional with new elements making an appearance: depiction of martyrs coming from European countries, excommunication issued against Arab governments, threats to countries allied with the United States, denunciation of a worldwide conspiracy against Islam, and hagiographies of martyrs with interviews filmed while they were still alive.[76] The Muslim holy places also made an appearance, while calls to jihad grew more systematic. This production would display the horribly mutilated bodies of martyrs—images that would not always be picked up and used by other jihadist groups. With the arrival of the Internet, the dissemination of these films accelerated to a new level after having previously been disseminated only via VHS tape. First, they were shared out of London in 1996 with the first jihadist cyber-network, azzam.com.[77] That same year, Qatar launched Al Jazeera, an Arab satellite television channel that disrupted the Arab audiovisual landscape, broke up the Western news monopoly, and provided Bin Laden with a major communication platform.[78] In Bosnia, and soon after in Chechnya (1999–2000), we find elements that would later emerge in Syria: exploitation of the religious variable for political ends by foreign powers and jihadist groups, as well as an uneven use of images, depending on the case. Where jihadists made intensive use of images, the strategy of the Islamic Republic of Iran was more complex: for example, the regime justified its presence to assist Bosnian civilians, opening an office of Iranian television[79] in Sarajevo and increasing the number of films and documentaries.[80] Alongside this high-profile presence, it was also intervening militarily, via Afghan refugees formed into militias in Iran, outside any media coverage. Fighters were thus recruited for combat—through the paramilitary organization Sepâh-e-Muhammad (i.e. the Army of Muhammad, or the SMP)[81]—in Bosnia, Chechnya, and then in Afghanistan (1996–2001). With few exceptions, these fighters made no use of images, and no official iconography testifies to their presence. One of them, however, came to grasp the importance of images to attest to their participation in these conflicts, heretofore entirely concealed. Himself a fighter, he took to photographing his brothers-in-arms in Afghanistan in 2001 in their struggle against the Taliban. Subsequently, when some veterans of the SMP, himself included, arrived in Syria in 2012 (in what would become the Fatemiyoun Brigade*), he filmed their fighting with a small professional video camera to keep a record of their engagement.[82]

The twenty-first century was ushered in by the attacks of 11 September 2001, the date marking the emergence of Bin Laden and al-Qaeda as world icons. The searingly powerful images of the planes slamming into the twin towers of the World Trade Center, filmed and streamed by Americans on the day of the event, guaranteed al-Qaeda and its leader a media strike force far superior to its military strength. Just like the testament videos of the martyred pilots made public in 2003, these images got worked into the jihadists' audiovisual productions as proof of their mastery and commitment to terror on a global scale. Shortly before, on 14 March 2001, another explosion had taken place five days after Mullah Omar, leader of the Islamic Emirate of Afghanistan since 1996, decreed the destruction of the Bamiyan Buddhas and all pre-Islamic representational art. This decision reveals the extent to which "iconoclasm, visibility and publicity are tightly linked":[83] in this Taliban regime that prohibited all photographic equipment, Al Jazeera was invited to come film this spectacular destruction. This event, like the September 11 attacks, produced images of unprecedented power. But these two recorded events speak to the deep divergence in how image is mobilized within Sunni

Islam. When Bin Laden retreated to Afghanistan as a guest of the Taliban in 1996, he tacitly benefitted from a statute of extraterritoriality for images in Kandahar province: until 2001, he appeared there in videos as leader of the mujahidin advocating a global jihad and inviting Muslims to *hijra*.[84] Meanwhile, the only media outlet authorized by the Taliban was Radio Sharia.

By 2005, when the insurrectional Taliban forces resumed fighting against the Afghan government and its international backers, with suicide attacks in urban settings as their mode of operation, they used to film themselves and their victims.[85] It was as if, overcome by the communication among jihadist movements and the triumph of the Internet, they could not help using images—even though they did not use them as intensively as the jihadist fighters, notably in Iraq during the same period. Where jihadist groups had been using video in Iraq since the late 1990s, it was from 2003, with the Second Gulf War, that the use of video reached an unparalleled magnitude. Al-Qaeda's audiovisual production, focused on high-profile, spectacular operations, had the effect of rallying isolated jihadist groups. But the videos of hostage executions—prompted notably by Abu Mus'ab al-Zarqawi, leader of different jihadist groups—proved to be counterproductive; they sparked disapproval in Arab public opinion and other Iraqi fighting groups, as well as from Osama Bin Laden and Ayman al-Zawahiri,[86] who succeeded him in 2011. In the Syrian context, execution videos would go on to represent a political resource and a stamp of identity for the Islamic State, differentiating them from the Nusra Front* affiliated with al-Qaeda. On the other hand, the Bashar al-Assad regime, among other tactics, would resort to videos of torture sessions to terrorize its own population.

Structure

This book is the fruit of a long thought process by its two coordinators, based on different perspectives and terrains. Since 2011, Cécile Boëx has been studying the practices and uses of video in Syria by various actors in the revolt and the subsequent conflict. Agnès Devictor has been working since 2005 on footage shot during several wars by actors in the conflict (the Iran–Iraq War, the Afghan wars, and the Holy Shrine Defense* in Syria). In dialogue for a number of years, especially for seminars they have team-taught at the School for Advanced Studies in the Social Sciences (EHESS) and the University of Paris 1 Panthéon-Sorbonne, they took up the challenge of gathering images from opposing camps into a single book in order to delve into the specificities of each side's audiovisual practices and culture: the way the images relate to one another and, when considered in aggregate, how they might render the Syrian revolt and conflict more intelligible. Given the multitude of actors and uses, this work was bound to be a collective effort. This plurality is also reflected in the variety of disciplines—ranging from anthropology and political science, to sociology and history—represented among the researchers, and in the actors of the revolt who filmed their videos and posted them online, or fostered their circulation. Likewise, the formats used are wide-ranging (interviews, articles, and shorter-form pieces), as are the approaches, since some have been surveying the audiovisual and digital landscape for quite some time, whereas others are venturing into working with this material to address a specific issue as part of their research. These manifold ways of dealing with image and digital media, along with the varying methods for doing so, demonstrate the heuristic impact of this study of videos coming out of Syria since 2011.

Our ability to meet up with some image-takers (either in person or virtually) to listen to the narratives of their daily lives during the events adds emotional heft to the analyses presented here. This proximity does not cancel out the requisite critical distance, just as empathy and emotion pose no obstacle to knowledge; on the contrary, they are an essential vector.[87] This book serves only to open up a workspace by proposing paths to explore and tools to deploy. It opens readers' eyes to understanding heretofore neglected aspects of the revolt and conflict, or proposes new ways of thinking about them. Every text comes with numerous illustrations and screenshots. Despite the poor quality of many of these materials owing to the conditions of their production, we deem it important to show them—the framing, textures, and pixelation are permeated by power relations.[88] The quality of the image is not only a function of the shot's context, but also involves issues of visibility embedded in the power relations that this work attempts to highlight. We have opted for a diachronic sequencing, starting with the earliest demonstrations through to the internationalization of armed confrontation, bringing to light the various phases of how revolt slipped into war even if it is not strictly chronological within each of the sections. Finally, we aim to provide the reader with various keys to understanding our texts by means of a glossary (notions and names are indicated with an *) and a series of five maps illustrating different phases of the conflict. The timeline included in this work is not intended as an appendix: because it is essential for understanding the scope of the conflict and how it evolved, we decided to locate it between the two parts of the book, as a cornerstone.

Part One of this work, entitled "Protest and Engagement," explores the various ways video accompanied peaceful activism and armed struggle among Syrians involved in the revolt. The opening chapters consist of two interviews with individuals who took an active part in filming. They asked to remain anonymous, since they still have family in Syria. These interviews, carried out in France and Sweden where the interviewees are now living, report a range of image-capture experiences in the very different locations of Homs and the suburbs of Damascus, showing how each neighborhood experienced revolt, repression, and militarization in a singular way. The third chapter, based on the experience of Chamsy Sarkis, founder of the agency Syrian Media Action Revolution Team (SMART), revisits the strategies implemented by the Syrian diaspora in France to support the production and dissemination of videos outside of Syria through logistics and training. It reconstructs the different stages of this form of media activism and addresses issues of veracity, while exposing the detrimental role played by NGOs as "supporters" of alternative Syrian media. The fourth chapter analyzes the various ways video has given rise to new forms of protest. Demonstrations, stealthy actions in public space, communiqués, military defections, and the formation of fighter brigades are also generated by images. Women, too, were speaking out on film, whether individually or collectively, opening intermediary spaces between the street and the security of the home. This is the topic of chapter five, which studies the communiqués as well as the at-home sit-ins—a mode of action never before seen on film. It deals with the specific lexicon utilized by women, along with the ways in which they affirm their identity as women despite the need to remain anonymous. The final chapter of this first part traces, via video, the epic journey of 'Abd al-Basit al-Sarut, an iconic figure of the revolution, at different stages of his involvement: his role as leader at the demonstrations, his engagement in armed struggle as head of the Islamist brigade, his travel to Idlib, and finally, his martyrdom. Before Part Two of this work, and by way of transition, we offer the reader the opportunity to gain some perspective with a timeline that recreates, if only partially, the sequence of events since 2011. We have designed this "wide shot" almost like a text, allowing for both an overall contextualization but also a concrete sense of the scope and density of the conflict.

Part Two, "Combat," goes on to explore the development and circulation of images within the different fighting groups on the ground in Syria. Since it would be impossible to produce an exhaustive cartography of image generation among all the armed forces, specific case studies were the obvious alternative. From the vast store of available images, each of the authors selected the most significant moving or still shots to study how combat experience relates to these images, and how the images are enlisted into the exercise of violence. This part opens with Chapter 7, which presents the actors, geographies, and temporalities of warfare, and studies the imaginaries of national armed struggle and global jihad. The next chapter deals specifically with al-Nusra Front's process of constructing audiovisual communication, heralding its break with the Islamic State, while Chapter 9 on the Saint Thecla Convent abduction affair shows how the Christian community of Syria has been at the heart of competing images and narratives, opening a more political than faith-based reading of the war. The competition for audiovisual production is also the subject of Chapter 10, which deals with the development of Kurdish military communication in Rojava: a requirement for its international credibility and its obtaining of political and military resources, but one which renders it torn between Western media expectations and the historical and political origin of this fighting group—a difficult line to walk.

Chapter 11 deals with how digital images circulate at the front, starting with photos and videos produced, disseminated, and received in the "Iranian camp." It also sheds light on new forms of circulating propaganda images between enemy camps. Chapter 12 analyzes videos produced by Hezbollah and shows how the party's audiovisual production was compelled to redefine its original set of representations and symbols back when it was filming its armed struggle against the historic Israeli enemy, thereby revealing all the ambiguities of its position in the Syrian conflict. The following chapter analyzes the opposing audiovisual terror tactics deployed by the regime of Bashar al-Assad and the Islamic State—the former based on the disclosure of amateur videos shot by Syrian soldiers and intended for the Syrian public, whereas the latter expended a sizable budget to stage productions that would reach the broadest audience possible. This part concludes with a *mise-en-abyme* that studies a blockbuster Iranian film produced by the Islamic Revolutionary Guard Corps*, in part devoted to the production of images by the Islamic State and the role such videos were believed to play within the combat strategy of this armed group. What these chapters share is an attention to the ways the various protagonists represent themselves in the territories in which they are fighting, and to the temporalities and religious and/or political implications of their actions in the future. For instance, certain contributions involve a circumscribed zone; others bear on the Syrian national territory as a whole; and some propose a more abstract, metaphysical relation to place. The same holds true for timescales. Although all these studies refer to the precise period in which a given audiovisual object was being produced, they also show how eschatological time slips into the perceptions and representations of this war. The contributions to "Combat," each from a specific angle, pinpoint the emergence of imaginaries specific to this conflict and sometimes single out visual cultures that face off and respond. All demonstrate how partisan, national, and international agendas fit into and shape this conflict.

NOTES

1. Ghalioun and Mardam Bey, "Un printemps syrien" (2003).
2. Perthes, *Syria under Bashar al-Asad* (2004).
3. Seurat, *L'État de Barbarie* (1989).
4. Heydemann, "Upgrading Authoritarianism in the Arab world" (2007).
5. Hinnebusch, "Syria: from Authoritarian Upgrading to Revolution?" (2012).
6. Hama, a hotbed of Islamist contestation, was meant to serve as an example to dissuade any form of opposition. The discrepancy in casualty estimates, ranging from 15,000 to 40,000 deaths, speaks volumes about the secrecy surrounding the carnage.
7. As Salwa Ismail explains in *The Rule of Violence* (2018), this silence reactivates humiliation and terror and fits into a governing technique based on the anticipation of massacre.
8. It was the most deadly of such attacks, claiming some 1,500 lives. Between 2012 and 2017, the Syrian army carried out over one hundred chemical attacks (chlorine and sarin gas). See the many reports online at the investigative site *Bellingcat.com*, which gathers evidence by means of videos shot and posted online by Russian press agencies, groups affiliated with the Free Syrian Army, and media activists, crosscut with satellite images and interviews with witnesses on the ground.
9. See Chapter 1: "The Neighborhood Camera." Interview in 2011 with F. B., twenty-three years old, native of Homs.
10. For examples see: Cimino, *Syria: Borders, Boundaries, and the State* (2020); Yassin-Kassab and Al-Shami, Burning Country (2016); Abboud, Syria (2018); Bichara, "Syria" (2013); and Burgat and Paoli, *Pas de Printemps pour la Syrie* (2013).
11. Munif, *The Syrian Revolution* (2020).
12. Baczko, Dorronsoro, and Quesnay, *Syrie. Anatomie d'une guerre civile* (2016).
13. Huët, "Quand les 'malheureux'" (2015), 31–75.
14. See notably those compiled by the online newspaper (in Arabic and English), Al-Jumhuriya.
15. For examples see: Maarouf, *Lettres de Syrie* (2014); Al-Dik, *À l'Est de Damas* (2016); Yazbek, *Les portes du néant* (2016).
16. Yazbek, *Feux croisés* (2012).
17. To define this writing, Yassin al-Haj Saleh, writer and former political detainee, speaks of "inhabited" writing, which emerged thanks to an unbridling of speech, fostered by social media and blurring the boundaries between professional and amateur writers. Cf. Mermier, *Écrits libres de Syrie* (2018).

18. Cf. Ferro, *Cinéma et Histoire* (1977).
19. White, "Historiography and Historiophoty," (1988), 1193–99.
20. Lindeperg, *Les écrans de l'ombre,* 1997.
21. Lindeperg and Szczepanska, *À qui appartiennent les images?* (2017).
22. Lindeperg and Wieworka, *Le moment Eichmann* (2016).
23. Cf. Delage, *La vérité par l'image* (2006).
24. Véray, *Avènement d'une culture* (2019).
25. Didi-Huberman, "Images malgré tout," (2001), 219.
26. Cf. Mirzoeff, *Watching Babylon* (2005).
27. Cf. Mitchell, *Cloning Terror* (2011).
28. Notably, Zelizer, "On 'Having Been There'" (2007), 408–428; and Frosh and Pinchevski, *Media Witnessing* (2009).
29. Andén-Papadopoulos and Pantii, "Media Work of Syrian Diaspora Activists," (2013), 2185–2206.
30. Wall and El Zahed, "Embedding Content" (2014), 163–180.
31. Al-Ghazzi, "'Citizen Journalism'" (2014), 435–54; and Wessels, *Documenting Syria* (2017).
32. Meis, "Mobile Death Videos" (2013); Della Ratta, *Shooting a Revolution* (2018); and De Angelis, "Controversial Archive" (2020), 69–88.
33. Üngör, "On the Multiple Uses of Video" (2019), 207–215; and Haugbølle, "Holding Out for the Day After Tomorrow" (2019), 229–244.
34. Saber and Long, "'I will not leave'" (2017), 80–99. See also Della Ratta, Dickinson, and Haugbølle, *The Arab Archive* (2020).
35. Notably, Boëx, "La création cinématographique," (2013), 145–56; and Wessels, *Documenting Syria* (2019).
36. See for example Zabunyan, *L'insistance des luttes* (2016).
37. Riboni, "Chercher, trouver, conserver" (2018), 45–56.
38. Weizman, "L'image en conflit" (2017).
39. Pastinelli, "Pour en finir" (2011), 38.
40. Castells, *Communication et pouvoir* (2013).
41. Exemplarily, the collectives created in the French Communist Party environment in the 1930s, such as Ciné-Liberté or Les Films populaires. Cf. Perron, *Cinéma du front* (1999).
42. Created in New York in 1967 by Robert Kramer, Allan Siegel, and John Douglas, this alternative film collective produced news via images, against network television. The collective, which thought of itself as an "urban guerilla" group, produced some fifty films documenting the 1967 march on the Pentagon, the 1968 occupation of Columbia University, the demonstrations at the Democratic Convention in Chicago, and the Black Panthers movement.

43. Starting in 1967, during the massive strikes at the Sochaux and Besançon factories, the Medvedkine groups assembled militant filmmakers and technicians to collaborate with workers. On amateur film production from this period, see notably: Layerle, *Caméras en lutte* (2008).
44. The documentary film by Ania Szczepanska, *Solidarność la chute du mur commence en Pologne* (2019) makes use of these archival images.
45. This extraordinary moment is visible in the film by Harun Farocki and Andrei Ujica, *Videograms of a Revolution* (1992), which uses archival images (amateur, televised, and journalistic) to retrace the audiovisual chronology of the events, while questioning how these images relate to power.
46. Mustata, "'The Revolution Has Been Televised'" (2012), 76–97.
47. Cf. Cardon and Granjon, *Médiactivistes* (2013).
48. Cf. Downing, "Film and Video" (2001), 192–200.
49. The militant film *Showdown in Seattle: Five Days That Shook the WTO* (1999) was produced with images shot by members of Indymedia during the demonstrations.
50. Cf. Coleman, "Les temps d'Indymedia" (2005), 41–48.
51. Blondeau, *Devenir Média* (2007), 61.
52. YouTube, acquired by Google in 2006, is a web platform where users can post, view, and comment on videos. In 2009, it was scoring around 350 million visits per month. By 2020, this number had reached 2 billion, with 500 hours of video content uploaded per minute. Cf. Salman Aslam, "YouTube by the Numbers: Stats, Demographics & Fun Facts." *Omnicoreagency.com*, February 10, 2020. https://www.omnicoreagency.com/youtube-statistics/.
53. Such as shouting "Allahu akbar" ("God is great") from rooftops, every night, in several large Iranian cities, both repeating and appropriating the defiant cry from the 1979 revolution against the Shah.
54. Kelly and Elting, "A Portrait of the Persian Blogosphere" (2015), 141–163.
55. Lim, "Framing Bouazizi" (2013), 921–941.
56. Cf. Snowdon, *The People Are Not an Image* (2020).
57. On surveillance and censorship on social networks and the digital counterattack in Syria, see notably: Bazan and Varin, "Le Web à l'épreuve" (2012), 595–606.
58. Véray, *Avènement d'une culture* (2019).
59. Bertin-Maghit, "Analyse des films de soldats" (2012), 60.
60. Riceputi, "Au-delà du mur" (2020); and Branche, *La torture et l'armée* (2001).
61. See Oxley, "'The Real Nasty Side of War'" (2016).
62. Christensen, "Uploading Dissonance" (2008), 155–175.
63. Beurrier, "La Grande Guerre" (2005), 162–175.

64. The question was raised as early as 1862, when a New York gallery exhibited photos of corpses taken at the Battle of Antietam that shocked visitors. See Brunet, "La critique des images," (2012).

65. Kleinberger, "Ruptures narratives" (2011), 185–205.

66. Stora, "Le cinéma américain" (1996), 149–155.

67. Virilio, *Guerre et cinéma* (1991).

68. Hallin, "Images de guerre" (1994), 121–132; and Fleury-Villate, *Les Médias et la guerre du Golfe* (1992).

69. Lindeperg, *La voie des images,* (2013).

70. Bozarslan, *Histoire de la violence* (2008), 98–149.

71. Devictor, *Images, combattants et martyrs* (2015).

72. El Difraoui, *Al-Qaida par l'image* (2013), 21, 359–360. See also: Hegghammer, *Jihadi Culture* (2017).

73. Devictor, "Massoud, le Commandant à la caméra" (2013), 29–47.

74. El Difraoui, *Al-Qaida par l'image* (2013), 97–109.

75. Naef, *Y a-t-il une question* (2015).

76. El Difraoui, *Al-Qaida par l'image* (2013), 119–141.

77. El Difraoui, *Al-Qaida par l'image* (2013), 141.

78. El Difraoui, *Al-Qaida par l'image* (2013) 171.

79. Observations of Agnès Devictor, Sarajevo, September 1, 1996.

80. Even films about Bosnia will be much less subject to censorship. Agnès Devictor, *Politique du cinéma iranien. De l'âyatollâh Khomeyni au président Khâtami.*

81. This army, about which there is little, is linked with the Islamic Revolutionary Guard Corps*. It was created in the 1990s to protect Iran's eastern borders, particularly against the Taliban.

82. Interview by Agnès Devictor and Shahriar Khonsari with some of those closest to this fighter-filmer who died in Syria, and with former members of the Sepâh-e Muhammad in Bosnia and Chechnya. Mashhad, 05/04/2019. There is still doubt as to whether, in the intervention in Bosnia, a structure called Sepâh-e Muhammad was actually involved, or whether this engagement took place in a less institutional fashion.

83. Centlivres, "Vie, mort et survie" (2009).

84. El Difraoui, *Al-Qaida par l'image* (2013), 149–153.

85. One such attack occurred on December 11, 2014 at the Institut Français d'Afghanistan (IFA), Kabul, during the theatrical performance of *Battements du cœur: le silence après l'explosion* [Heartbeats: silence after the explosion, 2014] whose subject happened to be the consequences of an attack in the Afghan capital. Two Taliban fighters who had infiltrated the IFA filmed the explosion, provoking a blurring between the subject of the play and the blast they caused. They broadcast the images shortly thereafter.

86. El Difraoui, *Al-Qaida par l'image* (2013), 179–233.
87. This is notably what Stéphane Audoin-Rouzeau witnessed when confronted with genocide in Rwanda. See: Audoin-Rouzeau, *Une initiation: Rwanda* (2017). In *Combattre* (2008), he interrogated the bond between researcher and the object of his/her research, particularly when the research bears on "loathsome subjects." More generally, Audoin-Rouzeau advocates for a more sensitive approach—one that for too long has been excluded from historiographic methods—to study fighting as a fact.
88. For a meditation on the power schemes at work in the choices of framing (both image and narration) in conflict zones, see Lebow, "Shooting with Intent" (2012), 41–62.

PART ONE
PROTEST AND ENGAGEMENT

1

"THE NEIGHBORHOOD CAMERA"

INTERVIEW WITH F., NATIVE OF HOMS

Interviewed by Cécile Boëx[1]

F.* was a master's student in Damascus in 2011. When the revolt broke out, he went back to Homs, his hometown, to "do the revolution." He spontaneously formed a group with his friends to organize demonstrations, trade news, and distribute aid. Even though he had no experience with image-making, he was designated by the neighborhood residents to document the demonstrations he was organizing. He didn't consider himself a media activist and filmed independently, using his cell phone. He would send his videos to a contact who would then post them online. F. also volunteered for the Red Crescent,[2] which was providing relief to displaced families, civilians in areas under siege, and those affected during bombings. After two weeks in detention in the spring of 2012, he stopped sending his videos to be posted to YouTube, though he would still transmit dispatches to a media group on Facebook that was a clearinghouse for daily news on Syria. He continued his activities with the Red Crescent until 2015. Knowing that he was wanted by the Syrian authorities, he left Syria, first for Turkey before finally arriving in France in 2016. At the time of this interview, he had recently begun working for an organization that assists disabled people. Throughout our exchanges, F. showed me videos and photos he found directly on YouTube, or otherwise in a digital folder that he had recently recovered and saved to his laptop.

First Demonstration, First Video

F.: Just before the start of the revolution, I was in Damascus. On Facebook, there were calls to demonstrate on 18 March, the "Friday of Dignity." We did what they did in Tunisia and in Egypt; we chose Friday because it's the day people go to the mosque to pray. In Syria, there was no political life, there was no place where you could gather people to start a demonstration. The only place was the mosque. Even people who didn't want to go to pray went there to demonstrate. On that day in Damascus, there weren't many people. I went home to Homs to see if something might happen there the following week. I wanted to make revolution in Homs because it's my town. I know the streets, which way to flee. I can move around and avoid police barricades. And in Homs, there were more demonstrations than in Damascus. On 25 March, it was the "Friday of Pride," I think. We didn't know whether it was going to work. The night before, I couldn't sleep. I went out to walk in the street. Strangely, I was completely alone that night; there wasn't a sound. I called a friend. We sat outside next to where he lives. We stayed like that without saying anything. Then he asked me: "Do you think something's going to happen tomorrow?" I answered: "I don't know. Well, see you tomorrow, *'a sa'a* (at the Clock Square)."[3] So, on the morning of the 25th, I left the house. Of course, my family asked me: "Where are you going?" I answered that I was going to get something. [*He laughs*]. On the way, I bought a sandwich, walking casually, like everything was normal. Little by little, without realizing it, my feet had led me to the square. I started hearing people shouting. I picked up the pace. The traffic cops had closed off all the streets leading to Clock Square. I passed in front of them and entered the square. There were lots and lots of people. The first thing I remember is a girl sitting up on a man's shoulders. She was shouting slogans that people repeated after her: "*Hurriyeh, hurriyeh!*" Freedom, freedom! She was not even veiled! We learned later that she was Christian. I looked at her like this [*He stands to mimic his astonishment*] and I joined the crowd. I looked all around me. [*He laughs.*] My legs were doing this [*He mimics trembling*] and . . . Wait [*He searches for a video in the files on his laptop—it's one that wasn't posted online.*] And at that point, I took out my old cell phone with a poor-quality camera. On the square in the center, there is a clock and a small platform. I climbed up and started filming the crowd. [*He launches the video. It lasts 24 seconds.*] (Figure 1.1).

1.1. First demonstration in Homs, 03/25/2011. Video shot by F., personal archive.

The demonstrators were around the square and on the other side, here [*he shows me on the screen*], in al-Quwatli Street; it was cordoned off by the police and the *shabbihas**. They had come to attack the demonstrators, chanting: "*Bir-roh, bid-damm nafdik ya Bashar*" (with our soul and our blood, we sacrifice for you, O Bashar). The demonstrators responded with: "*Allah, Suriya,* *hurriyeh wa bas!"* (Allah, Syria and freedom, that's all). They also chanted: "The people want the governor [of Homs] out" and *"Bir-roh, bid-damm nafdik ya Daraa!"* (With our soul and our blood, we sacrifice for you Daraa). You see the pixels [*He laughs.*] Look here, you can see the date and time: 25 March 2011, 11:19 a.m. [*He stops the video.*] The shabbihas started lobbing tear gas and beating us with clubs.

—Why did you film?

F.: I don't know. But I do remember that I was filming, my legs were shaking, and tears were flowing from my eyes. That was a very special day for me because it was the first time in my life that I heard my voice. I realized that I had a voice. I can say "freedom." Afterward, when they attacked, it was a mess, people started fleeing. What I did, to get away, is I walked slowly toward the shabbihas. [*He laughs.*] I figured that if I went straight for them, they weren't going to arrest me. I'd turned on my cell phone camera and tried, with my hand down at my side, to film how they were beating people and loading them into vans, but on the video, you can't really see much. A few minutes after the attack, the demonstrators started chanting: *"Ash-sha'ab yurid isqat an-nizam!"* (The people want to topple the regime). But from that point on, the square was totally cordoned off. For several weeks, we couldn't demonstrate there. Which is why we held our demonstrations in the neighborhoods. Sometimes, two or three neighborhoods, the closest together, would join up, depending on how large the security presence was.

When I shot that video, I wasn't thinking. Maybe I just wanted to keep it as a souvenir, because a revolution happens only once in a lifetime—or maybe not even that—and if it does happen, it means you're lucky to have experienced it. So saving this image, this memory, it was important. It's like when you have a photo taken as a keepsake. That's how it started: as memories for me to keep. Later, it became something else—we needed to show the world what was happening in Syria: Look, we're dying every day. We're demonstrating. You who talk about human rights, you who talk about freedom and principles, look, we're just like you, we want the same thing. It was also to get my message across, we didn't want to die for nothing. Okay, we were willing to die—I for one was willing to die—but we wanted to be sure at least that we weren't going to just die for nothing, we weren't going to go to prison for nothing. We agreed about dying, we weren't afraid, because it was worth it.

—You thought that the images, the videos, could change something?

F.: I did think so.

—For how long did you think so?

F.: I don't know. Actually, it's a bit complicated, because even though I say that I had hope that the videos and images were going to change something, at the same time, there was something deep inside me that little by little didn't believe in humanity anymore, in people's principles. When one year, two years have passed, you say to yourself: How come? What are you waiting for? You saw it. At first, there were the ambassadors present in Syria. They went to the demonstrations in Duma, Damascus, Hama. After them, observers from the Arab League and the UN came, and they saw, but nothing changed. When the UN international observers came on 23 May 2012, they came through our neighborhood. We stopped them, we gave them our USB flash drives with lots of videos, lots of images—we threw them into their vehicles. We thought they were there to help us. They didn't listen very closely, they answered "yes, yes" . . . They spent only 15 minutes in our neighborhood and didn't even get out of their vehicles. Even with foreign journalists[4] who saw the truth, nothing changed. So someone like me, with my little video, is going to change things? Of course not. Even if we had made millions of videos, it's not going to change anything, because they don't want it to. That's when you start to realize that, in fact, it's a political decision. It's not up to us. Before, we were excited, we went all in at the demonstrations. We were naïve, too. It was the first time we made a revolution.

—And yet, people continued to film.

F.: That's right, they didn't stop. On one hand, it's pointless, but at the same time, it's a duty—you have to do it. We did what we had to do.

Organizing and Contending with Repression

—How was your group organized?

F.: At first, you didn't know who to trust. It was very risky, even sometimes in your own family: all it took was one word and you went to prison, or died. But bit by bit, you started to learn who was on your side and who wasn't; those who didn't want to do anything, and those who needed to speak out and understand and were won over. Bit by bit, you start to find your friends, you start to meet people you didn't know before—but it's the revolution that connects you all. We started to make a group to work and organize things together. There were about fifteen of us. At first, we would meet up in a café, but that was too dangerous, so we met up in the apartment of one of the members, every day. We would meet there before going to demonstrate, sometimes in other neighborhoods. We'd also talk about the situation on the ground, and what was happening in other cities. Thanks to our contacts, we shared information to find out who needed relief, medications, food, and the like.

—Were you connected to a Local Coordinating Committee*?

F.: No, we didn't have a structure; we were a group of friends, that's all. We divided up the tasks. When we organized flash demonstrations that lasted only a few minutes, some attended while others took their cars to block the street to prevent the police vans from entering. We would jam up the streets. Women did that, too. It gave the demonstrators time to get away. We would arrange to meet by sending coded SMS messages. For example: "Sale at such and such a shop, 5 percent" [*laughter*] to indicate the place and time. You come, you pretend to be just walking and someone shouts "Freedom! God is great!" You'd see people rallying, and in two minutes, it would all be over. We had lookouts in front of branch offices of the security services who would warn us when they were coming, and everybody would disappear. It was kind of a smart way to survive, because by that time, there had already been casualties: they were firing at demonstrators and rounding people up.

But there were always big demonstrations whenever there was a funeral, as on 18 April 2011. There was a sit-in at Clock Square in tribute to 12 demonstrators killed the day before in the Bab as-Siba' neighborhood. The square was packed. The sit-in lasted from 2 p.m. to 1:50 in the morning. The police sealed the city. I'd had to go to Damascus at that time, so I missed the whole thing. People were celebrating; they thought the regime was about to fall. But the shabbihas opened fire. Dozens of people were killed. We weren't able to return to the square to demonstrate until the UN observers came. When the shabbihas attacked, they wrote "Bashar, we love you" along with their names on the clock. It was hard for us; we couldn't get there to demonstrate anymore. We did flash demonstrations in al-Dablan Street, right next to it. Once, we decided to have a demonstration on the square to erase the names of the shabbihas. It was really dangerous. There were police, snipers. At the appointed time, there wasn't anybody. I wore sunglasses to hide my face, and pretended to just be out for a walk. I saw a friend on the other side of the square. I started chanting a slogan and crossed over to the middle of the square. Then people started coming. There were a lot of us, twenty, maybe thirty . . . Someone came with a can of spray paint to paint over the names. We needed one or two minutes to film. [*He shows me the video (Figure 1.2). The person filming commented: "We broke the fear barrier."*]

1.2. "Cleaning up Liberty Square in Homs," posted on 08/22/2011 by glory4syriam, with 343 views by 08/18/2020. https://www.youtube.com/watch?v=NUJDXIBC4NA.

After that, we raced back to al-Dablan Street, and there were even more people. It was magnificent. The point of flash demonstrations—even if there weren't many people and they didn't last long—was to film them to show the world that we were still here, that we were still demonstrating. We organized one every day, even three times a day! Sometimes we had them transmitted live to Al Jazeera, like in Khalidiya, where you could hold demonstrations that lasted longer. Over there, it was possible because it was closed and the police didn't dare go in; whereas in my neighborhood, at the end of the street, there was a security branch.

— *How did that work, your cooperation with Al Jazeera?*

F.: The channel got in touch with people and sent them cameras, laptops, and money. One time, some activists suggested I do this, but I didn't want to, because it gets complicated—issues of money and honesty. There were a lot of problems. I had my cell phone, and that was enough.

— *You never got yourself a video camera?*

F.: No, I couldn't afford one and I didn't want to be working for somebody else; I wanted to be free. I bought another cell phone, a slightly better one. But in 2011, there weren't the phones like we have today. In our group, there were others who filmed (in other neighborhoods) or who were in contact with foreign journalists. In my neighborhood, I was the one who filmed the demonstrations because we didn't want everybody filming haphazardly, showing people's faces. I was the neighborhood camera. Things just evolved that way over time. I wasn't the one who posted the videos online; I gave my memory card to someone who had a secure computer [*with TOR, software that allows you to anonymize your connection location*] for posting videos on YouTube.

— *Did you know the owner of the channel?*

F.: *No.*

— *Did your videos circulate anywhere else?*

F.: They did: a few were posted online to ShaamNetwork S.N.N.,[5] but most of them are here. Look [*he shows me the page of a YouTube channel.*[6]] All the orange-tinted videos, shot at night, those are mine. The point was to film without showing any faces. I was careful not to film empty space. I positioned myself behind the demonstration and framed the people and the flags. Right in front of me, people were holding up signs written backward, facing me so that I could film them. They also gave me slips of paper with the place and date so that I'd place them in front of the camera (Figure 1.3).

1.3. On the paper is written: "Nighttime demonstration. Homs, al-Ghouta quarter, 10/19/2011." Posted by Syrian2011X, with 73 views by 08/18/2020. Cf. https://www.youtube.com/watch?v=3gUdVYfc8Ag.by 08/18/2020.

— *About how many videos did you make?*

F.: I don't know. A lot. I mean, every day for months, until I went to prison, on 22 March 2012.

On 16 March 2012, a week before I was arrested, I shot a video of the demonstration and another of the attack by security forces who fired at us. I was running and I heard shots. People were fleeing in my direction; there were some who were shot down, but I kept filming. Bullets were whizzing past. [*He imitates the sound.*]

— *So why did you keep filming?*

F.: I wanted to record the sound of bullets being fired. [*He shows me the video.*[7]]

It was longer than this, but the guy who posted it cut it down. Next, I entered an apartment building looking for safety. People had opened their homes so that the demonstrators could find refuge. I entered the apartment of someone I didn't know, and I filmed the attack from his place.

— Have you kept those videos?

F.: No! I never keep anything on me. I delete everything, it's too risky. One time, our meeting place was tracked down. Guys from security showed up, and they found signs and flags. They tore everything apart. I had to leave home. I went to Lebanon for a month with other members of the group. When we got back, we were summoned to appear before State Security. We paid to be let go, but we also had to make declarations to the effect that we hadn't wanted to demonstrate, we just happened to be there that day. That same night, we demonstrated [*laughter*]. That's why I would delete the videos from my phone. I kept a few hidden on my laptop, but my mother deleted everything while I was in prison. When I got out, I was too well-known in my neighborhood, and it was too dangerous for my family, so I stopped giving videos to be posted online. I made a few for myself. Photos as well. But I continued working on the sly. Every day, I would write a dispatch on what was happening—demonstrations, bombings, number of dead and wounded—for a media group on Facebook. I did that for a long time. I also kept working for the Red Crescent.

1.4. Photo taken by F. on 05/15/2014 in the Jurat al-Shayyah quarter, 200 meters from his house.

Living Memory versus the Archive

F.: A few months ago, a friend wrote to tell me that, while listening to some Fairuz on his computer, he found a hidden folder in my name. He sent it to me. It was the video folder that I had saved!

— *What things did you save?*

F.: They're the videos that I didn't give to be posted online—ones I'd filmed, or that friends had filmed. There's the one I shot during the first demonstration; I wanted to keep that one.

— *What about the others, why did you keep them?*

F.: I don't know. There are things I shot in the Khalidiya neighborhood. [*He shows me one of these videos*]. I was above it, looking down, and I filmed the skirmishes with the police. [*He clicks on another video. A demonstration.*] Look at this street, at the end, you see the police. It's one of the most dangerous streets in Homs because there were snipers up on an apartment tower right next to it. Over here is the State Security center, and over there is a police blockade. For a while, my neighborhood had been liberated. There were no more police. We demonstrated, we closed off the neighborhood—it was great. Then out of nowhere, they attacked the neighborhood with tanks and took it back. This was in June 2012. At that time, it was too risky to demonstrate. There were bombings.

— *Did you film any of the bombing?*

F.: No, because I was busy going to rescue people. I couldn't film at the same time. I did film the tanks, but I don't know what happened to that video.

— *Out of everything you filmed, all that remains are thirty videos, not even.*

F.: And the others are all on YouTube.

— *You're lucky that they're still there. Don't you want to save them?*

F.: I need to take the time to do that, because there are a lot of them.

— *When you were shooting, were you thinking of the archive, of history? Were you figuring that it might be useful later on?*

F.: No, I was only thinking in the present. Because I didn't know whether "later on" I'd be dead or alive. How can we talk about archives when things are actually happening? You talk about the World War II archive, because that war is over. I can't compare what's happening in Syria to the First or Second World War, it's something very specific. It isn't a war. We can't call it "a war," we can't call it a "conflict." Okay, the media called it that all the time. People say to me: "Oh, it's horrible, what's happening in Syria with the war and all." Then it's up to me to explain to them that no, it's not a war, it's not a conflict. You can talk about war when the parties involved are on an equal footing. But here, you have one side that wants to kill the other. When the people are just trying to defend themselves, it's not war—it's not even civil war either; it's worse still. Since 2012 and 2013, we've been hearing those words: "war," "civil war," "conflict." But they don't ever say "revolution." [*F. talks to me about a particularly difficult moment during a Red Crescent mission when, the day after the Houla Massacre*[8], *he found himself before a man in his fifties who had lost his wife and thirteen children.*] There are no words. Stories like that, you hear them every day. That's not a war. And that's why there are refugees; that's why people have taken up arms to defend themselves. It's too easy to judge. You live with anger. No one can ask me why I'm angry. It's just a feeling that never leaves me. But it's up to you to decide whether it's going to destroy you, or whether you can make something good out of it. No, it's not a war, it's not a conflict; it's just a revolution, and it's ongoing. It's not an archive, it's something in the here and now.

— *And yet, the videos that you recovered recently, what are they for you? A personal archive? A trace, a memory of what you experienced? Can you conceive of using the word "archive" for that, or is it different?*

F.: No, I don't know. For me, it's not an archive. In the end, when I look at those images, I can't even say that it's for remembering, because I've never forgotten. I can't put a word to it. It's just moments I've experienced . . . it's part of me, that's all. There's a time in people's lives when things happen, when things come to pass. Language and words are very far from the truth or from . . . I don't know how to say it, there isn't a word that's right enough to explain what I mean. Language is *'ajizeh*, how do you say?

— *It's powerless.*

F.: It's powerless, because here we're talking about feeling . . . you can't explain.
[*Going through the folders on the computer, F. opens a file that he has always kept with him. They are photos he took, or that friends took, from 2011 to 2015. He first shows me images of nearby neighborhoods destroyed.*] Here, that's the interior of the Khalid ibn al-Walid Mosque; it's very old, a historic monument. The dome is destroyed. This one here is our mosque. This is a camp for displaced people, in a school. Ah, this one is from January 2012. There were shortages: no electricity, no phone connection, no water.

That morning, it was snowing. Without really thinking about it, I grabbed a pail and collected some snow. I saw that everyone else was doing the same thing! That was the day we left home—when a tank arrived in front of our door. I have a folder here that's called "Dead." I included the photos of a few friends, not all. [*F. clicks on photos of smiling young men, from better times. He names each by their first name.*] That's M.: we were together at university. He went to do his military service, but he didn't want to. He took part in demonstrations. He was caught, and they killed him. This one is a friend: we were together at the Red Crescent. He was arrested and tortured to death. T. stayed back with the people under siege in the al-Waer quarter. He took up arms and decided to fight over there. This one is A.: he's been in prison since 2012 and no one has any news from him. Of our group, those who are still alive have all left. We went through some intense times together. We had fun. So many stories . . .

NOTES

1. This text is taken from two interview sessions conducted on June 26 and July 12, 2020 at F. B.'s place of residence, in a medium-sized French town where he has lived since 2016. At his request, our exchanges took place in French (which he has learned since arriving in the country). He wishes to remain anonymous because he still has family in Syria. I have known his uncle and aunt for quite some time, as I met them while I was living in Syria from 2001 to 2011.
2. A branch of the Red Cross in Muslim countries. This international organization is supposed to be neutral, but in Syria it is controlled by the regime, as are all NGOs. Still, within the context of the revolution, certain branches have distanced themselves from the regime, as in Homs, Hama, Idlib, and Duma—even though "to continue to do anything," as F. says, the volunteers are obliged to distribute aid in pro-regime neighborhoods that don't need it.
3. The main town square in Homs, renamed "Freedom Square" [Note: this is referred to as "Liberty Square" in the caption for Figure 1.2. Please advise] by the demonstrators. The clock tower located at the center would become the symbol of revolution in Homs.
4. He is referring to French journalist Gilles Jacquier and American journalist Marie Colvin, who both lost their lives in Homs in 2012.
5. Created on 26 February 2011: 220,315,485 views and 369,000 subscribers by 11 June 2024; still active by that date.
6. Syrian2011X, created on 25 March 2011: 2,952,027 views by 11 June 2024, with the last video posted on 17 May 2013. The 2,437 videos posted to this channel devoted to several neighborhoods in Homs (Khalidiya, al-Qusour, al-Waer, Baba 'Amr, al-Ghouta, al-Qarabis, Insha'at, etc.) show mainly demonstrations, martyrs, scenes of repression, deployment of security forces and, starting in 2012, air strikes and wreckage. Cf. https://www.youtube.com/user/Syrian2011X/videos?view=0&sort=da&flow=grid, accessed on 11 June 2011.
7. See Syrian2011X, "Homs, al-Ghouta district 16-3-2012. Shabbihas attack." https://www.youtube.com/watch?v=FXxhvCchI-I. Video posted on 16 March 2012. 2,302 views on 11 June 2024. In the video, https://www.youtube.com/watch?v=FXxhvCchI-I, F. comments: "Shots fired at demonstrators." This video was also posted on the YouTube channel ShaamNetwork S.N.N. on the same day.
8. On 25 May 2012, 108 people, including 34 women and 49 children, were massacred there by the Syrian army and the shabbihas.

2

FROM INFORMATION TO FILM

INTERVIEW WITH H., OF THE KAFR SOUSA COORDINATING COMMITTEE

Cécile Boëx[1]

H. was twenty-six in 2011. An enthusiast of cinema and theater, which he indulged in during his spare time, he studied at the University of Damascus and repaired dish antennae to pay for his education and support his family. This family hails from Kafr Sousa, a neighborhood near central Damascus where the headquarters of several ministries and security bureaus are located. However, after the 1982 Hama Massacre, H.'s family became mistakenly associated with a Hama family close to the Muslim Brothers, which led to the expropriation and incarceration of two of his uncles and his father. H.'s painful family history fuels a powerful sense of injustice for him. In the early days of the revolution, he dared to ask his family about their detention after 1982 and declared: "I had read the novel 'The Shell.' [2] I thought that a lot of it was exaggerated, but in fact, it wasn't at all." H. took part in his first demonstration in one of the neighborhood mosques, initiated into protest by a friend who helped found the Kafr Sousa Coordinating Committee*. With his rudimentary film training, he was designated to head the committee's media bureau, which included six photographers/filmmakers. The Kafr Sousa demonstrations drew a certain notoriety thanks to a live Al Jazeera broadcast. While complying with certain directives from the TV channel, H. invented new ways of filming the demonstrations as well as the security forces. He was also starting to work on his own film project. Arrested in August 2012, he had to complete his military service upon release. However, refusing to join the armed struggle alongside the Free Syrian Army (FSA), he saw departure as the only option. Within a month, he deserted and staged his own killing in a video, to protect his family. Refusing to join the armed struggle alongside the Free Syrian Army (FSA), he saw departure as the only option. Image production continued to affect his experiences of the revolt, even as he set out on the road to exile. Since 2013 he has been living in Sweden where, after working a number of menial jobs, he is doing a degree in prosthetics and orthotics to provide devices for war casualties. He also directed a play performed in several Swedish cities.

From Demonstrating to Image-making

H.: Some friends and I watched on live TV the fall of Hosni Mubarak in Egypt. It was unbelievable; we were so happy! My mother closed the windows, for fear our neighbors might hear us. Back then, we were thinking there would never be demonstrations in Syria. I didn't go to the first demonstration at al-Rifaʻi Mosque[3] [*25 March 2011*] because I was in a theater workshop. The following Friday, I was having coffee before going to the neighborhood mosque to pray when I saw one of my friends passing by. He seemed to be in a hurry. I asked him where he was going. He said: "If you want, come with me, but don't ask any questions!" I understood that he was going to demonstrate [*at a mosque located some 500 meters from al-Rifaʻi Mosque*]. Once we got there, I didn't understand what was going on around me. I watched, to register every detail: How does this begin? Where are the people? I was excited, my heart pounding. Prayer was starting. Al-salamu ʻalaikum . . . [*he makes the head movement from right to left that accompanies this phrase*]. I was clearly not in the mood for praying. At that moment, I heard someone shout "Takbir!"[4] People got up. At first, I didn't catch on, but four or five people had been waiting to shout the takbir. There was a kind of competition to be the first to shout it. We left and went out into the street. I was wondering whether I should be hiding my face. I had watched the first video of the 25 March demonstration, so as soon as I saw someone filming with a cell phone, I turned my head. In my neighborhood, everyone knew me because I repaired dish satellites. I didn't understand the slogans they were chanting. Instead of "Daraa, we are with you until death" I was hearing "Daraa, we can't die anymore" [*laughter*]. They were also chanting "Out! Out! Hoo! Hoo!" I was wondering why "hoo hoo"? They should have been saying Go! Go! So I started chanting "Go! Go!" at the top of my voice. Someone said no, it's "Hoo, Hoo." The atmosphere was fantastic, it was like being at a soccer stadium. We were all carried along. But right away, Abu Georges [*pseudonym*], my friend, told me to leave because the security forces were on their way. He didn't want me to be afraid at my first demonstration.

Afterward, we met up at his office where my friend was starting to organize a coordinating committee. We would meet people from different neighborhoods like Midan and Qaddam, who organized their own committees of ten to fifteen people each. We sounded out family and friends that we could trust, and we organized our first demonstration. Our choice of street was a function of the number of escape routes it offered. At Kafr Sousa, it's very dangerous because you're surrounded by nine security branches. On the appointed day, we all went to the mosque. We had designated the one who was to shout "God is great" [*Allahu akbar*]. I was in the same state as the first time, the same adrenaline rush. I was afraid. No one knew about our plan. Prayers began, continued . . . Then, at last, the takbir resounded. We put our shoes back on and dashed out. People were throwing eggs at us from their balconies. We got to the square. We stayed there six minutes until we spotted the security forces at a distance, moving in our direction. There weren't many of us: the residents of Kafr Sousa, who stayed inside at home, were watching us. Some filmed discreetly to find out who was there. We tried to find out who had filmed the demonstration so that we could post their clips on YouTube. I for one didn't film that day; I was too terrified. When we watched the videos, all the faces were recognizable. We couldn't post them. But it did help us to see who had demonstrated that day. We decided that we would film ourselves and create a YouTube channel to post our videos. (Figure 2.1) [*The channel is Kafar Sousah Revolt,[5] created on 19 June 2001, with 1,088 videos posted by 22 May 2016, and 108,944 views by August 2020*].

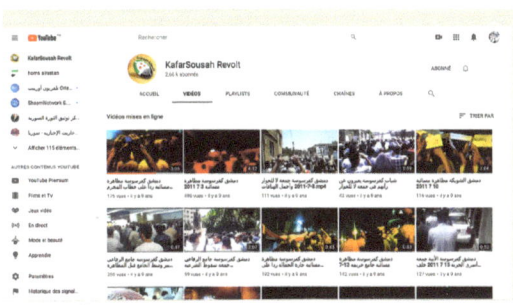

2.1. Channel "Kafar Sousah Revolt."
YouTube. Viewed on 08/27/2020.

Our coordinating group started to take shape. On Facebook, we created a dedicated account. We all had fake names; I had four different ones, including girls' names. We always communicated in writing, never orally. Sometimes we Skyped, but only with people we knew personally or who were recommended by someone we trusted. We divided up the tasks. One group was to give the time and place for demonstrations, and to send out a map taken off Google Earth that indicated in green the safest route and in red the likely positions of the security forces. In our neighborhood, we knew who was cooperating with the regime. We didn't have our own intelligence service, but over time we developed a network of informers—the local grocer, for example. There was also a group of four or five people who made signs and banners. When we'd get home from work at around 6 p.m. on Thursdays, we'd go to Abu Georges's office to come up with slogans. Organizing a demonstration in a neighborhood was a huge responsibility because we were getting more and more participants; we had to ensure their safety. At first, the security forces used rubber bullets when they shot at us. They didn't kill, but there were always other kinds of casualties. We set up a medical care station. For the first two or three months of mobilization in Damascus, the security forces resorted to violence less often than out in the provinces— even in detention. After a while, though, they were no longer restrained and shot with live ammunition.

— *How was the picture taking organized?*

H.: In central Damascus, there were only flash demonstrations because of the massive security force presence. Each lasted only a few minutes, and you could just film with your cell phone. To show that the demonstration did actually take place, we'd post the video online. We also started having demonstrations in the neighborhood almost every day. When I filmed, I thought, first of all, of my own safety [*picture-takers always wore balaclavas*] and that of the demonstrators: I filmed people from the back and told them not to turn around. But there were always those too curious to see whether they were being filmed. So, either I put my finger over the lens, or I blurred the faces before posting the video. I also tried to anticipate the movements of the demonstration leader. Even though the route had been determined in advance, there were always those who worked themselves into such a frenzy that they improvised. I also had to keep a steady hand and refrain from chanting slogans. It was frustrating because when I was filming I couldn't really participate in the demonstration. I had to focus on the picture, to the point where I didn't even hear what they were chanting. Once it was over and we could look at our videos, we were often disappointed: the image was jumpy, faces were recognizable. Blurring took too long, and we'd miss our deadline for sending daily updates to a television channel. We wanted our broadcast to be instantaneous. In addition, the regime claimed that we put fake dates on our signs to make people believe we were holding more demonstrations than we really were. That's why we wanted the demonstration videos to be broadcast live, which required a satellite connection and specific devices. All that was very expensive and we didn't have the means. We tried to get in touch with Al Jazeera, and especially the SMART organization,[6] which ended up giving us a BGAN (Broadband Global Area Network) and a laptop. We also got a video camera. That's how we were able to get a slot on Al Jazeera to broadcast our demonstrations live [*for about six months*] (Figure 2.2). Shortly afterward, we organized a ten-day camera training session with a photojournalist. This was in 2012, during Ramadan. We got together in someone's apartment after breaking the fast. This training was very basic, since those wanting to film had no previous experience at all. They trained on Smurf figurines on a table—they were the demonstrators—[*laughter*] for learning different camera angles.

2.2. Excerpt from the live broadcast of the demonstration on 06/05/2012 on Al Jazeera Live. Video posted to YouTube by FreeShamMidan on the same day, with 1,883 views by 08/27/2020.

Filming Differently

H.: After this training session, we set up a media bureau made up of six picture-takers. For security reasons, only they could film the demonstrations. Our role was to film the real-time action, but also to write up reports on the overall events in the coverage zone (deployment of security forces, acts of repression, arrests, martyrs, funerals, etc.). I was asked to be the local correspondent for Al Jazeera with a very attractive salary, provided I agreed to appear on camera. That was too risky in Damascus: I would have been immediately identified and my whole family would have been arrested. Television channels didn't take such considerations into account.

— How did your way of filming evolve over time?

H.: I realized that everyone was filming the same things in the same way. Live broadcasting involves a stationary camera that films the people, and often you can't understand the slogans. When the connection is too slow, the image breaks up. I wanted to come up with something new, to use several cameras to change the angle: one on the signs, one on the people chanting slogans, and another that would film the demonstrators from above, producing something more alive. We thought we were going to make videos like feature films. I cobbled together several booms out of extendable paint rollers, such that the camera could move among the demonstrators. One of the booms was three meters long. It was exhausting because the camera was heavy. In addition, you couldn't see what you were filming. I trained a lot. I filmed four demonstrations that way (Figure 2.3), but the other picture-takers weren't sold on the idea—it was too strange for them—so, in the end, we went back to a more classic style of filming, the one imposed by the TV channels. I gave in, but I didn't abandon the idea of filming my way. A project for a documentary film was taking root. I borrowed a small movie camera from a friend. One time, I was in charge of the live broadcast: with one hand, I held the camera that was cabled to the laptop connected to the BGAN, and with the other, my camera, with which I captured details: a woman who was throwing rice from her window, a man smoking on his balcony with his son, pointing things out to him in the demonstration. That day, my attention was drawn to a woman who was clearly showing her son how to demonstrate. I was so caught up in that scene that I forgot the Al Jazeera camera. Across from the rooftop of the building where I was filming, down below there was a hairdresser who was watching the demonstration on television—I don't know why, since the whole thing was happening right in front of him. He shouted: "Hey boss, your shoes look great on screen!" I felt ashamed; when people go out of their way to demonstrate, you can't act like that.

2.3. Demonstration on 06/22/2012, filmed with a makeshift boom. Hatem's personal archives.

We also invented new ways of filming in places where you couldn't normally bring a classic camera, such as anywhere the security forces were present. We got our hands on various models of spy cameras from SMART. We started with glasses: two buttons located on each of the stems allowed you to film or take photos. On us, they were too conspicuous, so we asked girls wearing hijabs to do it. The goal was to film the security forces in the street to detect how many there were and where they were positioned. We also used a spy camera in the form of a car key during the shopkeepers' strike [*they were protesting against repression*] when the security forces smashed the shops that were closed (Figure 2.4)—but it was hard to get a decent shot; we couldn't hold the camera still. The one we used most often was a "shirt button" camera, which was coupled with a ring. When you pass your hand in front of it, it takes a picture. If you pass it twice, it switches to video mode.

At first, we had trouble acting natural—a real camera would have been more discreet! [*He laughs and mimes how one of them would stick his chest out.*] One time, I put it on and started chatting to a member of the security force. But the image was too poor. Ultimately, our experience with those cameras wasn't very promising. We switched tactics for filming the security checkpoints, and we got better image quality. I used that little video camera I'd borrowed and I mounted it on a car dashboard inside a box of Kleenex with a hole for the lens. Before setting out, we recited the Fatiha [*the first sura of the Quran*] because it was really risky. We said goodbye to one another . . . It was a bit surreal. We used 16-gigabyte cards to shoot for longer. We had to document all the checkpoints in Damascus and its suburbs. The videos were not posted online: they were just for reconnaissance purposes. At first we went out in the morning, but we later varied the time of day to have different light. We played songs by Fairuz. We enjoyed shooting these videos and wanted to incorporate them into the film project (Figure 2.5).

2.5. Video filmed on 02/06/2012. Hatem's personal archive.

— *How did the idea to make a film occur to you?*

H.: One day, after a demonstration, a woman in a long coat and hijab came to see me. She thought I worked for Al Jazeera. She says to me: "Please, I'm asking you, my son was martyred four days ago. He loved Bashar al-Assad. I don't know why they killed him—he opened a window and was hit by a bullet to the head. Please, show him on Al Jazeera." I told her I didn't work for them, and that I could do nothing for her. She persisted. I ended up following her home and did an interview with her. She told me some unbelievable things. That was her only son; he was nineteen. Her husband was pro-regime, but she wasn't. She was in shock, bordering on madness. Their house was riddled with bullets. This is where the idea for a film on the revolution came from—one where we'd talk about how the movement began and its aims, in order to better understand the people it affected. I knew why I'd got involved in the revolution, but what about everyone else? With a friend, we started to search for people of all social classes who agreed to speak—from an illiterate mother to a judge. I learned how to shoot in silhouette to conceal faces. The film was to be entitled "Hirak" [*Movement*]. We did the shoot in 2012 but weren't able to finish because of hundreds of things on the side: the media bureau, humanitarian relief, medical aid. And then, the revolution was militarized. At first, I wanted to focus on the civilian movement, although for consistency's sake we also should have filmed those who took up arms—but we really didn't have time. For the editing job, I trained all by myself on Adobe Premiere, but it took too long. I contacted some professional editors. The problem is that they hadn't experienced what I had experienced; they weren't the ones who shot the footage. They wanted to work according to their own ideas, and we refused. Nor did I want people to be benefitting financially from these images. They are not for sale; they belong to the people I filmed. They were happy to express themselves, and they trusted me. Among those I interviewed, there are now three martyrs and six in detention. But I intend to make this film, no matter what. I want what those people said to be heard. Concurrently, we kept filming for television based on their criteria. It was either that or lose our satellite connection. But I did it against my better judgment. In addition, their attitude was changing [*he mentions the two main Arab satellite channels, Al Jazeera and al-Arabiya*]: there were a lot of massacres, but that didn't interest them. When we called them to let them know we were going to film and send them the videos, they would respond that the moment wasn't right. They were the ones who made the revolution work, they said. When the movement ran out of steam because of a hardening of repression and bombings, many revolutionaries took up arms. The media played a role here. They wouldn't do live broadcasts of demonstrations anymore, but they did want news of the armed struggle. When we told them we didn't have any, they looked elsewhere. They told us: "The revolution is over; it's turned into an armed conflict."

Detention, Military Service, Defection, and Departure

H.: The last major demonstration took place on 14 August 2012. I was arrested that same day. It was the 27th day of Ramadan—*Laylat al-Qadr*,[7] or "Night of destiny." There weren't the usual prayers and readings, since all the mosques of the neighborhood had been shut down by the security forces. We spread our prayer mats on the square, we demonstrated, we prayed, and then we demonstrated again. That day, I went straight home after shooting. As I always did, I hid my material and memory cards in a plastic container buried in the garden behind the house. At the checkpoint that I had to pass on my way home, I saw a guy who had said to me a few days earlier: "Are you the one who's filming? You didn't show up for your military service. You're wanted." I had a document that authorized a deferment because I was at university, but I'd stopped going to classes because I was too busy with the revolution, and I hadn't had time to renew my waiver. I was able to pass then by giving him some money. So, that night, I tried to circumvent the checkpoint. The men guarding the checkpoint saw me. I ran, but they caught up with me. They shoved me up against a wall, they filmed me with their cell phones. Apart from the fact that I hadn't shown up for military duty, they could file no charges against me because my name didn't appear anywhere (I was working under several aliases, and nobody had denounced me). I was swiftly transferred to a military tribunal. That day, a great number of convicts belonging to the Free Syrian Army* were transferred to the tribunal for terrorist cases. As luck would have it, my file was slipped in among theirs and we were all loaded into an armored vehicle that looked like a cage. There were 150 of us, piled in and chained together with the same cable. They beat us with batons. We were taken to the central military prison in Damascus. When I got there, there was an employee who was talking on the phone to his girlfriend. He switched on the camera, saying to her: "Look, they brought me another terrorist." I turned away. He started beating me with his shoe so that I would raise my head. Then he said: "Show your face, you animal!"

The torture started. Our cell measured three meters by two, and there were eight-five of us. You didn't have more than fifty centimeters of floor and there was excrement everywhere. I was always standing. We took turns sleeping, six by six in a corner. People were dying. I saw them . . . I saw someone, his name was Ibrahim—he was sixteen. He was accused of heading an FSA brigade, even though he had nothing to do with them. Bare-chested and his face bruised, he asked me to take his pants off. The blood had dried; you couldn't even see the fabric anymore. When I removed them, the skin came off, too. He was bleeding a lot. I looked for a doctor in the cell. There was one who had set up a clandestine clinic in Harasta, but there was little he could do. I banged on the cell door, which was forbidden, but I had arrived only three days earlier so I didn't know. I told them that someone inside was going to die. The door opened and I was hit. The guy said: "When he dies, put his corpse outside." After a week, I was called over the loudspeaker. For everyone else, that meant I was going to be released. I had to memorize lots of phone numbers to alert families that their loved ones were still alive and to let them know which prison. It was a huge responsibility. The walls of the prison were covered in writing. The detainees had inscribed their names and the place where they were transferred with the date, just to leave a trace. I had read all these words, and now I had to transmit the messages. I was afraid I wouldn't remember it all. I repeated over and over. But I wasn't released; I was transferred to another section. The others must have thought that I hadn't communicated the information to their families . . . Two weeks later, the ruling was made: I had to do my military service. Before that, I was transferred to the 'Adra prison, near Duma which was almost liberated. It was a civilian prison with more relaxed rules, and they didn't beat us. It was also very crowded. Half of the prisoners came from the FSA and the other half were activists. In our wing, there were 114 of us. All in all, I spent one month and ten days in prison. Next, I was transferred to the army. First to al-Qusayr* and very soon after to Damascus because I had been to university. There, I started officer training. They put me in a tracking unit. I wanted to defect immediately, but I figured that if I stayed a while, I could collect some intelligence. I acted all eager, showing that I fervently supported Bashar al-Assad. My experience as an actor came in handy. I did favors for high-ranking officers: got them cigarettes, repaired their game consoles, their TV sets. One day, I was sent out to change an electric socket in a building that no one was allowed to enter. It was reserved for Iranian experts in cutting-edge technology for tracing and bomb targeting. After some forty days, I started to prepare to go AWOL. I did everything I could to get sick and get myself hospitalized. I also made up a story about a fiancée that I was supposed to marry. I was very convincing and obtained a one-week furlough to go to the hospital. I had my civilian clothes underneath my uniform which I removed along the way.

Before my superiors realized I had gone AWOL, I left for a safe zone. I was supposed to get there through a tunnel, but it had been destroyed. I had no choice but to take a minibus [*moderately priced mass transit bus that makes stops on demand*], without my ID card. I was terrified. At the first checkpoint, the guy didn't notice that I had not given my ID to the driver. At the second, they made me get off. I showed them my furlough paper. They mistook me for a spy for the regime [*'aweyni*] on a mission into the liberated zone. At the third checkpoint, same thing. At the last one, I managed to pass under the protection of the Free Syrian Army. Around the same time, the security forces arrested my father and my brother; we never found out what the charges were.

I was afraid that my defection would make things worse for their detention. To protect my family, I decided to appear in a fake video to make believe that I had been forced to defect, and that later on, I had been executed. [*In this video, which Hatem kept in his archives, as he did the "making of version," he appears wearing a tank top, on his knees, kept at gunpoint by two masked men. On the wall in the background is the flag of the revolution. Off camera, a man announces the capture of one of "Assad's dogs." He shows the camera the furlough document. Hatem is ordered to state his identity. The man accuses him of participating in the al-Ghouta bombings and declares he will be judged. At the end of the video, he orders the two fighters to lead him away.*] [*This video was not posted online, in the end, because his fellow committee members didn't find it convincing enough.*] I also took photos of my fake death, on the banks of the Barada River. I put some sheep brains under my tee-shirt [*laughter*]. I lay down on the ground and they put branches and leaves over my body. [*Hatem kept all the shots. In some of the photos, spattered with sheep's blood and trying to look dead, he can't keep from laughing, nor can I.*]

When I joined the Free Syrian Army, I worked for two months in rescue and medical relief, in collaboration with a local coordinating committee. I didn't have my material anymore—no more video camera. They also wanted me to head a media branch, but I turned that down. Their camera people were filming gun battles and operations, but they weren't the ones who posted them online. For certain brigades, prior to an operation, for instance, the armed faction notified the person who sponsored them of the date and time. Next, that person was shown the video on a private YouTube channel to prove that the armed faction had done its job. In exchange, the sponsor sent money. The video was then posted to a public account. That's how it worked. All the FSA brigades also started putting their logo on the videos. Some filmed the same operation and showed it to several sponsors. This was detrimental to the revolution. Many also came to rely on outside sponsors [*coming from Saudi Arabia, Qatar, or Western countries*]. Damascene merchants or expatriate families who financed food relief also demanded videos of the purchases, storage, and distribution to prove that it really took place or to be able to claim the accomplishment. I didn't want any part of it; it wasn't ethical to display such distress. If I were a displaced person and someone came to film me, I'd spit in his face! The guys who worked with me shared my view. But one donor threatened to withdraw his financial backing. We were compelled to accept, although we filmed with spy cameras—we were too ashamed. And of course, these videos were not posted; we showed them only to the sponsor. As for me, I couldn't film. When the others brought back their videos, I watched them and cried. It really affected me, especially when some took salaries and skimmed off relief money. Even when the activists were perfectly honest, the whole thing made me sick. Nor did I want to take up arms. From the outset I was against that; I was a civilian activist.

My trek, organized in Syria with the help of an FSA faction, was especially long, in order to avoid the checkpoints and arrive at the Turkish border. I stayed in Istanbul for twenty days, then moved on to Izmir to take an inflatable motorboat with thirty other people. We nearly drowned. In Greece, I made it to Athens where I waited for a month and a half before being able to leave for Italy in the back of a truck transporting cotton. I was with another passenger, a Kurd who didn't speak any Arabic. The trafficker had told us that we'd be in there for an hour and a half: we spent forty . . . During this trip, I first filmed the slits that allowed us to breathe some air, and the very tight space around us. I was afraid. I figured that if I die, maybe someone will find this video and will learn who was here. And if I survived, it would be a souvenir of this experience. I gave my telephone to the other passenger so that he could film me. [*In this forty-second video, Hatem's words are inaudible, drowned out by the noise of the truck. I ask him what he said: "If I show you this video, it means I'm still alive. If you are fishing and you find this SIM card in the belly of a fish, perhaps you will be curious enough to watch its contents. That means I'm dead." At the end of the recording, he waves.*] In Syria, I wasn't afraid to die as a martyr, it's an honor for us, as Muslims. Martyrs go to paradise, to join the Prophet and his companions. Funerals during the revolution were like weddings. You weren't supposed to cry. When friends fell as martyrs, I looked at their faces. They were all smiling. Once, I, too, tried to be a martyr. I don't know whether I kept that photo. They brought a flag of the revolution and wrapped me in a white sheet. It was Abu Georges who took the photo. The first shots weren't great! And if you looked at my face, you could see I wasn't on my way to paradise [*laughter*]. We worked on the lighting and managed to get a great shot. He said: "What do you want to do with this?" And I answered: "Maybe put it on my Facebook profile, or if something happens to me, someone in the group will post it online." I'd lost my mind a little, and I wanted to see what I would look like as a martyr. I wondered: Who would come to my funeral? How many would be there? Who would carry my body to its resting place? Would the security services intervene? Would I be on Al Jazeera? [*Laughter.*] I was thinking of all those details. [*Silence.*] I would have liked to die as a martyr. Not as an escapee, but . . . We have to go back to Syria to honor the blood of our friends who are gone. [*His eyes fill with tears.*] May God keep them close.

NOTES

1. This interview, drawn from rushes (a little over 19 hours' worth), was shot between May 24th and June 1st, 2014 in a small town in Sweden, at Hatem's. At the time, I was working on a film project that never came to fruition. We were friends, having met in Damascus in 2008. Throughout this shoot, Hatem wanted to appear with his face uncovered. For this interview, he wanted to keep his first name but not mention his family name.

2. Moustafa Khalifé gives a largely autobiographical account of the prison experience of a young graduate in cinema studies who finds himself imprisoned in Palmyra. It was first published in 2007 by Actes Sud, then in Arabic in 2008 by Dar al-Adab in Beirut.

3. At the start of the revolution, before it was shut down, this mosque was one of the central locations where demonstrations in Kafr Sousa always started. On 27 August 2011, after a sit-in demanding the release of prisoners, it was violently attacked by security forces.

4. The act of shouting "God is great" [Allahu akbar] in defiance of the regime's worldly and ephemeral authority.

5. Cf. https://www.youtube.com/channel/UCdqy0MJox2GUa_9R_ILNbGQ. Between 2014 and 2016, only five videos were posted online. The channel was especially active between 2011 and 2013. The Facebook link indicated on the home page no longer exists.

6. See Chapter 3: "Free Syrian Media: The experience of Syrian Media Action Revolution Team."

7. On this night, the Quran is revealed to the Prophet Muhammad by the angel Gabriel in the cave of Hira.

3

FREE SYRIAN MEDIA

THE EXPERIENCE OF SYRIAN MEDIA ACTION REVOLUTION TEAM

Chamsy Sarkis

The SMART collective (Syrian Media Action Revolution Team), of which I was one of the founders, has been among the chief actors in Syria's media landscape since 2011. Created in Paris in March 2011 by a handful of Syrians living in France, back then it included young doctors, engineers, pharmacists, and attorneys between the ages of twenty-five and thirty. At the time, I was the eldest of the group (thirty-eight years old) and a biotech researcher at the CNRS, on leave to create a start-up specialized in vectorology and genetic engineering. A chance encounter at a demonstration for the Arab Spring in Paris brought together the future members of our collective, and we decided to form a support group for the Syrian revolution. I was the only one to have never lived in Syria. Son of dissidents who fled Syria as soon as Hafez al-Assad came to power in 1971, I was born in Lebanon and arrived in France at the age of five, without ever having the right to go to my country of origin. Educated in France, I am also steeped in the stories of my parents and their friends, all dissidents who testified to torture, political repression, corruption, and especially the 1982 massacre at Hama—a historic tragedy that has marked all Syrians of my generation. In fact, this is the point that united us in the group we had just formed: to prevent another blacked-out massacre from happening by bringing the country's repression to worldwide attention. Didn't Hosni Mubarak's political repression fail thanks to Al Jazeera's live, continuous broadcasts of the Tahrir Square demonstrations in Cairo in January 2011? Thus, naively, with no strategy and little forethought, our group believed we knew what to do: send out pictorial coverage of Syria and support the peaceful activists demonstrating in the public squares of Syrian cities.

First Steps: Networking and Media Connections

So, my nine acolytes set about getting in touch with the demonstrators, first through their friends and family on the ground. They quickly broadened this first contact to include activists, demonstration organizers, and members of little groups that coordinated the events. In a few weeks' time, several hundred contacts were sending us news or videos generally shot on cell phones. In summer 2011, our network included around 2,000 activists on the ground.

Organization of communications took place thanks to forums, Facebook groups, and especially Skype.[1] In this way, we created dozens of local or theme-based groups. Some were devoted to the news of one region, one town, or even one neighborhood; others to surveying and documenting the dead and wounded; and others to military intelligence. Most of these groups are closed, to ensure the safety of their participants. We relayed to the international media what we received from them: mainly videos of demonstrations and, more rarely, of repression. We also got videos of the first demonstrators killed and the funeral processions that followed. It was a period packed with events. We felt it was imperative that every demonstration, every casualty, every arrest, and every death be accounted for. We were all working on a volunteer basis. In Syria, the activists organized into Local Coordinating Committees*, media centers, documentation groups, and "logistics" groups tasked with getting cameras, satellite modems, and medications out to the other activists. Every Friday—the main demonstrating day—we would receive up to 6,000 videos. In one year, 700,000 videos were featured on the ShaamNetwork's YouTube channel alone![2]

Concurrently, political opposition inside and outside Syria was getting organized. Meetings were held in Egypt, Turkey, and Paris. The fact that we're based in Paris means we can be in contact with several of the main Syrian opposition figures in exile. In fact, they would often meet at my parents' house. We were able to channel information to them from the field, or fault them when we felt they were too slow to react. But our Paris group shrank quickly: with the massive repression and the first sieges of towns and villages by the army, within three months' time half our members had joined associations devoted to medical or humanitarian relief. Still, our network on the ground continued to strengthen. Many other collectives were also active, such as the Local Coordinating Committees, the ShaamNetwork, the Ugarit network, and many others. SMART quickly became an important conveyor for other media companies: France 24, Al Jazeera, the BBC, and al Arabiya, to mention but a few. One of our first actions was to send money to Syria for the local purchase of film equipment or "handy-cams"—handheld digital video cameras. We also had to secure the means of relaying images and information. By March 2011, the regime was quick to cut off communication in zones where it was carrying out repression operations. So, we bought satellite modems and delivered them to Syria. Our budget came from donations by members of the Syrian diaspora in Europe, the U.S., and the Gulf countries.

From the early months of the uprising, we faced the first set of obstacles. Many activists were arrested. The regime was using advanced means of eavesdropping and surveillance, and its many intelligence services were very active. When an activist was arrested, he was tortured until he gave the names of his fellow activists, who were in turn arrested. After talking with my father, a seasoned dissident, we understood that we had to interrupt the chain of activists so that they could communicate with each other indirectly and without knowing one another. We became a "network node": we played the role of intermediary between activists who had to interact—for example, to organize a demonstration or pass along a satellite modem, sometimes on muleback! Additionally, whenever we were able, we distributed VPN[3] accounts to activists, making communication tracing more difficult. One of our main activities consisted of installing independent means of communication, since the regime cuts and monitors the Internet and 3G. We weren't very tech savvy at first, but we did some research to find out which modems were the most high performing. We purchased BGAN[4] mobile satellite modems and satellite phones. This job required constant monitoring, as the regime could decrypt communications from Thuraya satellite phones, and so we purchased Inmarsat phones—more expensive but more secure. Between August and December 2011, we installed around 100 VSAT satellite modems (Very Small Aperture Terminal), which, unlike BGAN modems, aren't mobile; all you need is a dish antenna on the roof and a box at home, as you would for television reception. It's a major alternative in that the bandwidth is far less expensive than for BGANs. We chose the brand Astraconnect for our VSATs: powered at only one watt, and indistinguishable from the background noise of most electronic devices, their signal is undetectable. So, in late 2012, our network installed 350 VSAT Astroconnect devices all over Syria, giving Internet access to thousands of activists on the ground (Figure 3.1). Every modem was used by a media center, an underground hospital, or a local coordinating committee. For a little over a year, from summer 2011 to October 2012, we merged with the ShaamNetwork. We also attempted to bring together all the Syrian media networks under a single entity, Syrian Media Center (SMC), but that proved impossible because certain networks lacked the will—and especially the human resources—to implement such an operation.

3.1. Servicing of a VSAT in the countryside of Idlib, 2013. Credit: SMART NEWS AGENCY.

Another challenge was the issue of credibility. The regime would deny the information we circulated; when the mainstream media broadcasted images taken by citizens, they would always mention that these could not be verified. Our first quick response to this was to train the activists to authenticate their images by always filming in a recognizable place (a square, a government building . . .) and to mention the date of the event. Later, starting in winter 2011, we used Skype to train 400 activists in basic journalism, with three classes a week for almost a year. The instructor, Ghassan Ibrahim, is a professional Syrian journalist working for several Arab news channels. He first taught them the basics of journalism, then how to be a news commentator on filmed interviews. This is how hundreds of activists became commentators for Arab news channels.[5] But the regime still denied the scope of the revolt and repression, and the international media were reluctant to relay news coming from activists. We had to come up with a way to lend credit to our images, and so we decided to seek solutions that would enable us to broadcast our images live, in response to the doubts about their authenticity. In late April 2011, we broadcasted our first seconds of live TV from the town of Qamishli, in the province of al-Hasaka in northwest Syria. It was a real victory! In order to accomplish this, we used Bambuser, a new livestreaming app for smartphones.

In summer 2011, we did live broadcasts of demonstrations for about fifteen days in a row from the city of Latakia—a bastion of the regime—in the Palestinian camp of al-Ramil. The security forces threatened the organizers so that they would stop the live broadcasting. But they decided to move forward. In mid-August, the regime sent in the army and took back control, arresting a number of activists and compelling some to make false statements on Syrian television. Still, the live broadcasts resumed in Homs, and in Hama, Daraa, al-Rastan, and everywhere else in Syria. Alongside the local coordinating groups, we made sure to organize demonstrations during broadcast times. We would get on average five to ten minutes live for each demonstration, whose schedule was set that morning. Al Jazeera Mubasher (Al Jazeera's live channel) would broadcast most of these live telecasts; this guaranteed protection for the demonstrators for several months. We also posted online a tutorial video explaining the broadcast protocol (Figure 3.2). During this period, the activists of the Baba 'Amr neighborhood of Homs were particularly determined, and we supported them by supplying a BGAN modem whose communications cost up to 1,000 euros per day. The intensive communication coming in from Homs made it the capital of the Syrian revolution everywhere in the world.[6] Later, when repression in Baba 'Amr made organizing demonstrations impossible, the activists decided to film and broadcast live their "revolutionary soirées."

3.2. "SMART Live Streaming." Video posted online by Syrianmediateam on 01/31/2012. https://www.youtube.com/watch?v=y-DT3gDxN-8w&feature=youtu.be. [This video is no longer available].

Disenchantment: Intensified Repression and Militarization

The live broadcasts proved a massive success. The regime's spokesmen were ridiculed on Arab TV channels. When one of them, Talib Ibrahim, questioned the authenticity of the live broadcasts during a debate on Al Jazeera, protesters responded live on the same set with written messages held up in front of cameras.[7] The regime was losing the war of images. At the same time, soldiers in the Syrian army were defecting. The international community recognized the opposition and its Syrian National Council*. At that point, we thought victory was at hand. However, this was far from the case. The regime turned the situation around: repression was not curbed, but rather stepped up. The regime even facilitated the circulation of videos depicting torture and atrocities carried out by soldiers, militiamen, and officers,[8] some of whom would sell them back to the activists for several hundred dollars. The regime was also inciting the militarization of the conflict: army officers were selling weaponry—but very little ordnance—to their opponents. At the same time, thousands of defecting soldiers were starting to organize: first to protect the demonstrators, especially in Homs, and then to attack checkpoints and help other soldiers defect. The regime was committing more and more massacres of civilians, as in Darayya, Homs, and Daraa. For the first time, a bombing raid took place while demonstrations were being filmed live. On the night of February 3rd, 2012, we broadcasted live the images of the bodies of thirty-eight people killed in a massacre in Homs, in the Khalidiya neighborhood. The images were picked up by TV channels all over the world (Figure 3.3). But the next day, Russia and China vetoed a UN resolution to condemn the regime.

This was a major turning point: not only were images no longer protecting the demonstrators, but they allowed the regime to test the limits of the international community and raise the threshold of the so-called "red line" of its impunity. In spring 2012, one year after the start of the revolution, we came to the bitter conclusion that we were losing the information war. It even looked as if we were "helping" the regime via our images of the massacres.

Whereas a year earlier every death was identified and honored as a martyr, and every funeral procession became an occasion to demonstrate against the regime, the deaths were now mere numbers, totaling dozens every day; mass graves were becoming commonplace; and armed insurrection was prevailing over civil activism. For a few months we pursued our live broadcasts, but the more we covered repression and massacres, the harsher the regime cracked down on them. During the weeks leading up to the implementation of the "Kofi Annan Peace Plan"[9] in April 2012, the death toll was still on the rise. The regime was able to boost the level of tacit acceptance of its impunity even higher. It's my sense that by continuing to cover the massacres it was committing, we were allowing it to arrogantly defy a hamstrung international community. Even though we had taken the first round, by winning people's hearts, the regime took the second, through cynicism and realpolitik. We had to change strategies.

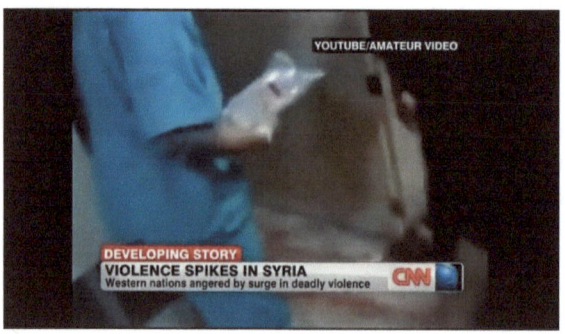

3.3. "Violence Spikes in Syria – 04/02/2012." Video downloaded and posted online by Jayeymedia-design on 02/04/2012. https://www.youtube.com/watch?v=x6pecGOYcE8.

It was around this time that I started investing more in the oversight of SMART. Earlier, my role was confined mostly to administrative and financial matters. In the second semester of 2012, I started up The Association of Support for Free Media,[10] which I registered in Paris in late 2011 with a strategic vision to develop media in Syria for Syrians, while supporting the civilian revolution and the army's rebellion against the regime. The goal was to sustain the freedom of expression that had emerged with the revolution. Myself and several colleagues developed a plan to create a sustainable media landscape with democratic pluralism in mind. Toward this end, we set up projects aimed at developing free media in Syria: print journalism, audiovisual press, and radio. In spring 2013 we created the first FM antennae in Damascus and Hama, then in Aleppo and Raqqa, and finally in Deir al-Zur. It was an uphill climb: they had to be located close enough to the fronts to target both camps so that soldiers in the Syrian army, whom we knew were cut off from the world, could hear the news on their walkie-talkies which could pick up an FM signal.

We called our FM band "Hawa Smart," and in 2014 we created a radio station with the same name. During this same period, we set up a printing shop out in the Idlib countryside, capable of printing 6,000 monthly magazines of twelve to fourteen pages, and we put together a distribution network to deliver the magazines to hundreds of outlets (pharmacies, grocery stores, local councils, local NGO headquarters . . .) in the provinces of Idlib, Hama, Aleppo, Raqqa, Deir al-Zur, Latakia (zones outside the regime's control), the Damascus suburbs (Ghouta), and north of Homs. We also brought together a team to oversee which content went where: for instance, when it was impossible to distribute magazines containing articles critical of the Islamic State in Raqqa or in Idlib, we would distribute them mostly to Hama and Aleppo.

We also supported—financially and technically—a dozen small local media activist groups (print journalism and radio). We didn't intervene in their editorial policy, but we signed an agreement on basic principles: diversity, independence regarding political parties or armed groups, and no hate speech or incitement to sectarianism. This is how we became the first Syrian media development agency. Our reference was the Reuters news agency, whose feature to have its working process made public we adapted to our particular situation. By January 2013, we were also training thirty-five war correspondents and supplying them with equipment, with a view to creating our own news service. Together we started doing our own video coverage, which we would then relay free of charge to a dozen Arab and Syrian TV channels[11] and post to our own YouTube page.[12] In the first three months, we produced on average ten reports per month. Six months later, we were producing between forty and sixty, reaching an audience of several million Syrians in Syria and tens of millions of Arabs all around the world. In August 2013 we launched our news service, Smart News Agency, composed of around six copywriters and thirty-five war correspondents. Within a few weeks we became a major information source in Syria and, especially, a source free of charge for the independent media projects we were supporting. We also developed partnerships with a dozen media centers in Syria, such as those in Aleppo, Hama, and Daraa, to both increase our source base and financially support these structures by paying around $500–$1,000 a month to each of them for their services.

It was in May 2015 that we added to our website a section devoted to videos and photos.[13] One of the problems with platforms like YouTube is that once videos are posted, they become YouTube's property. Furthermore, the metadata is lost when videos are downloaded to other accounts—data that is important for demonstrating their authenticity. For this reason, we save copies on our own servers. As a new agency, this is why we abandoned our work as mere aggregator and hub; we wanted to work with the activists that we knew and had trained. Here, again, the issue of credibility was crucial. We were able to verify and track images thanks to, for example, the serial number of the camera, which shows up on the video file. We banned compressed files—compression modifies the metadata and therefore the traceability—and none of our images were in any way modified, which made our photos less beautiful than those from other news agencies. We made this choice, though, because we were neither Reuters, nor Agence France Presse, nor Associated Press: we didn't have the same credibility at the outset. We also experimented with technologies to have a greater impact on hearts and minds by creating immersive reporting filmed in 360° on the first Russian bombings of Aleppo,[14] or on the destruction of the town of Jisr al-Shughur (Figure 3.4).[15] The "spectator," at the center of the image, can take the time to see what is happening all around, to discover things, unlike videos which move along too quickly. We also covered scenes of daily life: fishermen, markets, cherry picking . . . to show that life did continue despite the war. This aspect interested neither the legal authorities nor the journalists, but for us, as Syrians, it was important.

3.4. "The Battle for Northern Syria–360° Virtual Reality Report," 09/15/2015.

International Backing and its Unintended Consequences: The Political Neutralizing of Media Activism

In 2013, the countries that self-proclaimed as "friends of Syria"[16] took an interest in Syrian media. Prior to this, since 2012, only American and British secret services had arranged media training for around 3,000 Syrian activists in Turkey—a pretense for cultivating possible informers. They also handed out equipment (satellite modems and phones, and semi-professional video cameras), some of which was sold on to armed groups, with the result that this "non-lethal" aid was in fact falling into the hands of what amounted to Islamist groups. As for European foreign ministries, recent arrivals to the issue of aid to Syrian civil society, they mandated media development agencies such as International Media Support, Free Press Unlimited, Canal France International (the French Foreign Ministry media development agency), Irex, and Internews, which all supported independent media by imposing their notion of journalism. For example, the term "martyr" was prohibited. Likewise, from their standpoint, it wasn't conceivable that someone could be both an activist and a journalist: they demanded "neutral and impartial" editorial policies, disregarding media activism's *raison d'être*, born of the revolution with the express objective of working to bring down the regime. Further, not considering security constraints caused by the rise of Islamist groups such as Ahrar al-Sham* and the Nusra Front*, they would not accept that local media were able to work thanks to the support of factions of the Free Syrian Army* (FSA) that provided protection and logistical help. Finally, international aid in Syria, including support to media and civil society, was based on the notion of "resilience," as opposed to that of resistance. In order to qualify for the backing of these agencies, you had to renounce resistance and accept being a passive actor whose sole objective was survival. It was also deemed appropriate to please the funders by dealing with such taboo subjects as homosexuality and caricatures of the Prophet Muhammad.

Within a year, the action of these media development agencies had completely undermined media activism in Syria, turning it into a series of "potboiler" projects. Syrians even have a term for these: *dikakin*, which translates to "shops" or "grocers." SMART had come into conflict with these agencies, refusing to comply with their directives. One day, an official from one of them said to me: "How can you be a media development agency in Syria when you're Syrian? It's dangerous and it's a conflict of interest!" So, I retorted: "What seems dangerous to me is when a development agency directly under a foreign chancellery is working in Syria. It's dangerous, and it's a conflict of interest!" None of these agencies would back us, apart from Canal France International in 2018 for a training project for our editorial teams. In order to raise their profile in the Syrian media landscape, these outside agencies began distributing financial aid. As it turned out, the overwhelming majority of the media projects they backed were the same ones we were supporting. But unlike the financial aid that we apportioned, theirs was earmarked for specific items: equipment, office rental in Turkey, and salaries. For the first time, activists were earning substantial salaries in dollars.[17] Although we hadn't ever paid out salaries until then, by March 2013 it had become standard practice. But the considerable sums of money in circulation, against the backdrop of war, abetted corruption. Fake projects emerged. Furthermore, it was the agencies themselves that took most of the funds earmarked for the media, spending it on operating expenses or monitoring and evaluation: an average of 50 to 70 percent of the allocations.[18] It would appear that this system of international aid is first and foremost designed to be able to announce that massive aid is being granted to a cause, while at the same time allowing these funds to be funneled back into the agencies' own development, preventing projects from thriving independently or sustainably. When certain directors of such agencies would ask me how they might better help us, I would reply pragmatically: "Stop aiding us, pull out of Syrian projects altogether, and let us get on with our work."

While they might have been useful in 2011 and 2012, these media development agencies didn't arrive on the scene until militarization, once the regime could claim it was waging war against Islamist terrorists—enemies that it created itself by releasing jihadists from its own jails—with the participation, active or passive, of the international community that had failed to support and protect the civilian population that was slaughtered. In less than two years, this foreign aid had dismantled the activist networks by introducing a pernicious competitiveness among people who used to work together, and by "de-patriotizing" the militants, turning them into mercenaries or agents of donors from the West or the Gulf. Ultimately, they indirectly contributed to strengthening the regime. Today, our collective has changed radically. We have moved from field-based activism—what I call hard-core activism—to a more society-oriented activism. Our media projects have gone professional, and now aim not only at bringing down the regime, but also at providing information to those most in need, just to help them survive. It's also a matter of preserving the memory of this period of Syrian history, in real time as it is unfolding. In 2017, SMART, along with other activist YouTube channels, was erased by Google's software that deletes violent images.[19] Backup storage is critical. This task is important for both transitional justice and for the social reconstruction of the country. Within the scope of our news agency we have developed our own system of archiving the media content we have produced, which amounts to around 450,000 videos, 150,000 photographs and 50,000 articles. Thus, every article, photograph, and video is saved with its metadata, and annotated thanks to a thesaurus specifically designed for our needs. Part of this structured archive has been entrusted to the International, Impartial and Independent Mechanism (IIIM),[20] a UN mechanism created in 2016 with the purpose of supporting investigations and legal proceedings for crimes committed in Syria since March 2011. We are also studying the possibility of preserving all this archived material with a French institution, thereby making it available to researchers. The activism of SMART and the thousands of other Syrian activists, whether high profile or anonymous, could provide a model for other protest situations elsewhere in the world. Likewise, in the coming war waged by states deploying unbridled surveillance of their citizenry, Syrian activists will undoubtedly be at the forefront of civil resistance.

NOTES

1. After four years of using Skype, we opted for Viber, WhatsApp, and then Signal and Telegram, which are more secure.
2. The YouTube channel that has collected the greatest number of videos since its creation on 26 February 2011. Still active, it had recorded 220,315,485 views by 11 June 2024. Cf. https://www.youtube.com/c/SHAMSNN/ featured.
3. A VPN (Virtual Private Network) is a system that allows for the creation of a direct link between remote computers, isolating their exchanges from the rest of Internet traffic taking place on public communication networks. Notably, it makes it possible to modify the IP address, making it hard for security services to identify the connection.
4. BGANs (Broadband Global Area Network) are satellite modems that allow an access point to mobile Internet, while also serving as a satellite phone terminal. They operate on the satellite communication network Inmarsat.
5. An activist broadcasts live on a news channel: https://youtu.be/jBr-mVXnauo. "Activist Omar al-Telawy reports on the situation in Baba 'Amr" [in Arabic]. SOS Homs. Archived and posted to YouTube on 18 February 2012. Every day, SMART would coordinate an average of twenty televised reports with Arab news channels.
6. An example of a live broadcast relayed by SMART, and picked up by Al Jazeera Mubasher, is archived on the YouTube account of Jaber 'Athrat al-Karam, posted on 21 October 2011 (this account has been suppressed in 2024).
7. "Talib Ibrahim and the Syrian Regime." Video posted online by Al Jazeera Mubasher on 29 September 2011. https://www.youtube.com/watch?v=COdYPSe11kA.
8. See Chapter 13: "Terrorizing and Killing with Images: Amateur Videos by Syrian Army soldiers and Execution Rituals of the Islamic State Organization."
9. Backed by the UN Security Council, this plan was presented in March 2012 and provided, notably, for a halt to combat and "an open political process led by the Syrians."
10. ASFM is a non-profit association (Law 1901) whose purpose is to develop Syrian media and to promote freedom of expression in Syria.
11. Al-Jazeera Direct, Suria Al Ghad, Orient News, Al Mustaqbal, Al Aan, Deralzor, Syria al Shaab, Shadha Alhuriya, Al Arabiya.
12. Active between 11 June 2013 and July 2020, it has recorded over 64,000 subscribers and 9,200,794 views by 11 June 2024. Cf. https://www.youtube.com/c/Smartnews-agency/videos.

13. https://smartnews-agency.com/en. [This site is no longer accessible].
14. "Nobel's Nightmare. An immersive experience with the Syrian White Helmets in Aleppo." SMART News Agency, 15 June 2016. This report won a prize in the "Virtual Reality" category at the New Media Film Festival in 2016.
15. "The Battle for Northern Syria – 360° Virtual Reality Report," posted to YouTube on 15 September 2015, https://www.youtube.com/watch?v=aTTzKwLPqFw, 598,206 views as of 15 July 2020.
16. Established after a meeting in Tunisia on 24 February 2012, this group is comprised of regional and international organizations as well as some sixty countries, including the United States, the UK, France, and Germany. In the communiqué issued after their first meeting, they called upon the Syrian government to "immediately cease all forms of violence" and to "allow free and unimpeded access to humanitarian agencies." The group committed to "take measures to apply and strengthen sanctions on the regime." Cf. Mardam Bey F., "Qui sont vraiment les 'Amis de la Syrie,'" Blog in *Libération*, (2016).
17. Hallin, "Images de guerre" (1994), 121–32; and Fleury-Villate, *Les Médias et la guerre du Golfe* (1992).
18. The salaries of those working with NGOs and international agencies can reach $7,000 a month for a project lead. One project with American backing, for instance, paid $3,000 per month to field reporters—ten to thirty times the salary of a bank employee or a high school teacher.
19. For SMART and ASFM, our operating costs and monitoring and evaluation expenditures came to about 4 percent, the remainder being devoted to structure projects or media support. We organized training sessions for an overall cost of €1,500–€2,000, whereas agencies would spend from €25,000–€50,000 for identical training.
20. Cf. Omari Mansour, "YouTube's Artificial 'Intelligence' Obstructs Syria's Justice," Justicehub.org. I tried, myself, to contact YouTube administrators, unsuccessfully. It was Eliot Higgins, founder of the investigation site Bellingcat, who managed to convince them to put the videos back online.
21. https://iiim.un.org.

4

REVOLT WITH AND THROUGH IMAGES

FROM RAW RECORDING TO EMBODYING COMMUNITY

Cécile Boëx

Documenting the demonstrations was the initial step in counteracting the official propaganda that sought to downplay the scope of the revolt and cover up the repression. Nevertheless, between 2011 and 2013 demonstrators also filmed to defy the regime and take to the street, whether collectively or on a smaller scale, with their covert and creative actions. In the span of minutes, in broad daylight or under cover of night, it was all about staking out their territory with their bodies, words, and symbols. This physical reclaiming of public space was also visual and sonic: the image and its posting online publicizes and perpetuates the performance, enabling its conservation, however fragile and illegible that trace may be. Video was thus an active partner in the excitement of protest that invented a unique culture of defiance full of theatrics and humor, despite the violence. This creativity was all the richer for deriving from local culture and talent (song, poetry, dance, and signage) and for the Internet enabling the spread of certain skills. This creativity would fluctuate depending on the degree of repression, which was more intense in the larger cities. Meanwhile, video opened up new protest scenes in more secure private spaces. Spoken word predominated, most notably to solemnly declare the break with the regime and its institutions, whether military or civilian. Defection in this manner, often with faces uncovered, amounted to staking one's life as testimony to a commitment to the revolt and as condemnation of the repression. This chapter explores the different ways video accompanied the revolt and people's commitment to it by documenting protest actions and lending substance and shape to collectives, whether in the street or in private settings. It retraces the stages and contexts of how the video camera was used, which in turn helped shape the protest performance and innovative speech. This analysis will address first of all the spontaneous recording of the first demonstrations, concluding with training videos of fighting brigades. It will also shed light on this slip toward armed struggle that would eventually supplant the protest actions and spaces, starting in 2013.

Filming in the Thick of Things: Body, Emotion, Opacity

At the first demonstrations in March 2011, most protesters were brandishing their cell phone cameras. These videos were shot in the heat of the moment, with no communication strategy. Filmed at ground level, the framing is shaky, the image is out of focus, and most often there are very few clues as to the spatial organization and timeline of the event. Posted to the Internet unedited, this raw footage is an extension of the act of demonstrating. Viewers get a very strong sense of being there, since they are propelled into the fray, but the images are unclear due to breaks in the visual field, erratic camera movement, and poor resolution.[1] Hence, they reveal a paradoxical tension between the intensity and authenticity of lived experience on the one hand, and on the other, the abstract form of their audiovisual translation.[2]

"3/25/2011: Hama Demonstration in support of the inhabitants of Daraa[3]" 1'18"

4.1. Hama demonstration, 03/25/2011.

Shot in the town of Hama only ten days after the first demonstration in Daraa, this video gives a particularly vivid account of spontaneous filming practices early in the revolt. Most notable is the sonic saturation: the cameraperson and the other demonstrators are shouting things like "freedom," "peaceful," "There is only one God," and "With our soul and with our blood, we sacrifice for you, O Daraa." The force behind these words and the intensity of the chanting transcribe the demonstrators' emotional state. After years of forced silence, taking to the street to shout these slogans out loud is an extraordinary event. These euphoric voices are also broken by fear, for just outside the frame the security forces are monitoring and taking note of the demonstrators—when they aren't firing on them with live ammunition. Hama is not just any city: in 1982, Hafez al-Assad crushed a protest movement by bombing the city for three days straight, with a death toll between

20,000 and 30,000. This massacre, committed with total impunity in the interest of the struggle against Islamism, took place in a complete news blackout.[4] When the people of Hama took to the streets to demonstrate in 2011, many thought that filming the event would curb the repressive reaction by exposing it to outside witnesses. But in this video recorded during the first Hama demonstration, the videographer is filming while demonstrating and eventually forgets that he is filming. In the end, the image is synchronized with the arm movement that accompanies the chanting of slogans. Here, the camera is clearly an extension of the body in action. Held at arm's length, the cell phone's angle of filming conveys an exhilaration directed more by movement than by sight.[5] The spontaneity of these videos shot by ordinary demonstrators thus stems from the corporeality of the shot involving minimal setup. In effect, it is the intensity of the lived event that constrains the space and movement inside the frame.

Although videos of this kind do get reused by international television channels, they cannot be reduced to "citizen journalism." Filming is an act of defiance that involves taking to the street to demand regime change. Video also enables a visual reclaiming that amplifies and extends the mere physical, time-constrained moment. In this context, filming is a highly transgressive act. Filming is also an event unto itself, as it testifies to this breakpoint where what was inconceivable moments before is suddenly happening. Of little information value, this film fragment gives but a patchy account of the event. Not much is visible: men marching in a somewhat erratic street demonstration (car horns can be heard). Some look back nervously. Buildings and palm trees are also visible. Without the caption (in Arabic), it would be hard to tell what is being filmed. The documentary value of this video lies elsewhere: precisely in its illegibility. The chaos of the images and sounds makes visible and immediately palpable the emotion of the image-taker and those around him. It documents this extreme experience of demonstrating in a repressive setting and produces a kinetic and embodied vision of the event, too radical to be represented coherently. This articulation between the body, camera, and action shifts the visual perception toward something more sensorial.[6] This video as a form of trespassing provides a living record of an intense moment, dissolving the border between the intentionality of the filming act—consistent with a commitment to testify—and the lack of control in such contingent circumstances. Here, the demonstrator is filming the event and in the end gets so swept away that he forgets that he is filming. The image resulting from such a tumultuous moment, at once embodied and mechanical, remains as a living imprint of that relation between historical event and the way it is personally experienced.

When All the Street's a Stage

In 2011, the spontaneity of the early videos quickly yielded to film techniques directed toward news and awareness-raising. With the passing months, demonstrations were also being organized on the basis of their being filmed, giving rise to more theatrical protests[7] deployed as performances (modes of occupying a space, individual speech acts, chanting, dancing, etc.) and as specific objects (banners, posters full of imagery, emblems, and portraits of martyrs killed during demonstrations). This quest for legibility brought about a gradual control of the shots: the act of filming was uncoupled from the act of demonstrating in order to capture the event in its spatial and temporal unity. As a result, the camera view grew increasingly autonomous as regards the protest action, becoming an activity in its own right. Things professionalized, giving way to "best practices." Many of these self-styled videographers would take care not to reveal the demonstrators' identity by filming them from the back or from a safe distance. If faces were to appear, they were often blurred out. This professionalization can also be explained by the demand for images from foreign media that have no on-the-ground access, but also by the gradual organization of demonstrations through the local coordinating committees* that cover logistics, documentation, and media coverage (Figure 4.2). Contextualization devices and staging of protest actions aimed to render the videos more legible and eye-catching. For instance, the cameramen set a placard in front of the lens to indicate the date and place, or to highlight a slogan. The demonstrators were also called upon to angle their signs or portraits of martyrs toward those who were filming from strategic locations. The protest space was circumscribed, framed by the camera but also by the banners on the walls of the surrounding buildings, as if to reclaim a portion of public space. The effort to capture the revolt in more professionalized images contributed to the general drive to prove the existence, energy, and peaceful nature of the demonstrations. Though this effort was quick to affirm itself, it did remain somewhat random depending on where the filming was happening, which in turn determined the availability of equipment and exchange of expertise.

4.2. Demonstration in al-Sanamayn*, 4 November 2011. A singer, a drummer, and people brandishing portraits of martyrs are standing on an improvised stage. A façade is entirely draped in a sign reading "LIAR" in large yellow lettering. On the leaflet presented by the photographer, a spoof of the TV show Who Wants to be a Millionaire, we read: "For Bashar al-Assad, choose one of the following: resignation, trial, death sentence, getaway." Signed "The revolutionaries of Sanamayn, 4 November, Friday, Allah is great."

Certain protest actions were staged entirely for filming purposes, such as the one at Binnish, in Idlib province, where several human tableaux were organized.[8] Making such performances happen implies tight coordination between demonstrators and camera operators who, from their elevated position, would zoom in and out at precise moments. One of these tableaux, posted online on 22 June 2012,[9] depicts a soccer match with players displaying the flag of the revolution and others wearing the Syrian flag, which had become the symbol of the Assads' power (Figure 4.3). The clapping and beating of a *tambal* drum kept rhythm with the chanting of slogans such as: "May your soul be cursed, Hafez [al-Assad]" and "Victory." Seven signs flank the upper side of the tableau, the way advertisements encircle a soccer pitch. One of them shows a TV screen with the caption: "Tune in to the Syrian Revolution." Others announce ironically: "1,000 deaths for one Russian ship," "Conscience for sale on the markets," and "NEW. Demonstration at 2,000 Syrian pounds per person." Two logos from the 2012 UEFA European Football Championship, which was taking place at the same time, also appear. These statements denounce the lack of interest at the international level, just as they make fun of the accusations of manipulation of the demonstrators by the regime. After a few instants, the tableau starts to move. The revolutionary team's ball scores against the opposing side. The participants, in joyful disarray, flip their giant cards to create a second tableau in black and white. Around a scale showing that UEFA Euro 2012 weighs heavier than the massacres committed in Syria (represented by a blood-stained map), we can read: "Shit/Woe to the world." Despite its light-hearted atmosphere, this tableau represents the political break that was at work in Syria and fiercely calls out the international community. This performance subverts two cultures: that of the soccer stadium (entertainment, saturated media coverage, and national unity) and that of the political and ceremonial displays to the glory of the leader, so valued by Hafez al-Assad in the 1980s and 1990s.[10]

4.3. Binnish tableau, 06/22/2012.

The use of video not only shaped protest events but also fostered more individualized actions, giving rise to some rather original staging. In the early days of the revolt, there was an almost euphoric reclaiming of the street. A special gleefulness was expressed through emotion, body language, and speech in unprecedented performances. Depending on the place, and determined by exposure to the danger of security force presence, playfulness and creativity were possible to varying degrees. These new protest practices in public space were met by the whole range of risk: they took place day and night, with faces both covered and uncovered. Video contributed especially to furtive, underground actions. Graffiti tagging, for instance, became a filmed performance, and the graffiti artist, "the man with the spray can" (*al-rajul al-baghagh*), an icon of the revolt.[11] These ad hoc actions also sought to disrupt urban space. In 2011, fountains in the capital were dyed red to denounce the repression.[12] Revolutionary slogans ("Out!" "Freedom," "Down with sectarianism," and "Pacifism") printed onto ping-pong balls tumbled down the sloping streets of the capital. This action, called "Freedom Balls," filmed and broadcasted, was subsequently repeated in different neighborhoods of Damascus, as well as in Aleppo and Latakia. Other performances involved more elaborate staging, with contributions by improvisational actors. In Hama in June 2012, for example, the locals staged a parody of parliamentary elections, broadly denounced as a farce.[13] At the start of the video,[14] the person filming announces the date and adds: "The Parliament does not represent us. Here is how we vote in Hama, freely and democratically." We then see a dozen people taking turns walking on a stenciled graffiti of the face of Bashar al-Assad, forming the words: "Trample here."

On 6 March 2012 the people of al-Rastan, near Homs, put out a call for help to the inhabitants of the planet Mars[15] to denounce the inertia of the international community and the travesty of the UN emissaries present during that period. The video starts with a panoramic view shot from above, showing a portion of street inscribed in large white letters, written in English and Arabic: "S.O.S. Call for help to Martians." The person filming mentions the date and indicates that the Martians have indeed landed in Rastan. A reporter provides live commentary on the event with, in place of a microphone, an enormous bone on which is written "Radio Shame-on-you." He notes that the Martians, who have come to help the inhabitants, "have no vocabulary for war or violence," and that due to "space barriers erected by the regime that understands only the language of death and destruction," they had to dig a tunnel to get to the people of Rastan. The reporter then explains that the Martians have come to bring plastic flowers to the city's families in mourning, and that they wish to give "one last chance to the regime by sending it, for example, before the tribunal of planetary psychoses to seek medical attention, and before the High Council of the Universe, that it might rule on the issue in order to send one day a space emissary to stop the violence." One of the Martians then gives a flower to the reporter, and in a solemn tone, says: "Sir, we are with you heart and soul." The reporter smells the flower and gives it back, looking jaded, and says that it has no fragrance (Figure 4.4). The humor of this scene should not overshadow how "radical" it is, given the context of extreme violence where it is taking place. During this period, the city was under siege and pounded daily by the Syrian army. The person playing the reporter, Walid 'Abid[16] (Abu Salah), in his late forties, led several demonstrations and worked for the Rastan media center where he did live broadcasts of a number of bombings.

4.4. The Martians of al-Rastan, 03/06/2012.

Breaking with Institutions, on Camera
Military Defections

On 30 April 2011, the first defection video was posted online on YouTube via different channels.[17] He was a soldier in the Republican Guard[18] who had defected the previous week. Walid 'Abd al-Karim al-Qasha'mi, somewhat hesitant, at medium shot distance, states his identity, his rank, and his unit number (Figure 4.5). When the person filming, whose voice we hear off-camera, asks him to provide proof of his status, he shows an ID card and his dog tag to the camera, which zooms in. At the request of a second person off-camera, the soldier tells how his unit (250 men) were mobilized on the grounds that armed gangs were attacking the citizens of the city of Harasta, near Damascus. Once on site, all they saw were peaceful demonstrators and members of the intelligence services firing on them with live ammunition. When they received orders to fire, he refused and, along with four fellow soldiers, fled to join the protesters. They were themselves fired upon, but they managed to escape with the help of the protesters. At the end of the video (he has trouble finding his words), he calls upon the military not to shed the blood of civilians. A man off-camera thanks him. The first defection videos in circulation between May and June 2011 served as testimony that countered official propaganda. Before long, they were codified as their numbers increased.[19] They harness words, objects, and acts to formalize the break with the military as an institution, to testify from within the apparatus of repression, and to call on other members of the military to come forward and dissent.

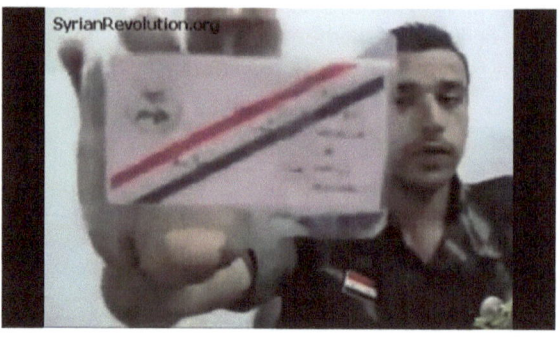

4.5. First defection video, 04/30/2011.

This codification is consistent with the gradual organized defense of demonstrators, then with the armed struggle, and the creation in June 2011 of the Free Officers Brigade [*Liwā' ad-dubbāt al-ahrār*] by Lieutenant Colonel Hussein Harmush, the first high-ranking officer to appear in a defection video.[20] Here, the tone is more martial: self-assured, even if he looks down occasionally at his text, he is speaking in classical Arabic and no one off-camera asks him any questions. For the first time, the Syrian flag appears in the background. In military fatigues, displaying his ID card to the camera, he condemns the regime's deadly repression against demonstrators and urges his fellow officers to join them and to use their weapons to protect them. In a communiqué posted online on 14 July 2011, he announced the formation of the Free Officers Movement with its own leadership structure. On 29 July, at the behest of Colonel Riyadh al-Asaad who had publicized his defection two weeks earlier, seven members of this movement, dressed in their military uniforms, announced the formation of the Free Syrian Army* (FSA) (*al-Jaysh al-Suri al-Hur*).[21] This video of a little over three minutes is shot non-professionally in a cramped space (Figure 4.6).

4.6. Announcing the formation of the Free Syrian Army, 07/29/2011.

As the FSA got more organized, announcements of defection came in quick succession in a codified format. They also involved members of security services. The ritual display before the camera of identity—either spoken or by showing a military ID card—marks the passage from one camp to another, or more precisely, from one way of being a fighter to another, inducing a moral break with the military institution. Generally filmed indoors by members of the media teams of the Local Coordinating Committees*, these videos start off with the presentation of the name and rank of the person defecting, always in military attire, sometimes with his weapon, who then declares his defection (*inshiqaq*) from the Syrian army, often referred to as the "Assad army," likening it to a militia subject to the interests of the clan in power. Each explains the kinds of things he has witnessed in his city or town and the reasons for his decision. The flag often appears in the background to make the declaration official.[22] Some videos open with a Quranic verse, as a way of calling on God as witness to attest to the veracity of the statement. Despite the revolutionary context, military hierarchy remains: each declares his rank. Likewise, the people filming never ask questions of the more highly ranked, while they do so with ordinary soldiers, thereby effecting a radical inversion of power relations between those filming and those filmed—also a part of the switching of camps.

4.7. "Defection of Colonel ʿAfif Sulaiman with a number of officers and soldiers," 02/21/2012.

With the passing months, defection announcements increased steadily and collectively.[23] Some gave way to the formation of fighter brigades made up of both military personnel and civilians. The register of these videos, in a more explicit warrior mode, involves other codes. It is more about exhibiting men and weaponry by displaying the effective organization of the armed struggle, but it is also about laying down the principles of this new entity and renewing the oath of allegiance to the revolution. These videos are shot both outdoors (in liberated zones) and indoors. Some are filmed in public, as with the video of soldiers defecting to join the ranks of the Shield of the North Brigade (*Dirʿ al-Shamal*) under the command of Colonel ʿAfif Sulaiman[24] at Idlib in February 2012 (figure 4.7).[25]

Suleiman speaks, citing a verse from the sura of "al-Imran" that calls for union.[26] This recourse to the Quranic lexicon[27] by factions of the FSA during the earlier declarations, though not systemic, is meaningful in several ways. Firstly, religious identity had to be included in a military institution where its expression had been previously prohibited in line with the nationalist Baathist ideology. This was despite the regime strategically striking a sectarian balance within the army in order to favor the Alawites, to the detriment of the Sunnis. Accordingly, many factions of the FSA distanced themselves from this supposedly secular culture within the Syrian army. Furthermore, it was about invoking divine justice to seal the commitment to the armed struggle and delegitimize the regime's authority. Finally, certain factions explicitly foreground Sunni references, often to ensure the support of sponsors from the Gulf States.[28] The thousands of brigade creation videos posted online between 2011 and 2017 (with the highest concentration of videos posted between 2011 and 2013) constitute an invaluable resource for understanding the diverse modalities of how to train an alternative military entity when the balance of power is so asymmetrical, and why such an entity becomes so fragmented and volatile in the midst of conflict.

Civilian Defections

Civilians soon took on the theatrics of defection. Between 2011 and 2013, judges, lawyers, senior civil servants, ulemas, members of the Baath Party and the Parliament, police officers, sports champions, journalists, schoolteachers, doctors, and senior managers of state-run companies announced, either individually or collectively, that they were resigning from their positions. These declarations marked an "official" break with different structures answerable to the regime that governed them, and those who stepped down then joined the ranks of the revolution (often referred to as "people of honor," or *al-shurafa'*). The political roots of the network of professional activities becomes indirectly apparent here: a particularly dense set of connections in Syria. Some announced that they were joining free alternative structures. For instance, journalists joined media groups siding with the revolution, while some athletes engaged in armed struggle alongside the FSA. Identities were revealed in the same manner, with professional ID cards or, for the athletes, their awards (Figure 4.8). They employ the same solemn tone as the military defectors as they articulate their reasons for breaking with their institutions and urge their colleagues to follow suit. Each explains, from their own viewpoint, the manipulations, violence, and abuses they witnessed. An example is a video posted on 31 August 2011, in which the public prosecutor of Hama province denounced the execution and mass burial of seventy-two demonstrators on 30 July. The demonstrators had been detained in the central prison of Hama and buried in a common grave near the village of Khalidiya.[29] He also denounces the increasing number of mass graves in public parks that are believed to contain over 420 corpses of those murdered by the security services and the regime's henchmen (*shabbiha**). He declares that he was compelled to draft a report affirming that these people had been killed by "armed gangs." Another resignation video showed a journalist, who was a member of the Presidency's own press service and director of several television channels, denouncing media machinations as well as secret meetings and transactions held with Iranian and Russian representatives and members of Hezbollah.[30]

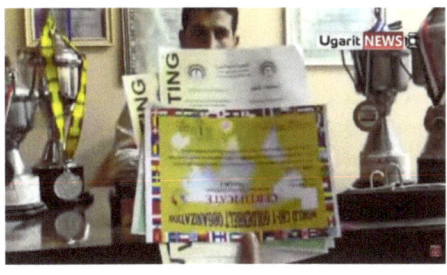

4.8. Defection of the coach of the national kickboxing team, 08/13/2012. "Ugarit. Importaaaaaaant. Defection of national Kickboxing coach and referee Ghazal Mohammad Hilal and his rallying to the Ghuraba' al-Sham." YouTube video posted by Ugarit News-Syria on 13 August 2012, with 750 views by 30 June 2020. https://wwww.youtube.com/watch?v=uWB9fV1XH_Y.

Students also had a hand in modifying the codes: they drew inspiration from these military defections to announce their own commitment to the revolt, denounce the surveillance and repression they were being subjected to, and declare their withdrawal from the Student Union (a Baathist organization). Their announcements (often including male and female students) took the form of communiqués that specified the reasons for their decision, their solidarity with their detained comrades, and the specific actions they were carrying out. These actions, including demonstrations, sit-ins at university, strikes, and relief to displaced families, were carried out under the auspices of Free Student Unions—alternative organizations that emerged in late 2011 in university towns like Damascus, Aleppo, Homs, Hama, Deir al-Zur, Raqqa, and Daraa. The students often appear masked with flags of the revolution, keffiyehs, or balaclavas. Despite this attempt at anonymity, they continue to symbolically brandish their student cards, though always from a distance, so that they remain illegible. Some crossed out their names with Sharpie permanent markers as a way of destroying these cards, while declaring their refusal to show up for classes and exams. In the same style as the at-home sit-ins,[31] hand-painted signs and flags appear, most often affixed to the walls in the background of the videos. In one video posted on 3 March 2012,[32] students in Daraa announce their defection from the Student Union and the creation of a Daraa branch of the Free Student Union (Figure 4.9). Seated at a computer, in the manner of a spokesperson announcing the formation of fighter brigades, a young, masked man denounces "the transformation of the National Student Union into a branch of the intelligence services, and its members into thugs of the regime." He asserts his refusal to be enlisted into repression. He then enumerates the organization's goals: Pursue peaceful mobilization within the framework of the student movement, post updates of the regime's manipulations, and support actions to bring it down. He calls for a halt to the repression, especially toward the (particularly active) students at the University of Aleppo. He also declares their intention to ferret out and neutralize the colleagues who are terrorizing other students. He emphasizes that their organization is not affiliated to any party or political alliance other than the Syrian people and all revolutionary factions. He adds that what they want is democracy, without regard to community or religion. He ends his statement with the line also heard among the military defectors: "Victory to our revolution and mercy for our martyrs; healing for our wounded and freedom for us and our prisoners. Long live free Syria!"

4.9. "Declaration of the formation of the Free Student Union of Syria, Daraa section," 03/03/2012.

Conclusion: The Emergence of, and Engagement in, a Culture of Revolt

From the early demonstrations to the protest performances or recorded declarations, video does more than just document: it is part of the experience of revolt and engagement, and gives voice to the various forms of expression. Most of these videos were not widely seen, though some remained online until today. This visibility is a crucial issue, to the extent that it risks the lives of those who appear in them, whose purpose is at once to justify their commitment, convince others of the legitimacy of the revolt, and bear witness to the violence exerted against them. Protest actions, performances, lexicons, and images were invented from within this unprecedented ferment of unbridled speech and collective expression, in the street where it was uttered playfully or more solemnly for the defection declarations. Video gave rise to modes of occupying public space, and contributed to turning private spaces into places where people could have their say. The defection announcements in particular marked a new standard: because the individuals involved belonged to larger institutional entities, these videos created alternative entities whose conventions need to be structured and actions organized, as counters to the previous models. While these videos made sense individually from the moment they were shot, together they account for a particularly rich revolutionary culture that circulated throughout the territory and beyond. As the conflict was further engulfed in violence and protest actions were increasingly marginalized, especially after 2013, these videos also contributed to safeguarding the memory of that period, one that was still very much alive and quick to reemerge years later. Between 7 and 15 June 2020, hundreds of men and women of the town of al-Suwayda (majority Druze) took to the streets—not to protest against the critical economic situation as they had been doing over the previous months, but to call for an end to the regime[33] (Figure 4.10). The revolutionary slogans, such as "Freedom," "Dignity," "Rather death than humiliation," "Bashar Out," "The Syrian people are united," and "Why are you afraid? God is with us!" were chanted at the same rhythm and with the same fervor. Within a few days, placards started emerging, along with scraps of paper in front of cell phone camera lenses attesting to the date and location. A series of arrests put a (temporary?) end to the movement.

4.10. "Further mass demonstrations in the province of Suwayda for the second day and renewed calls for the fall of the regime," 06/08/2020.

NOTES

1. Andén-Papadopoulos, "Media Witnessing" (2013), 341–357.
2. According to Roger Odin, this paradoxical tension underpins the aesthetic of films shot with cell phones. Cf. Allard, Creton, and Odin, Téléphone mobile et création (2014).
3. Posted to YouTube on 25 March 2011. The original link has disappeared, but the video was reposted as an archive on 18 August 2012 to the account of Abu Fahd al-Hamwi, as well as on 27 March 2020 to the account of Archif al-thawra as-suriya. Both links are no longer available at the time of publishing.
4. Only a dozen or so photos taken by journalists and by inhabitants after the siege was lifted—very few of which were seen at the time—document the massacres and the destruction.
5. Regarding videos of the Tunisian revolt, Ulrike Lune Riboni calls this type of image "bodymage" to highlight the peculiar imbrication of the body and the photographic act. She compares the cell phone camera to the "Paluche," a miniature camera invented in the early 1980s that freed the eye from the photographic device. Cf. "Note pour une définition: 'Bodymages'"(2013): http://culturevisuelle.org/window/archives/102.
6. In what he refers to using the term "mobilographie," which encompasses filming practices that use mobile devices, Richard Begin emphasizes the shift from the event to the experience of the event, which also engenders a shift away from seeing toward feeling. Cf. Bégin 2015.
7. Traïni, "Dramaturgie des émotions" (2010).
8. A group of amateur actors devised these tableaux. Cf. Boëx, "La grammaire iconographique" (2013), 65–80.
9. The link is no longer accessible in 2020, as the YouTube account was ended.
10. Modeled on North Korean pageantry, thousands of performers had to execute these precisely choreographed human tableaux to the glory of the "eternal leader." See Wedeen, Ambiguities of Domination (1999), 20–24.
11. Even though the graffiti is not particularly stylized, this form of activism required a specific kind of organization, particularly widespread among young people who formed collectives in certain cities such as Damascus, Tell, al-Suwayda, and Qamishli. Video guarantees visibility and longevity to these graffiti that are often erased the same day by security forces. Cf. Boëx, "La grammaire iconographique" (2013), 65–80.
12. See for example the video "Damascus revolutionaries dye Damascus fountains the color of blood." Posted by Dimashqiiiii on 10 May 2011, with 10,641 views by 10 June 2024. https://www.youtube.com/watch?v=PhQPz411vs8.

13. There are over sixty videos parodying elections all throughout Syria.
14. "Hama. Free and fair elections take place." Video posted by Syrianman9000 on 7 May 2012, with 576 views by 11 June 2024. https://www.youtube.com/watch?v=eT1FXVzTAK4.
15. This video circulated on several accounts but was inaccessible in 2020.
16. In an Orient News report devoted to him, we learn that he spent eleven years in prison for "treason" due to his engagement with the Popular Front for the Liberation of Palestine, founded by Georges Habache. Cf. https://www.youtube.com/watch?v=x7mkKttHzP0, posted on 22 December 2012, with 719 views by 11 June 2024.
17. Including Ugarit News and ShaamNetwork, the most popular, as well as various individual accounts such as Syrianagent2011: https://www.youtube.com/watch?v=6U1o7a2Y5-Q&t=149s. 57,193 views by 28 June 2020. Some are subtitled in English. This account has since been switched to private mode.
18. Elite unit of the Syrian army, the Republican Guard [al-Haras al-Jumhuri] is in charge of protecting the capital, Damascus, as well as senior officials. Many members of the Assad family have served in it, including Bashar al-Assad, who commanded one of its brigades before becoming president in 2000.
19. The corpus that I have assembled to date includes 215 videos from 2011 through 2013. They likely number in the several thousands.
20. Posted on 9 June 2011, notably on the YouTube channel Freedomforeveryone20: https://www.youtube.com/watch?v=mLAa9NSC9fo (with English subtitles). It is also available at the satellite channel al Arabiya. Hussein Harmush began organizing his battalion at Idlib. He went to Turkey in an attempt to consolidate, with other dissident soldiers at the border, the free officers' movement. He was abducted there in September and resurfaced on Syrian national television in a staged confession during which he declared, under duress, that it was not the Syrian army that was killing civilians, but armed gangs, notably the Muslim Brothers* coming from abroad. Since then, he has gone missing.
21. "Announcement of the formation of the Free Syrian Army." Video posted on YouTube by al-Muthana al-Ahmad on 29 July 2011, with 21,879 views by 30 June 2020: https://www.youtube.com/watch?v=SZcCbIPM-37w&t=74s. This link no longer exists in June 2024.
22. In July 2011, a Libyan pilot used the same process to announce his defection.
23. Syrian Human Rights Watch was able to document 2,625 of them in a paper published online on 15 May 2020. Cf. https://www.syriahr.com/en/157193/.

24. He was affiliated with data security in the Air Force. He defected on 26 October 2011 and directed the military revolutionary council from 2012 to 2014. Detained since August 2019 by Hay'at Tahrir al-Sham.

25. "Defection of Colonel Afif Sulaiman along with a large number of officers and soldiers." YouTube video posted by Nazem Almansour on 21 February 2012, with 31,944 views by 11 June 2024. https://www.youtube.com/watch?v=_ssu3tufO2A.

26. "Cling one and all to the faith of God and let nothing divide you. Remember the favor that God has bestowed upon you: how after your enmity, He united your hearts so that you are now brothers through His grace."

27. We find it in various forms in other videos with, for example, a Quran placed on a table or leaning on an open laptop computer, and on banners declaring the profession of faith.

28. See Chapter 7: "National Armed Struggle and Global Jihad in the Public Imagination."

29. "Resignation of the public prosecutor of Hama province 31–8." YouTube video posted by Syrianagent2011 on 31 August 2011, with 560 views by 30 June 2020: https://www.youtube.com/watch?v=YLvmDFrKvR0. This account was switched to private mode in 2024.

30. "Defection of Abdallah al-Omar, director of several Syrian channels." YouTube video posted by UnitedPressOffice on 13 August 2012, with 38,310 views by 30 June 2020: https://www. youtube.com/watch?v=0EUVjiJSKIA. This link no longer exists in June 2024.

31. See Chapter 5: "The Women Speak: Declarations on film and sit-ins at home."

32. "Declaration of the formation of the Union of Free Syrian Students, section Daraa." YouTube video posted by Susfdaraa on 3 March 2012, with 742 views by 11 June 2024: http://www.youtube.com/watch?feature=player_embedded&v=SOi5Ar4eJjc.

33. "Further mass demonstrations in the province of al-Suwayda for the second day and renewed calls for the fall of the regime." YouTube video posted on 8 June 2020, with 570 views by 6 July 2020. https://www.youtube.com/watch?v=SIvN9Fw5OmA&t=1s. This link no longer exists in June 2024.

5
THE WOMEN SPEAK

DECLARATIONS ON FILM AND SIT-INS AT HOME

Emma Aubin Boltanski and Cécile Boëx

Though far less covered by the media, women's participation in the revolt movement was significant. While their presence at demonstrations[1] (Figure 5.1) was smaller than men's owing to the repressive violence, many took part in less visible activities such as supporting the families of detainees and martyrs, and the displaced; or performing such undercover operations as conveying medications or film and communications materials (they were less likely than men to be searched at checkpoints).[2] In liberated regions, a great many of them took part in managing day-to-day life, particularly when it came to education and medical emergencies.[3] Some filmed the protests and the fighting.[4] They also had a hand in preparing the demonstrations by designing placards, flags, and banners. A few even took up arms.[5] Although most were working underground, certain figures emerged, such as the attorney Razan Zaitouneh the physicist Fatin Rajab, the human rights militant Muntaha al-Atrash, actresses May Skaf and Fadwa Sulaiman, schoolteacher Soaad Nofal, media activist Zaina Erhaim, and writer Samar Yazbek. Women engaged in the revolution at various levels and in a number of fields, structures, and modes of action.[6]

5.1. "Damascus, al-Midan. Demonstration of free women calling for the fall of the regime," 09/28/2011. Video posted on ShaamNetwork S.N.N on 28 September 2011, with 616 views by 8 June 2020: https://www.youtube.com/watch?v=2MMysBy1ftU.

Some expressed themselves through videos filmed in their homes. Home was a safer space they could transform into a stage; engagement with the revolt was their performance, which manifested in different ways:

declaring support for the demonstrators or the Free Syrian Army* (FSA), denouncing the atrocities committed by the regime, demanding the release of prisoners, chanting slogans, reciting revolutionary poems composed for the occasion, singing, displaying handwritten signs, and paying tributes to martyrs. The register and staging would vary, inspired by a demonstration that the women would translate and make their own. This chapter explores these performances of women's protest by employing a (non-exhaustive) corpus of around 250 videos designated in their titles by the words "communiqués" (*bayans*) or "home sit-in" (*i'tisam manzili*), posted online between March 2011 and October 2016. We attempt to capture what is specific to these modes of expression and ways of articulating private and public spaces, anonymity and affirmation of diverse identities, grievances, and events. What discursive, textual, and corporeal lexicon do these women use to lend form to their speech, and what roles do they assume for themselves in the revolt? Whom are they addressing? Our analysis starts with the declarative form and moves toward a more marked theatricality, typical of the home sit-in. We also examine how these peaceful modes of action evolve as the repression increasingly militarizes and shifts into warfare.

Home Video: "Daughter of the Syrian Revolution"

On 24 March 2011, nine days after the first demonstration in Daraa, a video of a girl, her head wrapped in a Keffiyeh revealing only her large, kohl-lined eyes, was posted on YouTube.[7] Likely shot at home on a webcam, for twelve minutes, in one take, and without a stumble, she is sending a message to the men of Damascus—for in her view not enough of them are daring to defy the regime. She speaks softly, most likely so that her neighbors won't hear her. Choking up ever so slightly, she starts by reciting the bismillah: "In the name of God, the Most Gracious, the Most Merciful." This recitation that opens most of the suras in the Quran lends a solemn feeling to her speech, and provides a way to overcome fear. She first hails those who have demonstrated elsewhere in Syria—in Daraa, Homs, and Baniyas: these are "free revolutionaries," "heroes," "they struggle nobly to defend themselves and their country." "They have gone out and broken through all the fears that paralyzed them for fifty years. Today, tens of thousands of them are out in Daraa, they are being gunned down, blood is being shed." A muted rage is heard in her voice, and the tone becomes accusatory: "And we watch them and we say, 'My God.' Alright, it's one thing to ask for God's protection, but it's not enough [. . .] This is not the time for calling upon God to protect us, we must act, we must be in the streets. We must go out to say no." She sets the example by declaring her willingness to face danger. She challenges the men: "It's not normal that a girl goes out into the street and you stay at home." She tells how, during a rally in front of the Ministry of Interior (which she attended), demonstrators were arrested: "Imagine your sister, [. . .] your wife, or your mother gets arrested: Imagine what goes on in there, [. . .] and you, what are you doing? You implore God?" Her anger rises: "It's shameful that I confront my own fear by making this video that can be seen by millions of people and you, you're content just watching it [. . .] You who are watching this video, wherever you may be, go out and express yourself, say no [. . .] People of Damascus, where are you? People of Damascus, where are you? I'd rather be in Daraa."

Three days later, a second video (13 minutes) of the same girl was posted online.[8] The shot of her face is even tighter (Figure 5.2). She had taken part in a demonstration a few hours earlier. It is 27 March 2011: "Pride Friday."[9] Damascenes responded to the call in large numbers. Her delivery is as steady as before, but the tone is more playful: "Hey everybody!" she starts out. "Today was great, just great. Never did we think anything like this could happen in Damascus," she explains before eating humble pie: "My apologies for ever doubting that this could happen." "But I'm begging you, we have to keep going until the regime falls," she implores at several points. She is addressing girls here in particular: "There weren't enough of us. But don't go thinking we don't have a role. We can support, encourage and motivate people to take to the streets. I'm asking you, let's not just settle for Facebook." In the first video, she foregrounds her status as a girl to provoke and shame the men. In the second, more grateful this time, she calls for the movement to continue. By choosing to conceal her face with a keffiyeh—the emblem of the Palestinian struggle—she is summoning the symbols of resistance by also refusing any religious grounding. But this particular symbol, which hinders her in the end, is transitory. In the second video, she confidently announces: "The day will come when I will be able to remove this keffiyeh from my face and say 'it's me.'" Furthermore, video and the Internet make it possible to circulate and borrow forms of protest expression. Statements made by the Syrian Revolution Girl were most likely inspired by a viral video shot two months earlier by the Egyptian activist Asmaa Mahfouz, calling for a rally on 5 January 2011 in Tahrir Square.[10] The shoot is framed in the same way, with similar wording and arguments urging mobilization. Her Egyptian counterpart, however, does not conceal her identity—a sign that in Syria, fear is still present, and that the degree of repression is not comparable. Genuine web-based speakers, these two young women reclaim and refresh the role of orator, while constructing a new revolutionary role model that challenges male virility.

5.2. "The Daughter of the Syrian Revolution. Revolution 15 March 2011," 03/27/2011.

The Communiqués: Affirming Commitment and Challenging Power

While individual declarations were somewhat rare, many women's collectives used video to publicize their communiques (*bayanat*; sing. *bayan*). A few minutes long, these always display date and location on cardboard signs, as during the demonstrations. It was during the April 2011 revolt against Muammar Gaddafi in Libya that this form of declaration, blending spoken word and "exposed writing," was invented.[11] In Syria, they started appearing in June 2011. The staging is codified: a dozen participants, faces covered and self-identifying as "revolutionary women" (*nisa' tha'irat*) or "free women" (*hara'ir*),[12] speak with placards on behalf of a neighborhood or town as a spokeswoman reads a communique in an official tone. The purpose is to explain the reasons for their commitment and the legitimacy of the revolt. On the placards are slogans (often borrowed from the demonstrations) written with Sharpie permanent markers, and grievances (notably calling for the release of detainees arrested during demonstrations) as well as appeals for people to take to the streets. The camera is always careful to zoom in on the placards and allow time to read the different messages. Here, the staging is plain and static: the participants are standing in tight formation next to one another or sitting around a table. The tone is determined, serious. Anger is palpable in the timbre of their voices, and sometimes, participants freely sob when martyrs are mentioned. These filmed declarations are addressed first and foremost to Bashar al-Assad, to defy him and show that all over Syria a political body that also includes women is taking shape—in person, through images; in spaces opened up by the revolt; and all the way into the privacy of homes. The videos are also about thwarting the regime's propaganda and violence by denouncing its ploys to discredit the revolt.

On 21 June, Bashar al-Assad delivered his third speech to the University of Damascus. He attempted to preempt the protest movement by promising reforms, while threatening "the criminals and terrorists who are targeting the agents and property of the State." The following day, The Free Women of Damascus retorted in a "hard-hitting" two-minute communiqué.[13] They are gathered, sitting in front of the walls of a room covered in white sheets (Figure 5.3). The flag of the Arab Republic of Syria[14] is displayed at the back of the room. Below, written on a dozen signs set end to end are slogans, and a thank-you message to the TV channel Al Jazeera.[15] These signs, which feature the logo of Young Syrians for Freedom, give the scene the look of a press conference. In front of the table where the spokeswoman sits in the center, we read: "We demand freedom, we refuse sectarianism, we call for national unity." Other participants hold signs that read such slogans as "No, no, no to the power of the security apparatus over our lives," "He who kills his own people is no longer legitimate," "Where are your tears, Asma al-Assad, for the children of Syria and the blood of martyrs?" The girl at the center reads, in classical Arabic, a declaration that begins with the bismillah. The solemn tone of her intervention contrasts with the virulence and irreverence of the statements addressed directly to Bashar al-Assad: "Your third speech was a treacherous attack and a false promise. You still believe that Syria is the Assad family's private property. Well, Bashar, you are stealing with the left hand what you gave with the right. Watch out! We are not your slaves. We shall wrest our rights back from you [. . .] Bashar al-Assad, we shall not forget the crimes committed by your henchmen [shabbihas*] and by your security services in tormented Daraa, in splendid Homs, in bereaved Talkalakh, in long-suffering Baniyas, beloved Rastan, Jisr al-Shughur where blood flows endlessly, and the martyred Hama." This listing, to be found in various forms quasi-systematically in all of these communiqués, is a way of showing solidarity with other regions and of "nation-making," in response to the threat of fragmentation and chaos constantly put forward by the authorities. The spokeswoman completes her declaration by affirming that no negotiation is possible with "your tanks and your repressive regime." To conclude, the staging shifts into demonstration mode: the participants get up, and with fists raised, they intone the chief slogan of the revolt: "The people want the fall of the regime!"

5.3. "Declaration by the Free Women of Damascus. First Communiqué," 06/22/2011.

These communiqués reflect the concern at the increased intensity of violence: the point was to defuse sectarian tensions being stoked by the regime that equated insurgents with Islamist terrorists and was thereby slipping toward stigmatizing the entire Sunni majority community. In this type of video, it is not uncommon that women display their membership in the Alawi, Druze, and Christian minorities, while foregrounding their Syrian identity to more strongly underscore inter-community sisterhood and the peaceful basis of the revolt. These videos are often made in reaction to specific acts of violence that need to be condemned. They are also included among acts of resistance to terror, such as a declaration issuing from Free Women of the Coastal Alawi Community[16] that reasserts the uprising's peaceful intent and denounces the violence exerted against "the Syrian people" that threatens to lead to "a civil war and foreign interventions." On 28 May 2012 some young women of al-Suwayda, invoking the legacy of Sultan al-Atrash,[17] dressed in the transparent, off-white veils typical of the Druze (Figure 5.4), emitted "a cry of suffering and condemnation" to denounce the violence and massacres against civilians.[18] They called on people to refuse sectarian dissension. This declaration came at a time when repression was being militarized, cities were being bombed and put under siege, and fighting between the Syrian army and factions of the FSA was raging. A few days earlier, 108 people, including thirty-four women and forty-nine children, were massacred by the Syrian army in the locality of Houla near Homs. In this shift toward war, dissonance and even disagreement started to emerge: while the women of al-Suwayda held to the pacifist line, other women's collectives expressed their support for the FSA and armed struggle.

5.4. Communique of the revolutionaries of al-Suwayda, 05/28/2012.

Starting in 2012, the organization of armed struggle went hand in hand with that of the civilian movement. One video posted in July announced the creation of the Consolidated Free Women (Hara'ir) of Homs.[19] The tone and staging of this declaration recalls the FSA brigades creation videos.[20] Thirty women gather in a room, standard-bearers of the enormous flag of the revolution draped across the walls, surrounding a spokeswoman who reads a declaration from a computer screen (Figure 5.5). In a staccato voice, she solemnly announces that the Consolidated Hara'ir of Homs will be coordinating actions with other women's collectives at the regional and national levels. Other videos lament the fragmentation of the opposition camp and urge fighters to stay united and faithful to the principles of the revolution. In 2013, these communiqués grew scarcer. With pacifism now out of the question, it was all about resisting to honor the blood of the martyrs.

5.5. "Call by the Free Women of Homs to heroic revolutionaries," 06/11/2012.

Home Sit-in: Invention of a Subversion Ritual

In addition to filmed declarations, in May 2011 a less formal and more theatrical form of speech appeared: the home sit-in. While it involves certain elements of the filmed declarations, the sit-in more closely approximates a demonstration in that it uses the same songs, movements, slogan chants, scenography, and self-staging by individuals and collectives. Whereas in communiqués speech tends to be uttered by a single person, in sit-ins speech is shared. This mode of action developed as a space of mobilization by default,[21] at times and in places where the grip of the security services was such that demonstrations were practically impossible, as in Damascus and Aleppo, or locations where support of the revolt movement was in the minority: "In Salamiyeh, the take-over by the security services was so overwhelming that we stopped going into the streets," explains an activist from Salamiyeh. "And besides, the revolt was not widely supported by the general public. The home sit-in became our way of carrying on the struggle and expressing our viewpoint on what was happening in the country [. . .] every i'tisam was a reaction to a specific event."[22] Like the communiques, these sit-ins would bring together a dozen female participants in a living room rendered unrecognizable. Their faces were also concealed. Still, even with this anonymity came an opportunity to assert individual and collective identities. The apparel, fabrics, or accessories they chose were eloquent: they transformed the women's bodies into a medium for claiming collective identity. Once again, regional identities are foregrounded. These elements indicate a counter-discourse by showing that the revolt is multi-faceted, political, and non-religious, affirming resistance to attempts at division and sectarian polarization. This mode of protest action was itself becoming an institution: despite a few variants, codes were quickly set. It lasted until 2016—the height of the war.

First Sit-in in Damascus, 30 May 2011

Thirteen women gathered in a closed, white-walled room. Standing motionless, most are masked with fabric in the colors of the Syrian flag.[23] They form a half-circle, each holding a sheet of A4 paper. Shoulder to shoulder, together they create a long banner (Figure 5.6). They start with a minute of silence in tribute to the martyrs, then intone the national anthem. The camera moves from one to the next, pausing on the written messages and the smiling portraits of 13-year-old Hamza al-Khatib, kidnapped by the security services while he was demonstrating with his father in Daraa. His mutilated body was returned to his family a few days later. Images of his corpse went viral, making this adolescent an icon of the revolution.[24] The participants in the Damascus sit-in assert that they viscerally feel the shock of this violence and loss: "We are all the mothers of Hamza" one of the signs reads. On another, the face of the child appears set against a map of Syria filled with the colors of the Syrian flag and the phrase in Syrian Arabic dialect "*min-hibbak*" (we love you). This montage is a play on Bashar al-Assad's campaign poster for the presidential election of May 2007, with the young boy's face replacing that of al-Assad. Moreover, by taking up familiar slogans of the revolution, including "The Syrian people are but one and the same" and "Freedom," these women are also showing that despite (or because of) the violence, they are determined to pursue their mobilization. Countering the official discourse and its language of violence, they make the point: "We are not Salafists nor infiltrators."[25]

5.6. "Home Sit-in in Damascus 30 May," 05/31/2011. Final movement before the zoom to the TV screen.

While the symbolic register of the demonstration is indeed present with flags, slogans, and banners, certain elements—some of the women wearing black, and the rather elaborate staging—recall a funeral ritual. The camera movements are slow and precise, heeding a choreography that reinforces the impression of solemnity. This ritual is deeply subversive: they are replacing the presidential figure with that of a child tortured to death, visually reversing the official rhetoric by displaying a range of appearances and sensibilities, whether religious or secular: "This video was shot somewhere in Damascus," explains one of the participants now exiled in Paris. "I arrived there with a friend; I didn't know the others. There were veiled girls. We had to find a way to hide our faces while making it clear that we were not veiling for religious reasons. So that the regime wouldn't say: 'See, this proves that the revolution is Islamist; they're all veiled.'"[26] As the camera focuses in on the written sheets of paper, it frames the women's torsos. Between the signs, details catch the eye: hands with manicured nails, long sleeves or bare shoulders, a low-cut top, a strictly tied headscarf, or a cap that seems to speak to the wearer's refusal to veil. These clothing clues assert the group's cohesion in diversity. This sit-in also spoofs regime propaganda, as shown by a TV set in the back of the room tuned in to the national channel, with the women standing in a line on each side of the screen. At the end of the video, the cameraperson zooms in on the screen which announces the results of the national lottery, even while the country is in turmoil.

The Outbreak of War: The Sit-ins in Salamiyeh

Salamiyeh, a town located some thirty kilometers from Hama and whose population is majority Ismaili, is where the home sit-ins were most numerous (our corpus includes some fifty) and the video recordings lasted the longest online: starting in 2012, the last one we were able to find on YouTube was dated 15 October 2016. Along with its neighbor Hama, Salamiyeh shares a reputation for being anti-authoritarian. However, unlike "conservative" Hama, it is considered a progressive stronghold, where "all the leftist movements have been represented since independence," explains K.D., a woman activist from Salamiyeh exiled in Lebanon at the time of the interview. She goes on: "The people of Hama have been oppressed because of the Muslim Brotherhood*, and us because of the secular and leftist political positions of several prominent families of our city. The campaign of arrests against the Communists started in 1987, which was the year my father was put in prison because of his membership in the Communist Workers Party. Salamiyeh was economically strangled by the regime in order to quash any political ambitions. In the nineties, the local people were thinking of one thing only: getting enough to eat. They didn't want to hear about politics anymore. But the families of prisoners, like ours, didn't forget." In Salamiyeh, the first demonstration took place on 25 March 2011: "There weren't many of us, a few dozen, but the shabbihas were sent in to attack us. They even went after elderly people like my mother. We ended up organizing home sit-ins. My mother didn't miss a single one."[27] From the very first videos, the Salamiyeh sit-ins stand out for their resolutely feminist tone. It is worth noting here that since the 1970s, the political feminism that accompanied the struggle for Syrian independence, and which was determined to fight for women's rights among the working class (both urban and rural), was supplanted by a "State feminism."[28] This regime-sanctioned feminism had two objectives: to channel the economic and political backing generated by the attention accorded to gender issues at the international level; and to favor the feminism of an elite, considered easy to control and impervious to outside influence, and thus countering the growing impact of political feminism.[29] The regime had to prevent this more radical brand from gaining popularity among women in rural settings and underprivileged social categories. In this context, it is not insignificant that a small provincial town like Salamiyeh should become, in 2011, the spearhead of a two-pronged combat: against the regime and against the entrenched patriarchal society. The hundred or so members that made up the women's branch of the Local Coordinating Committee* were faithful to both these goals, while the consensus view in the ranks of the opposition—from the earliest months of the uprising—gave priority to the struggle against the regime and postponed the addressing of women's grievances.

On 1 July 2013, a dozen women got together in a dimly lit room in solidarity with the women prisoners on hunger strike.[30] Facing the camera, they hold panels that call for revolutionaries to unite and denounce the cowardice of the Syrian army, as well as placards which read: "A society without free women is a society doomed to failure" and "Anyone who believes that women and freedom are two parallel lines never meant to meet is mistaken." One of the participants shows a drawing in the style of manga: we see a girl holding the flag of the revolution and breaking a chain whose links are the letters of the words "customs and traditions" (Figure 5.7).

5.7. "Home sit-in by women of the Salamiyeh Local Coordinating Committee," 07/01/2013.

The actions of the Salamiyeh women also stand out for their boldness, their caustic humor, and, sometimes, the rawness of the statements chanted and displayed on their placards. "How ugly you are, how dirty you are, how cowardly you are. It's beyond belief"[31] can be read on one of the signs of a sit-in organized in reaction to the Houla massacre of 27 May 2012. On another, a play on words borders on blasphemy: "There is no Houla nor power except in God," where, instead of the word "power" (*hawla*) is the name of the martyred locality. Meanwhile, the woman reading the declaration dares to compare the regime to Israel: "A massacre like this, even the Zionists wouldn't do it." The sit-in of 16 June 2013,[32] on the other hand, marked a local event against the backdrop of a ramping up of armed confrontation. On the image of a woman whose pose (she's making the V-for-victory sign with both hands) and clothing (a keffiyeh and a tight T-shirt that reads "get high") recall that of a combatant, an intense voice announces the withdrawal of the Free Syrian Army from villages east of Salamiyeh (Figure 5.8). "But," she adds, "this is not a defeat; they will return and will be victorious." Then, she shifts into grievance mode: "Freedom for our prisoners. Give us back Manal Farha (a detainee hailing from Salamiyeh)."

5.8. "Home sit-in by women from the Local Coordinating Committee of Salamiyeh," 06/16/2013.

In a second stage, the participants begin to move about, holding their signs in such a way that hides their faces, while leaving their short-sleeved shirts visible. They start walking in a circle, chanting in unison: "Freedom, freedom, we're through with pacifism, we want bullets and Kalashnikovs." Followed by "Watch out, the Assad clan is on its way! They're going to ruin your party!" Without entirely abandoning their femininity—hinted with their voices, outfits, pink placards, carefully rounded handwriting, but also, in another way, the oilcloth-covered table around which they are circling—they are deliberately adopting a masculine, warrior-like register of expression and repertoire of action. The insult register dominates, whether addressed to the leader of Hezbollah: "May your soul be cursed Nasrallah!" or to Hafez al-Assad: "May your father be damned Bashar al-Assad," or to the Syrian army that loots the villages where they take control: "The shabbihas purged the houses [. . .] of their furnishings and women's clothing." A final placard is intended to wound the soldiers' male pride, and to ward off the fear of social abjectness resulting from the detention of women "suspected" of having been tortured and raped by their jailers: "How weak and empty is your manliness when you arrest a woman."

Conclusion: Reversing the Stigma of Fear

In several videos, women explain that they don't demonstrate in the street for fear of being arrested and put in prison, while at the same time hundreds of demonstrators chant "*ma fi khawf ba'd al-yawm*" (no more fear starting today). In an article about the home sit-in phenomenon in Syria, the poet and novelist 'Umar Qaddur[33] pays tribute to this fear assumed with "painful courage." He feels it provides the key to explaining the majority's silence in the face of oppression: "The camera sees through the secret of the silent houses [. . .] These women turn the weapon of terror back upon those who have been abusing it for decades [. . .] fear is no longer the sign of their weakness, but the shameful proof of cowardice on the part of the snipers and truncheon-bearers." To this observation, Qaddur adds a second: these sit-ins are a challenge and a warning to the regime, for they reveal that in countless silent homes "demonstrators, both women and men, are ready to take the leap"; they are a way to assert that "the majority's silence does not mean consent or submission." There are women who demonstrate with flags, slogans, and banners in living-rooms; others who make their commitment public and defy government authorities in their communiqués delivered in private homes; and one girl who calls for uprising from her bedroom. Each time, the camera "transports" the private, fleeting protest onto the Internet where it becomes public and more lasting. These modes of protest action are reminiscent of the English suffragettes who, in the 19th century, made their bodies a site of protest by transposing their struggle into images by means of widely distributed postcards.[34]

By March 2011, the Internet had become one of the stages where revolt, repression, and war were deployed. The Syrian women involved in the uprising stepped onto this stage and occupied it in a way that was all their own. In the maze of Facebook pages, YouTube channels, and Twitter (known as "X" since 2023) accounts, the fate of these videos varies widely. While "Daughter of the Syrian Revolution" garnered 44,000 views, the Damascus home sit-in got only 2,888, and the home sit-ins of Salamiyeh were watched only a few hundred times. Whatever their impact, these filmed documents with their polyphony of songs, proclamations, and writings cast a stark light on the history of the revolt and the war in its local iterations. They also compel a rethinking of women's involvement in the revolt, running counter to images of doves and victims. They present women of different generations "speaking up" and "writing down,"[35] who mix together various registers: femininity and motherhood with warrior violence and insults, or emotions with politics. In doing so, these women not only leave behind the social conventions of respectability, modesty, and reserve so often imposed on them, but they shift the expression of political speech into the privacy of domestic space.

NOTES

1. Mixed demonstrations, which largely took place in Damascus and al-Suwayda, were rare. Either women demonstrated without men, or their march was grouped together within the demonstration to shield against the violent repression and against improper behavior by the male demonstrators.
2. On the various forms of women's engagement, see the testimony gathered by Samar Yazbek in her work *19 femmes* (2019).
3. Gilbert, "Sister Citizen" (2020), 552–79.
4. For example, the video "Damascus, Qadam train station, violent clashes between FSA and regime forces" (YouTube, 2013) analyzed in Chapter 7: "National Armed Struggle and Global Jihad in the Public Imagination."
5. A notable mention must go to Alma Shahud, who founded an armed group called "Mothers of Martyrs" in eastern Ghouta, Cf. Yazbek, *19 femmes* (2019), 82.
6. On the specificities of women's involvement during the revolt, see Kahf, "Two Nonviolence Campaigns" (2020), 58–67; Saleh, "'The Factory of the Revolution,'" (2020), 354–362; and Kannout, *In the Core or on the Margin*, 2017.
7. "A Syrian girl calls upon all those who still have honor." YouTube video posted by freedomarab2011 on 24 March 2011, with 45,650 views by 11 June 2024: https://www.youtube.com/watch?v=34fYOkMm3Nc.
8. "The daughter of the Syrian revolution. Revolution of 15 March 2011." YouTube video posted by freedomarab2011 on 27 March 2011, with 37,385 views by 11 June 2024: https://www.youtube.com/watch?v=0SlUfFR6Rqs&t=3s.
9. The attribution of a Friday slogan (Friday, the weekly day off, being the main demonstration day) was borrowed from the 2011 revolt in Egypt. In Syria, it was organized by vote on a Facebook page (The Syrian Revolution 2011, https://www.facebook.com/Syrian.Revolution?fref=ts) with many followers in Syria and outside, from the earliest weeks of the mobilization. This system makes it possible to coordinate demonstrations all over the country and to feature a common slogan, but also to attest to the actual date of the demonstrations.
10. This video made Asmaa Mahfouz an icon of the Egyptian revolution. The activist and blogger already had political experience. In 2008, she joined the April 6 Youth Movement that lent support to the textile workers strike in the industrial city of al-Mahalla. This movement worked intensely in cyber-activism and was in the front line of those calling for the fall of Hosni Mubarak. In 2011, Asmaa Mahfouz and Razan Zaitouneh received the Sakharov Prize for Freedom of Thought awarded by the European Parliament.
11. Artières, *La banderole* (2013), 19.

12. Adopted by numerous collectives of revolutionary women starting in 2011, the word hara'ir has a religious connotation that aroused heated debates: certain secular activists associated it with an Islamist deviation that was discriminatory toward women, while others felt it was a "neutral" term equivalent to "revolutionary" (tha'irat). On this point, cf. Aubin-Boltanski.

13. "Declaration of the Free Women of Damascus. First communiqué." YouTube video posted by damascusvideos on 22 June 2011, with 2,872 views by 11 June 2024: https://www.youtube.com/watch?v=ja_pDAqU9VU.

14. Starting in November 2011, the flag called "flag of the revolution" made its appearance and was adopted by the rebels. It is a revival of the independence flag of the pre-Baathist era: it presents black, white, and green stripes (instead of black, white, and red), and three red stars (instead of two green ones).

15. At the start of the revolt, this very popular Arab satellite news channel based in Qatar was considered by the protesters as a media ally because of its broad coverage of the revolts in the Arab world and of the demonstrations in Syria (via activists on the ground, most notably). However, as the months passed, many activists criticized its coverage, which focused strongly on the militarization and clashes.

16. "Declaration by the Free Women of the Coastal Alawi Community, Latakia News." YouTube video posted by aboamro ammar on 29 June 2011, with 3,852 views by 11 June 2024: https://www.youtube.com/watch?v=EMrllu9hqbQ.

17. An important figure in the Druze community, Sultan al-Atrash led the 1925–27 revolt against the French Mandate. He became the symbol of national independence, in Syria and the Arab world.

18. "Declaration of the revolutionaries of al-Suwayda." YouTube video posted by Tansiqiyat al-Suayda' on 28 May 2012, with 4,075 views by 10 June 2020: https://www.youtube.com/watch?v=GhmiBQWoT0Y.

19. "Announcing the creation of the Assembly of Free Women of Homs." YouTube video posted by alabeya on 7 July 2012, with 332 views by 11 June 2024: https://www.youtube.com/watch?v=nIzF_bZR5Xc.

20. See Chapter 4: "Revolt With and Through Images."

21. "Appeal by the Free Women of Homs to its heroic revolutionaries." YouTube video posted by scripter2011 on 11 June 2012, with 2,555 views by 11 June 2024: https://www.youtube.com/watch?v=ljmncKSPurA.

22. On this subject, see the article by Rosa Yassin Hassan: "Women in the wings. The effective and sustained presence of Syrian women in the revolution," online, 23 December 2011.

23. Interview by E. Aubin-Boltanski, 25 March 2019, Beirut.

24. "At-Home Sit-in in Damascus, 30 May." YouTube video posted by tasniqi-yatdamascus on 31 May 2011, with 3,014 views by 10 June 2024: https://www.youtube.com/watch?v=iv7CdmLkURs.
25. This last phrase comes in response to a speech by the president delivered on 30 March 2011, in which he called the uprising a "foreign plot" and the demonstrators "undercover agents" and "Salafists."
26. Interview conducted by E. Aubin-Boltanski, 15 June 2020, Paris.
27. Interview conducted by E. Aubin-Boltanski, 25 March 2019, Beirut.
28. On this subject, see the testimony of Hama feminist Hazâmi Adi in Yazbek, *19 femmes* (2019), 331–63.
29. State feminism is not unique to the Syrian regime. Most authoritarian states in the region adopted it during the same period. For an in-depth analysis, cf. Latte-Abdallah, "Vers un féminisme politique" (2009), 177–95.
30. "Sit-in by the women of the Salamiyeh coordinating committee." YouTube Video posted by Syrian salamiahrevolution on 1 July 2013, with 246 views by 10 June 2024: https://www.youtube.com/watch?v=5y3P2ssOjVE.
31. These words addressed to the president are borrowed from the lyrics of a popular song of the moment: *"Ma arwa'ak"* (You are so prodigious) by the Kuwaiti singer Nabeel Shuail.
32. "At-Home" sit-in by the women of the local coordinating committee of Salamiyeh 06/16/2013." YouTube video posted by Syrian salamiarevolution on 17 June 2013, with 277 views by 11 June 2020: https://www.youtube.com/watch?V=kma-RPj9jIs. This link no longer exists in 2024.
33. "I'tisâm Manzilî!" al-Awan Collective , 8 December 2013, online, accessed 22 June 2020.
34. Artières, *La banderole* (2013).
35. Ibid.

6

FROM PACIFIST MILITANT TO ISLAMIST BRIGADE LEADER

'ABD AL-BASIT AL-SARUT: THE MAKING OF AN ICON

Cédric Labrousse

Born in Homs in 1992 into a working-class family, the goalkeeper of the up-and-coming Homs soccer team al-Karama (Dignity), 'Abd al-Basit al-Sarut, was one of the most famous figures of the Syrian revolution. His life was closely bound up in images, whether filmed by local activists, circulated by various international press agencies, or brought to the big screen. A considerable body of visual productions accompanied him along his path through the revolution and into war, until his death in combat in June 2019 in northwest Syria. Pages on various social media platforms have posted and reposted content of his performances at demonstrations, his outspokenness, and his actions within the armed struggle. Archived documents are regularly posted to various networks, servicing the myth that has gradually built up around him. How did a promising young athlete come to lead numerous peaceful demonstrations in his birthplace, the Homs neighborhood of al-Bayada, and take up arms with the Army of Glory* (*Jaysh al-'Izza*), an Islamist formation? This chapter retraces 'Abd al-Basit al-Sarut's trajectory based on videos shot by activists—some of whom were his friends and others members of local coordinating committees—as well as documents shared by people in the opposition press. The videos provide an insight into the different stages of a revolutionary engagement that evolved over eight years, and how it was transformed when exposed to violence and war.

Learning to Perform Before a Camera

Although 'Abd al-Basit al-Sarut took part in demonstrations as early as spring 2011 in Homs, he did not take a clear position until July, as is visible in a series of short videos posted to YouTube. Sitting on a sofa, presenting an issue of *The Revolution* (one of the official dailies) in order to authenticate the date of the shoot (7 July), and then his licensed athlete card in the manner of the military deserters, he asserts his commitment to the revolt and denies accusations made in the official Syrian media that claim he is a Salafist* and is being paid, distributing this money to incite people to demonstrate (Figure 6.1).[1] In this filmed sequence, he speaks out about the peaceful and non-sectarian character of the demonstrations and denounces acts of violence by the security services. He also pays tribute to Ibrahim Qashush, also known for having mobilized crowds in Hama through his satirical songs against the Assad clan, and who was found murdered, his throat slit, a few days before this video was shot. Three days after this first recording, the young goalkeeper made a more official appearance in another video,[2] again to debunk accusations by the regime that he wished to establish a Salafist emirate in Homs (Figure 6.2).

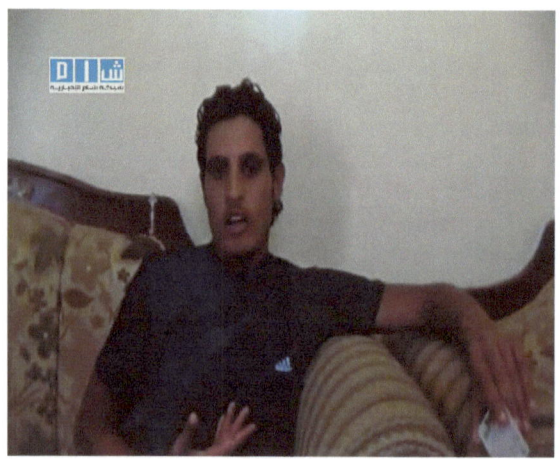

6.1. "Sham – Homs – 'Abd al-Basit al-Sarut – 7–7," 07/07/2011.

6.2. "Sham-Homs-Statement by 'Abd al-Basit al-Sarut singer of the revolution in Homs," 07/10/2011.

The staging style borrows from the defection videos of army soldiers and officers that were proliferating in the early summer of 2011.[3] Sarut is standing, his pose and tone solemn, in front of a large Syrian flag. While making it known that he is being hunted, and that there is a price on his head, he still comes forward as spokesperson for the revolutionaries' grievances. He talks fast. He is not at ease in front of the camera, but he seems determined. His plain-spoken-ness would add to his popularity. Sarut's image would very quickly transform: he was no longer on the defensive, but more defiant during his performances at the demonstrations, filmed at the center of large crowds (Figure 6.3) by the Local Coordinating Committees* in Homs, most notably by the media branch of the Khalidiya neighborhood. By August 2011 these videos of mass demonstrations, shot both by day and by night,[4] depict the young goalkeeper as enthusiastic, stoking the crowd's cheers with revolutionary songs. The atmosphere at these events he was leading at that time resembled the atmosphere of a soccer stadium.

6.3. Demonstration in the Khalidiya neighborhood of Homs, YouTube, 08/30/2011. Video broadcast on 30 August 2011 by an anonymous account, syria homs, "Homs, Khalidiya. First moments of Eid, extraordinary, with the hero 'Abd al-Basit al-Sarut," Cf. https://www.youtube.com/watch?V=TbZtJPWaNoM, accessed on 26 May 2020 [video no longer available].

The slogans were deeply hostile to the regime and the intelligence services that are particularly invested in the repression. Calls for Syrians to unite and to arm the fledgling Free Syrian Army (FSA)* were also numerous. Always inclined to exploit his popularity to draw attention to the situation in Homs as the repression continued to intensify, Sarut urged opposition figures such as the actress Fadwa Sulaiman, an Alawi, to help him head up demonstrations in early December 2011 and chant together "the Syrian people are united, united, united, united!" (Figure 6.4).[5] Sarut became the "nightingale" (*bulbul*) or the "singer" (*munshid*) of the revolution, thanks to his songs, whose refrains the crowds would repeat. The most famous one was a tribute to the martyrs, "Jannah, Jannah, Jannah" (paradise, paradise, paradise), a song taken up by people all over the country, and which he even recorded in a makeshift studio.[6] By fall 2011, Arab and Western media were airing an increasing number of features on the young man. His popularity allowed for more focus on the fate of Homs.

6.4. Fadwa Sulaiman and 'Abd al-Basit al-Sarut, YouTube, 12/07/2011.

Singing to Celebrate, Defy, and Mobilize
Fighting to Survive

As Sarut's fame grew during the spring of 2012, he became a symbol for all Syrians engaged in the revolt, but also more locally for the Homs insurgents who invited him to several neighborhoods where they had regained control. He was called upon to sing at revolutionary concert events, where he would meet with commanders of the FSA and activists in al-Qusayr, Khalidiya, Bab as-Siba', Bab Dreib, and al-Waer, the latter being a somewhat isolated neighborhood on the western periphery of Homs.[7] His appearances were filmed and shared by the local coordinators who also used his image to enhance their visibility and, beyond this concern, expose their own health, security, and social hardships. These "tours" in the different neighborhoods of Homs continued throughout the entire time the main rebel neighborhoods were under siege, from spring 2012 until the last bastions had fallen in May 2014.[8] In late November 2013 he made an appearance at an evening event in the neighborhoods of the Jurat al-Shayyah and Qarabis, to intone another of his now famous songs entitled "Who will revive the glory of the Arabs, if not Homs" (Figure 6.5).[9]

6.5. 'Abd al-Basit al-Sarut singing among fighters, YouTube, 11/24/2013.

More than willing to perform, 'Abd al-Basit al-Sarut was in full charge of his own communication. From early on he was present on social media, notably Facebook, where he posted opinion pieces and video messages, often about people he wanted to showcase.[10] These included the highly popular figure 'Abd al-Razzaq Tlass, a deserting non-commissioned officer, leader of al-Faruq brigades*, and a native of the Homs region. His links with the Local Coordinating Committees, especially with those activists working in media, go beyond cooperation: many are his friends, like Abu Adi or Abu Saleh (Figure 6.6) from Khalidiya and Baba 'Amr, who would follow him to the demonstrations as well as into the thick of combat and bombings.

6.6. Several Homs activists, with 'Abd al-Basit al-Sarut and Abu Saleh (center), gathered to celebrate the first anniversary of the Syrian revolution on 15 March 2012 behind a scale model representing the Khalid ibn al-Walid Mosque and the Clock Tower Square in Homs. YouTube. (Video broadcast on 15 March 2012 by the Coordination of Khalidiya, "Memories of the battle of Baba 'Amr during the festivities marking the first anniversary of the revolution" [translated from the Arabic]. Cf. https://www.youtube.com/watch?v=32pYyyh_A-M, accessed on 26 May 2020.)

By summer 2012, 'Abd al-Basit al-Sarut was increasingly appearing with weapons, at the head of his own battalion, al-Bayada Martyrs* (*Katibat Shuhada' al-Bayada*), created in May 2012 in response to the increasingly bloody escalation in the repression of the demonstrations. The members of the Khalidiya Coordinating Committee, as well as the friends and family who followed him, were now filming his armed engagement. He is shown on the front amid blown-up buildings, denouncing the Syrian army's air strikes. On several occasions he was wounded in combat, notably in July 2013—an incident that gave rise to videos of him on a bed, in pain or convalescing. The film *Return to Homs*, directed by Talal Derki, documents and weaves a narrative around the different stages of his journey into the armed struggle and his daily life as a combatant. This film would go on to be distributed internationally.

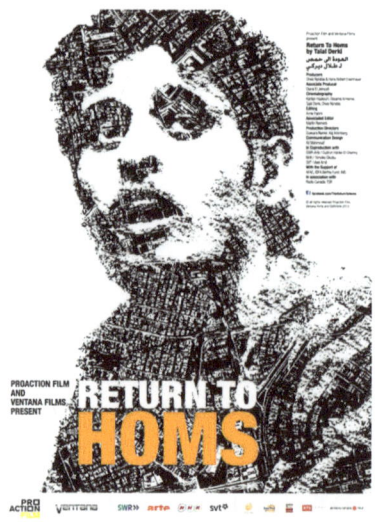

6.7. Poster of the film Return to Homs, Talal Derki, 2013. The high-contrast dark areas of 'Abd al-Basit al-Sarut's face are aerial views of Homs, which he embodies.

The Siege of Homs and the Metamorphosis of 'Abd al-Basit al-Sarut

As the siege intensified, the image of Sarut began looking more and more like that of a battalion commander. With his men, he took part in "the battle of the silos" in January 2014—an operation aimed at using tunnels to get out of besieged neighborhoods and rallying a farm product storage zone on the city's northern edge to resupply the neighborhoods choked off by months of hardship. But intelligence on the operation reached the regime, which then carried out a veritable massacre. Dozens of fighters were killed, among them two of Sarut's brothers. He bore witness to this military disaster, and experienced despair at not yet seeing a victory for Homs, appearing on-screen in a military jacket and with a Kalashnikov, looking thoroughly dejected (Figure 6.8).[11]

6.8. "'Abd al-Basit al-Sarut on the reality of what happened during the battle of the silos to break the siege," 01/17/2014.

The situation of the rebels was increasingly precarious in Homs, but 'Abd al-Basit al-Sarut could still be seen leading a few demonstrations, on a smaller scale, where most participants were combatants. In these videos his speeches were more religious, more sectarian, hurling abuse against the Alawi-majority neighborhoods of the city that he declared he could no longer abide, and calling for the military unity of all combatants, including the jihadists of the Nusra Front* which at that time was still an official branch of al-Qaeda* in Syria. On 18 February 2014, he was filmed giving a speech, then singing, in one of the last neighborhoods held by the rebellion in western Homs (Figure 6.9).[12] In this poor-quality video Sarut looks weary, but his voice still carries. Flags of the revolution have disappeared, replaced by banners professing the Muslim faith. The images are filmed from above to give the impression of a larger crowd.

6.9. "A song for your eyes Homs, with al-Sarut. Besieged Homs is still alive," 02/18/2014.

Apart from these few appearances, Sarut was only looking increasingly exhausted and angry—notably in one of his more famous videos, posted on 29 January 2014 (Figure 6.10), in which he rails against how combatants were being marginalized in political negotiations.[13] He refuses any compromise and comes across as totally unaccepting of defeat. By that time, talks had already begun between rebel forces—besieged and famished—and the local representatives of the regime, with a view to evacuating the combatants and their families to the north of Homs province. An agreement was finally sealed in early May.

6.10. Coordination of Khalidiya, YouTube, 01/29/2014.

'Abd al-Basit al-Sarut finally reemerged on 8 May 2014, as he was leaving central Homs, denouncing the divisions within the rebellion and the abandonment of Homs and its defenders to their fate.[14] He was greeted as a genuine hero in al-Dar al-Kabira, in the countryside to the north of Homs, as he and others got off the green busses chartered by the regime. After this point, his videos were increasingly rare and short. Appearing terribly gaunt, he accepted the defeat but swore to return to Homs.

From Disappearance from Screen to Isolation on the Ground

Little by little, the one that many nicknamed the "Keeper of the Revolution," referring to his past as a goalkeeper, disappeared from people's screens. During the summer of 2014 he reappeared in a video that proclaimed a new rebel group—Islamist this time—the Homs Legion* (*Faylaq Homs*). After that, the trail all but vanishes bar a few stolen images, like the celebration in September 2014 where he once again sang his song "For Your Eyes Only, Homs" in the region of Talbisa, according to the name of the channel broadcasting these very amateur images, most probably shot by one of the combatants.[15] Between late 2014 and spring 2016, though less and less visible, he was mired in controversy. A tweet by a Homs militant, Ziad al-Homsi, posted on 25 December 2014, asserted that al-Sarut's battalion, al-Bayada Martyrs, had sworn allegiance to the Islamic State*.[16] The regional press picked up the story, with international agencies soon to follow. Sarut's silence served only to amplify the rumor. It was not until summer 2015, looking right into the camera, that he denounced these allegations[17] (Figure 6.11). In his brief statement, he asserts he is unaffiliated to any organization, advisory board, or political party. He warns anyone who might be spreading false allegations that could harm his battalion. This fighting unit, geographically isolated and without the military backing of any other rebel groups (all of which fear the wrath of Sarut's adversaries), found themselves unable to hold a position, and 'Abd al-Basit al-Sarut disappeared from screen coverage altogether. Taking advantage of the situation, the Nusra Front* launched an attack against him. In late November 2015, al-Bayada Martyrs were driven out of Homs province.[18] This trying time ended with exile in Turkey. There, 'Abd al-Basit al-Sarut gave numerous interviews and took part in a few opposition demonstrations.[19] But he did not attract crowds, despite the strong presence of Syrian refugees hostile to the regime.

6.11. STEP News Agency, YouTube, 08/31/2015.

The Song, Allah, and the Kalashnikov: Construction of a Myth

In late 2016, 'Abd al-Basit al-Sarut returned to "Greater Idlib," that vast rebel-held zone in the northwest of the country. There, he founded a new faction, the Homs Brigade "for good" (*Liwa' Homs al-'Adiya*), swelling the ranks of the Army of Glory (*Jaysh al-'Izza*). This historical revolutionary group, established in 2012 in the north of the governorate of Hama, and many of whose fighters are native to the region, gradually came to espouse a religious discourse, abandoning the iconic referents (banners and logos) belonging to the FSA. It is instructive to observe that the leaning of Sarut—an activist with no particular ideological allegiance—toward an Islamist discourse, seems to closely match the ideological evolution of that group. This new period yielded a substantial quantity of images. In two years, a distillation of what comprised 'Abd al-Basit al-Sarut's public life is on display: the militant and singer, the activist, the commander, and even the athlete. At his first appearances, he is leading the demonstrations. In Idlib in late December 2016, he intones revolutionary chants for hundreds of demonstrators (Figure 6.12).[20]

6.12. Baladi News Network, YouTube, 12/16/2016.

When he is far from the front lines, he laces up his soccer cleats. Filmed training, during games, or celebrating a win, Sarut is once again presented as a major athlete. We see him smiling and enthusiastic, playing in a game with a local team composed of civilians and fighters, assuming his position as goalkeeper (Figure 6.13)[21] or as captain of a team of Homs natives a year later.

6.13. Report from the Edlib Media Center, YouTube, 05/12/2017.

His popularity now regained, 'Abd al-Basit al-Sarut was brought to the fore on several occasions by the local coordinating committees, during demonstrations protesting Syrian army offensives in the region of Idlib, notably in 2017 and 2018. These videos were intended to draw attention to civilian mobilization, totally absent in international media. But seeing Sarut in such a high-profile capacity right in their heartland, the jihadists from the group *Hay'at Tahrir al-Sham**, an outgrowth of the Nusra Front, finally arrested him on 29 May 2017, accusing him of conspiracy and, once again, of allegiance to the Islamic State. Nevertheless, his renewed popularity, thanks to his revolutionary commitment to the region, in discordance with the jihadist domination, was what saved his life: confronted by protests demanding his release, Hay'at Tahrir al-Sham finally freed him on 24 June 2017.[22] In his final appearances, he at times boosts the morale of his brigade fighters with his songs,[23] reposted to YouTube or Twitter ("X") on the accounts of famous activists or anonymous followers. In late May 2019 he also appears in a few interviews filmed on the battlefield, providing news from the front to the north of Hama, most of the time surrounded by his brothers in arms (Figure 6.14).[24] These videos were filmed by media bodies now more experienced in shoots of this sort. They are of good quality, and the stage direction is often more professional (choice of frame and background, posing of the people filmed, sound capture, etc.).

6.14. Syria News Net, YouTube, 10/22/2019.

When he was wounded in combat in early June 2019, 'Abd al-Basit al-Sarut did not recover. Videos flooded social media, showing him being loaded into an ambulance then lying unconscious on a respirator in a hospital in Turkey. He died a few hours later. The same day, local media and activists posted reactions taken from spontaneous street interviews, notably in Idlib,[25] but also tributes in the form of retrospective compilations of videos and stills. That evening, the STEP News Agency filmed demonstrations in Idlib organized in his honor. His songs were broadcast over loudspeaker all around the city, accompanying prayers in the street (Figure 6.15).[26] The songs he performed in 2011 and 2012 are now part of the culture of the Syrian revolution and provide the soundtrack of many video tributes posted to the Internet. The countless videos of his funeral, also shot by amateurs who followed the cortege from Turkey, testify to his popularity. Thousands of people converged on 9 June 2019 in al-Dana, a small town in the governorate of Idlib near the Turkish border, where his burial was recorded by innumerable smartphones and cameras. Each sought to capture his final image, as a relic (Figure 6.16).

6.15. STEP News, "Goodbye Sarut," YouTube, 06/08/2019.

Conclusion: The Posterity of a Figure of the Syrian Revolution

The life path of ʿAbd al-Basit al-Sarut slowly evolved toward an Islamization of his discourse and grievances, with a turning point in 2014 as a result of the absence of support for the revolution despite the ever more ferocious repression. In this respect, al-Sarut is both a symbol and a symptom of a paradigm shift involving a great number of activists and fighters. From leader of peaceful demonstrations to battle-hardened warrior, he embodied a version of the revolution that many Syrians subscribed to. An entire narrative of the hero (*batal*) and martyr (*shahid*) sprang up after his death. The activist Abd al-Jalil Orabi, who had followed him in Homs, was among the first to post a tribute video to his deceased friend on his personal YouTube account.[27] Anonymous individuals created entire channels devoted to Sarut. Since then, thousands of videos have been posted, recycling photos and archival video footage. To mark the one-year anniversary of his death on 8 June 2020, the number of tributes grew exponentially, sometimes revealing images seen for the first time. The visual production, especially video, generated by ʿAbd al-Basit al-Sarut has had a decisive impact on the construction of a genuine heroic figure, an icon of the revolution whose aura has shone far beyond Syria's borders. For over a decade, a large portion of his life has been shared, viewed, and known by all. Over this period, each has sought to obtain a part of Sarut as his various stances evolved, be they secular-minded activists or Islamist warlords. Still today, they share in his legacy as they reconstruct a consensus figure closer to the 2011 revolutionary than the Islamist fighter.

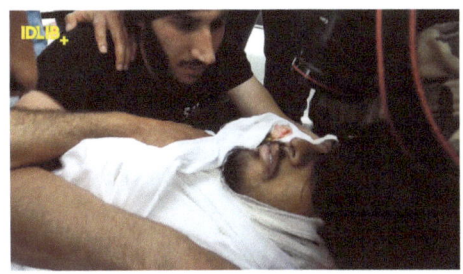

6.16. "The funeral of the martyr 'Abd al-Basit al-Sarut in his final resting place, the town of al-Dana, north of Idlib," Idlib+, YouTube 06/09/2019. Cf. https://www.youtube.com/watch?v=09_ULnm3a7Q, 129,353 views by 29 October 2020.

Sarut has thus become the "glue" still able to bind opponents of all persuasions, as activist Hadi al-Abdallah recalls at the first commemoration of his death.[28] A sign that a lineage is taking shape, another figure has emerged during these tributes to the "keeper of the revolution" since 2019. The young Muhammad al-Sarut, one of his nephews living in Idlib who performs some of his uncle's songs before cameras and at times sizable crowds, further ensures 'Abd al-Basit's posterity.

NOTES

1. Video broadcast on 11 July 2011 by the militant channel ShaamNetwork S.N.N, "Sham – Homs – 'Abd al-Basit al-Sarut – 7–7" [translated from the Arabic]. Cf. https://www.youtube.com/watch?v=sfMR-MfLkkY, accessed on 3 May 2024.
2. Video broadcast on 10 July 2011 by ShaamNetwork S.N.N, "Sham – Homs – Declaration by 'Abd al-Basit al-Sarut Singer of the Revolution in Homs" [translated from the Arabic]. Cf. https://www.youtube.com/watch?V=TmQx7O40Teg. Link no longer available.
3. See Chapter 4: "Revolt With and Through Images."
4. Video broadcast on 15 September 2011 by the anonymous militant account Syrian2011X: "Homs, al-Qoussour, 09/15/2011 with the hero 'Abd al-Basit al-Sarut" [translated from the Arabic]. Cf. https://www.youtube.com/watch?v=caplu5naZKw, accessed on 12 May 2024.
5. Video broadcast on 7 December 2011 by the Coordination of Khalidiya at Homs: "Homs, neighborhood of Khalidiya, 12/07/2011, beautiful demonstration led by al-Sarut and actress Fadwa Sulaiman" [translated from the Arabic]. Cf. https://www.youtube.com/watch?v=nT329nbsVXs, accessed on 6 May 2024.
6. Thousands of demonstraters sing the song along with Sarut in the Khalidiya neighborhood. Video recorded on 13 January 2012, then broadcasted on 8 June 2012 by activist Aous al-Mubarak: "Homs, al-Khalidiya, the song Paradise, Paradise, Paradise, with al-Sarut" [translated from the Arabic]. Cf. https://www.youtube.com/watch?v=_12ISLIwF28, accessed on 26 May 2024.
7. 'Abd al-Basit al-Sarut singing a revolutionary hymn beside militant Omar Abu Abdo during an event in the al-Waer neighborhood, Homs. Video broadcast on 28 April 2012 by the Coordination of the Syrian Revolution in Homs – al-Waer: "Homs the unshakable, al-Waer, 'Abd al-Basit al-Sarut and the hero Omar Abu Abdo, with Ahrar al-Waer" [translated from the Arabic]. Cf. https://www.youtube.com/watch?V=X-uR5W29_lS8, accessed on 5 May 2020. This link no longer exists in 2024.
8. The only neighborhood to remain under siege was al-Waer, until 2017 when it was retaken by the Syrian regime.
9. Video broadcast on 24 November 2013 by the account of the coordination of the Qarabis and Jurat al-Shayyah neighborhoods managed by Abu Jamal: "Fantastic: The glory of Arabs is elevated by singer 'Abd al-Basit al-Sarut, from the siege" [translated from the Arabic]. Cf. https://www.youtube.com/watch?v=ZpHylDIvVBY, accessed on 13 May 2024.

10. These pages no longer exist but traces remain, notably through communiqués and other elements reposted on other pages. 'Abd al-Basit al-Sarut created at least five on Facebook between 2012 and 2014.

11. Declaration by 'Abd al-Basit al-Sarut for the Coordination of the Khalidiya neighborhood, broadcast on 17 January 2014: "'Abd al-Basit al-Sarut on the reality of what took place during the battle of the silos to break the siege" [translated from the Arabic]. Cf. https://www.youtube.com/watch?v=ucPng-BoY4sQ, accessed on 5 May 2024. This video is no longer availabe.

12. Video posted on 18 February 2014 by the local militant channel Abu Jamal: "A song for your eyes, Homs, with al-Sarut. The resilience of besieged Homs is still very much alive" [translated from the Arabic]. Cf. https://www.youtube.com/watch?v=ElSrD1oRFYU. Accessed on 6 May 2020. The speech can be heard on an adjacent video. Cf. https://www.youtube.com/watch?v=9yOLoY-Cw8g, accessed on 6 May 2024.

13. This video got over 1.2 million views: "'Abd al-Basit al-Sarut, Homs under siege, this is not a political game and his fate depends on the besiegers" [translated from the Arabic], broadcast on 29 January 2014 by the Coordination of the Khalidiya neighborhood. Cf. https://www.youtube.com/watch?V=KRpL-6oNXb4. Link no longer available.

14. Statement by 'Abd al-Basit al-Sarut, as he was getting off the bus in the countryside north of Homs, filmed on 8 May 2014 and broadcast the same day by an account under the pseudonym Ash Ras, partisan of the opposition: "A word with 'Abd al-Basit al-Sarut after his arrival in the northern countryside" [translated from the Arabic]. Cf. www.youtube.com/watch?v=jhwj3NcGQWY, accessed on 26 May 2020.

15. These images, of very poor quality, were broadcast on 9 September 2014 through the account of a local militant under the alias, Kenan Ter Malaa: "For your eyes only, Homs" [translated from the Arabic]. Cf. https://www.youtube.com/watch?v=1sztQqHDQRg&t=165s, accessed on 7 May 2024.

16. Tweet posted on 25 December 2014 by Ziad Homsi, on his personal account. Cf. https://twitter.com/ZiadHomsi/status/548223889147711490/photo/1. This page no longer exists in 2024.

17. Statement broadcast on 31 August 2015, notably by media activists Halab Today TV and STEP News Agency. Cf. https://www.facebook.com/watch/?ref=external&v=1211361608881275, accessed on 7 May 2024.

18. On this event, refer to the detailed summary of the opposition media outlet Zaman al-Wasl, "Sarut: the Martyrs of Bayada belong to no organization and we shall not abandon the revolution to the Nusra Front" [Translated from the Arabic], published online on 17 November 2015, accessed on 12 May 2020.

19. Video broadcast by ShaamNetwork on 30 April 2016: "Sham, the voice of the Syrian revolution, 'Abd al-Basit al-Sarut leading a demonstration in Istanbul to denounce the destruction of Aleppo." Cf. https://www.youtube.com/watch?v=JVEOXUMioig&t=5s, accessed on 14 May 2024.

20. Video by media outlet Baladi News Network broadcast on 16 December 2016: "A demonstration in Idlib, led by Sarut" [translated from the Arabic]. Cf. https://www.youtube.com/watch?v=ZXtQZBfVUf8&feature=emb_title, accessed on 7 May 2024.

21. Interview with 'Abd al-Basit al-Sarut in a report by the agency Edlib Media Center, broadcast on 12 May 2017: "Sarut is back in the stadium with the al-Nouman team facing the home team Saraqeb, in first division" [translated from the Arabic]. Cf. https://www.youtube.com/watch?v=1CDgmdaWYeQ, accessed on 7 May 2024. This video is no longer available.

22. "Tahrir al-Sham releases 'Abd al-Basit al-Sarut" [translated from the Arabic], Enab Baladi, published online on 24 June 2017.

23. In a video, 'Abd al-Basit al-Sarut, surrounded by his men, sings amidst fighting north of Hama: "'Abd al-Basit al-Sarut 4/16/2019" [translated from the Arabic], broadcast by activist Mohannad al-Said on 16 April 2019. Cf. https://www.youtube.com/watch?v=Zkt9MLi0AhM, accessed on 12 May 2020. This account is now closed.

24. Interview broadcast by SYRIA NEWS NET SNN on 22 May 2019: "Hama: 'Abd al-Basit al-Sarut entering Kafr Nabuda after its liberation, among the commanders of Jaysh al-'Izza" [translated from the Arabic]. Cf. https://www.youtube.com/watch?v=XzPRv5Cv5ng, accessed on 7 May 2024.

25. News reporting and street surveys in Idlib, on the evening of Sarut's death. Video broadcast on 8 June 2019 by the local media outlet MMC (Macro Media Center): "A demonstration in Idlib to keep alive the memory of 'Abd al-Basit al-Sarut, singer and keeper of the revolution" [translated from the Arabic]. Cf. https://www.youtube.com/watch?v=4HikNdAfo58, accessed on 26 May 2024.

26. Demonstration in the heart of Idlib, after the news of the death of 'Abd al-Basit al-Sarut, filmed by STEP News Agency and broadcast on 8 June 2019: "Demonstration in the town of Idlib in memory of 'Abd al-Basit al-Sarut, singer and keeper of the revolution" [translated from the Arabic]. Cf. https://www.youtube.com/watch?v=GcVFmeNDnQ0, accessed on 7 May 2024.

27. "Mourning for the martyr 'Abd al-Basit Sarut in the words of one of his friends" [translated from the Arabic], broadcast on 11 June 2019. Cf. https://www.youtube.com/watch?v=BllPO8iMUn0, accessed on 12 May 2024.

28. Speech by Hadi al-Abdallah, broadcast by his own YouTube channel on 8 June 2020: "Hadi al-Abdallah's speech at Idlib to commemorate the guardian of the revolution 'Abd al-Basit al-Sarut" [translated from the Arabic]. Cf. www.youtube.com/watch?v=gJ8uUKlckFQ, accessed on 11 June 2024.

SELECTIVE CHRONOLOGY

*This selective timeline cites events which are mentioned in various chapters, or are somehow connected to them.

2011–2020

2011. The Popular Uprising and its Repression

18 March 2011
First demonstration in Daraa. The security forces fire on the demonstrators, killing four.

24 March 2011
Bouthaina Shaaban, advisor to Bashar al-Assad, announces at a press conference economic measures designed to quell the people's anger. In response, the demonstrators chant the next day: "Hey, Bouthaina Shaaban, the Syrian people are not hungry."

25 March 2011
First demonstrations in Aleppo, Homs, Hama, Salamiyeh, Latakia, Baniyas, and Damascus. The demonstrations took off from the Grand Umayyad Mosque, and from the Rifa'i Mosque in Kafr Sousa.

26 March 2011
260 prisoners, mostly Islamists, are released from the prison of Saidnaya.

30 March 2011
President Bashar al-Assad's first speech before the Parliament.

5 April 2011
Siege of the city of Daraa.

7 April 2011
President al-Assad issues a decree for the naturalization of 300,000 Kurds who had been deprived of Syrian nationality by a 1962 decree.

13 April 2011
First student demonstration in Aleppo.

16 April 2011
Bashar al-Assad's second speech before the ministers of his new government that had been appointed two days earlier.

18 April 2011
Sit-in at the Clock Tower Square in Homs is violently repressed. The death toll is still unknown, but some sources put it in the hundreds.

22 April 2011
The Local Coordinating Committees* publish their first declaration calling for freedom and dignity through a peaceful transfer of power. One of their demands is the release of all prisoners of opinion, as well as the dismantling of the security apparatus.

25 April 2011
The Syrian army sends tanks into Daraa to crack down on protests, killing at least eighteen people.

27 April 2011
More than 230 members of the Baath Party resign in protest of the violence against civilians.
A UN Security Council resolution condemning the repression is blocked by Russia, who states that the situation in Syria "does not constitute a threat to international peace and security."

30 April 2011
In Damascus, women undertake a silent march in solidarity with Daraa under siege. The first filmed defection, of Walid 'Abd al-Karim al-Qasha'mi, member of the Presidential Guard, is shared.

6 May 2011
The siege of Homs begins. The old city will fall in May 2014 and the al-Waer neighborhood in March 2017.

25 May 2011
The family of Hamza al-Khatib, a 13-year-old missing since 29 April in Daraa where he had been taking part in a demonstration, recover his body mutilated by the armed forces. He becomes the symbol of the revolution.

31 May 2011
Bashar al-Assad decrees a general amnesty.

10 June 2011
Creation of the Battalion of Free Officers [*Liwa' al-Dhubbat al-Ahrar*] by Lieutenant Colonel Hussein Harmush.

17 June 2011
Fifty-one demonstrations are organized throughout the country to mark "Men of Honor" Friday.

20 June 2011
Bashar al-Assad's third speech at the University of Damascus.

1 July 2011
The largest demonstration of the revolt movement takes place in Hama, with several hundred thousand protesters.

29 July 2011
Creation of the Free Syrian Army*.

31 July 2011
Offensive in Hama on the eve of Ramadan, with the Syrian army shelling residential neighborhoods. Bombing begins the following day and lasts until 4 August.

13 August 2011
The Syrian army starts bombing Latakia, the country's main port, with tanks and naval warships. Between 5,000 and 10,000 people flee the city.

27 August 2011
Attack on the al-Rifa'i Mosque in Kafr Sousa.

2 October 2011
Announcement of the creation of the National Syrian Council in Istanbul. After several days of combat and dozens of fatalities, 250 tanks retake control of the city of Rastan.

4 October 2011
A draft resolution is submitted to the UN to subject Syria to a series of targeted measures. The resolution is vetoed by Russia and China.

4 November 2011

The Revolutionary Committee of Homs and the National Syrian Council adopt the former flag of the Syrian Republic, used between 1932 and 1963, as the official flag of the revolution.

22 December 2011

Arrival of an Arab League observer mission made up of 166 observers from thirteen Arab countries.

2012. Militarization of the Repression and Armed Struggle. Violence Intensifies.

6 January 2012

493 demonstrations take place throughout the country on this Friday dubbed "If you love God, He will rescue you and guide your steps," the watchword drawn from verse seven of the sura entitled "Muhammad."

24 January 2012

First communiqué from the Nusra Front*.

26 January 2012

The Syrian army shells Homs, killing several hundred.

4 February 2012

The Syrian army bombs the Khalidiya neighborhood of Homs, killing 260 civilians.

Russia and China veto a UN draft resolution condemning the repression and calling for the removal of Bashar al-Assad, under the terms of the crisis plan drawn up by the Arab League.

21 February 2012

Largest military defection operation (over 350 men) led by Colonel Afif Sulaiman in Ma'rat al-Nu'man in Idlib province, forming the Northern Shield Brigade.

1 March 2012

The regime takes back the Baba 'Amr neighborhood of Homs after a twenty-six-day siege.

10 March 2012

Siege and bombing of the city of Idlib.

2 May 2012
Over 11,100 people killed since the start of the uprising in March 2011, according to Syrian Human Rights Watch.

25 May 2012
Massacre in Houla, a few kilometers north of Homs, killing thirty-four women and forty-nine children.

1 June 2012
939 demonstrations throughout the country—a record number—to mark the Friday dubbed "Children of Houla, torch of victory" as a tribute to the massacre victims.

20 June 2012
First defection from the ranks of the Syrian Air Force.

12 July 2012
Massacre at Tremseh, a Sunni-majority town located north of Hama. The town was bombarded by tanks and helicopters, first stormed by the army then by the shabbihas*. The death toll rose to over 150.

15 July 2012
Offensive by the Free Syrian Army* in Damascus.

18 July 2012
First use of barrel bombs by the Syrian Army—makeshift weapons composed of barrels filled with explosives, shrapnel and/or fuel oil. The bombs are dropped from helicopters; their targets are random and their effect particularly devastating. They were deployed massively between 2014 and 2016. In March 2020, the Syrian Network for Human Rights estimated the number of drops since 2012 at 81,916.

19 July 2012
The Syrian army partially withdraws from northern Syria, allowing the Kurdish political party *Partiya Yekîtiya Demokrat* – Democratic Union Party (PYD)* to take control of the Kurdish zones along the border with Turkey.

Third veto by Russia and China of a draft resolution by the UN Security Council condemning "the increasing use of heavy weaponry by the Syrian authorities, including indiscriminate artillery shelling carried out by tanks and helicopters on the civilian population."

20 July 2012
Offensive by the Free Syrian Army* in Aleppo that takes control of the eastern part of the city.

6 August 2012
Defection of Prime Minister Riyad Hijab, who takes refuge in Jordan.

20 August 2012
Speech by Barack Obama warning against the use of chemical weapons in Syria, which he calls a "red line."

25/26 August 2012
Massacre in Darayya, located 6km from Damascus, with a death toll of over 700. This causes most of the civilian population to flee.

17 October 2012
Creation of the Citizens Council of Darayya that runs the city autonomously and oversees military operations.
First sarin gas attack by the Syrian army in Kafr Takharim and Salqin, in Idlib province.

8 November 2012
Start of the siege of Darayya that lasts until 27 August 2016, and during which 90 percent of the city will be destroyed.

2013. The Armed Conflict Goes Transnational

11 January 2013
The Taftanaz airbase (the largest in northern Syria) is taken by the Nusra Front*, Ahrar al-Sham*, and factions of the Free Syrian Army* after two months of combat.

4 March 2013
Raqqa is taken by Ahrar al-Sham*, the Raqqa Liberation Front, and the Nusra Front*.

9 April 2013
Abu Bakr al-Baghdadi announces the formation of The Islamic State in Iraq and the Levant (ISIL)*. This group gains a foothold in Raqqa.

30 April 2013
The General Secretary of Hezbollah, Hassan Nasrallah, officially acknowledges the party's presence in Syria.

1 June 2013
ISIL* begins its control of Raqqa.

5 June 2013
The Syrian army and Hezbollah take back control of the town of Qusayr*.

9 July 2013
Destruction of the historic mosque Khalid ibn al-Walid, in Homs.

29 July 2013
Kidnapping of the Jesuit priest Paolo Dall'Oglio in Raqqa.

21 August 2013
Large-scale chemical attack carried out by the Syrian army on several towns in the Ghouta area near Damascus, causing nearly 1,400 deaths. These towns were besieged and bombed for eight months. Between 2012 and 2020, the Syrian army carried out 217 chemical attacks (chlorine gas and sarin gas).

28 August 2013
Barack Obama announces imminent strikes in retaliation for the Ghouta chemical attacks—strikes that ultimately fail to materialize.

4–15 September 2013
Fighting for control of Maaloula between rebel forces and the Syrian army. The Syrian army will gain the upper hand, but in early December the rebels will take the town once again.

3 December 2013
Thirteen nuns are evacuated from the convent of Saint Thecla in Maaloula after the Nusra Front* and groups of the Free Syrian Army* took control of the city.

24 December 2013
The Islamic State* kidnaps Jordanian pilot Mu'adh al-Kasasba after his fighter plane crashed in Syria.

2014. The rise of the Islamic State

8 January 2014
Members of the Bayada Brigade, affiliated with the Free Syrian Army*, attempt to break the 600-day siege of the city of Homs. The operation fails, with a death toll of over 60.

14–16 March 2014
Loyalist forces and Hezbollah recapture Yabrud, a strategic town in the Qalamun region bordering Lebanon.

14 April 2014
The Syrian army, backed by Hezbollah, retakes control of Maaloula, which had been captured five months previously by the Nusra Front* and brigades of the Free Syrian Army*.

30 April 2014
ISIL* offensive in Deir al-Zur.

7 May 2014
First forced removal operation since the regime regained control of Old Homs. Nearly 2,500 combatants and civilians are evacuated into northern zones held by the opposition, after Iranian and Russian mediation and under UN monitoring.

26 May 2014
Advance of the Nusra Front* and the Free Syrian Army* brigades into Idlib, where they take control of the town of Khan Shaykhun.

3 June 2014
Reelection of Bashar al-Assad to the presidency of the Syrian Republic, with 88.7 percent of the vote.

29 June 2014
The Islamic State in Iraq and the Levant (ISIL) becomes the Islamic State (IS)*, as its leader Abu Bakr al-Baghdadi proclaims the restoration of the Caliphate*.

14 July 2014
The governorate of Deir al-Zur comes under the control of IS*, which drives out the Nusra Front* and Ahrar al-Sham*.

16 September 2014
IS* offensive on the city of Kobani, on the Syrian border with Turkey.

23 September 2014
First strikes by the International Coalition*, led by the United States, against IS* in the region of Kobani. The coalition had begun its strikes in Iraq on 8 August. It carries out 4,530 strikes in Syria through 2016.

After 2015. Total Transnational Conflict

26 January 2015
The IS* is driven out of Kobani by the Kurdish People's Defense Units (YPG)* backed by factions of the Free Syrian Army* and International Coalition* airpower, after a battle that lasted nearly four months.

25 March 2015
Conquest of the city of Busra in the Daraa governorate by the Southern Front, a coalition composed of various factions of the Free Syrian Army*.

28 March 2015
Conquest of the city of Idlib by a coalition composed of the Nusra Front*, Ahrar al-Sham,* and other rebel factions.

21 May 2015
The IS* takes over Palmyra.

2 June 2015
While the Syrian regime is beleaguered by successive military defeats, Iranian president Hassan Rohani declares his support "until the end." A few days earlier, it had dispatched to Syria some 7,000 Iranian, Iraqi, and Afghan fighters under the command of the Islamic Revolutionary Guard Corps (IRGC)*. The Fatemiyoun Brigade*, consisting mainly of Afghan Shiites and created in 2013, boosts its recruits and becomes the Fatemiyoun Division.

25 June 2015
Massacre by the IS*, with a death toll of nearly 300.

30 September 2015
In a speech, Bashar al-Assad calls for help from Russia. Russia has been preparing since May 2015 and is able to act immediately; as of 2020 Russian intervention is still ongoing in the region of Idlib, though to a lesser degree.

24 November 2015
A Russian plane is shot down by a Turkish aircraft, setting off a diplomatic crisis between the two countries.

21 February 2016
Backed by Russian airpower, loyalist forces advance to the east of Aleppo.
27 February 2016
Russian-American ceasefire agreement.

4 March 2016
Taking advantage of a lull in fighting, demonstrations break out in the governorates of Aleppo, Idlib, Rif Dimashq, Daraa, and Homs.

27 March 2016
The Syrian army regains control of Palmyra, under the command of the Islamic Revolutionary Guard Corps and backed by Shiite militias from Iraq, Lebanon, and Afghanistan.

13 April 2016
Legislative elections in the territories under regime control (around 30 percent). The opposition considers this ballot to be fraudulent. It is not recognized by the UN.

24 August 2016
The Turkish armed forces and Syrian opposition groups, allied with Turkey, launch "Operation Euphrates Shield" against IS* and the Kurdish People's Defense Units (YPG)*, which are considered by Turkey as terrorist groups. Military operations are carried out in the governorate of Aleppo, between the Euphrates and the zone held by the rebels around the town of A'zaz, backed by coalition warplanes led by the United States.

25–26 August 2016
Retaking of Darayya, under siege since 2012, by the Syrian regime. 8,500 inhabitants are evacuated. Rebel fighters are sent to Idlib, with the remainder of the population sent to zones under regime control. Darayya, once home to 250,000 people in 2011, is 90 percent destroyed and emptied of its population.

12 September 2016
New ceasefire agreement under the auspices of the United States and Russia.

20 September 2016
Intensive bombing campaign over Aleppo by Russian aircraft. 377 civilians are killed between 20 and 26 September.

11 December 2016
IS* retakes Palmyra.

13 December 2016
After four months of clashes, East Aleppo is retaken by the Syrian army with the backing of Russia, Islamic Revolutionary Guard Corps* (Iran), and Iraqi, Lebanese, and Afghan Shiite militia. Rebel fighters, estimated at around 7,000, and nearly 30,000 civilians are evacuated to Idlib province between 15 and 22 December following a Russian–Iranian–Turkish agreement.

28 January 2017
Creation of the Organization for the Liberation of the Levant (*Hay'at Tahrir al-Sham*)*, an outgrowth of the Nusra Front*, which was itself renamed the Fath al-Sham Front after its break with al-Qaeda* in 2016 and its fusion with five other Syrian Islamist groups.

2 March 2017
The Syrian army retakes Palmyra after three months of fighting against IS*. It is backed by Syrian paramilitary groups, Hezbollah fighters, and Russian special forces.

4 April 2017
Chemical attack by Syrian planes on the town of Khan Shaykhun in Idlib, where groups of rebel fighters and jihadists have been engaged in an offensive north of Hama since March. The death toll is upward of one hundred.

21 April 2017
Evacuation of the last rebel fighters holed up in the al-Waer neighborhood of Homs to rebel zones in the provinces of Aleppo and Idlib. Homs is now entirely under the regime's control.

4 May 2017
Russia, Iran, and Turkey sign an agreement providing for "de-escalation zones in Syria" that should allow for an end to fighting. Neither the Syrian regime nor representatives of the opposition are invited to the signature of this agreement.

12 September 2017
Hassan Nasrallah, Secretary General of Hezbollah, declares: "We have won the war in Syria." '

19 September 2017
An offensive is carried out by the Organization for the Liberation of the Levant (Hay'at Tahrir al-Sham)* and several rebel factions in Hama. In retaliation, the Syrian army and Russia launch air raids against Idlib.

7 October 2017
With the approval of Russia, Iran, and the Organization for the Liberation of the Levant (Hay'at Tahrir al-Sham)*, the Turkish army deploys across several positions in the Idlib region to establish a buffer zone, with a view to containing the influx of refugees and impeding a possible advance of the YPG*.

17 October 2017
Raqqa, under IS* control since 2013, is taken back by the Syrian Democratic Forces (SDF)*, backed by the International Coalition*.

2 November 2017
After several years of fighting against IS, the regime takes back the town of Deir al-Zur.

21 November 2017
Iranian general Qasim Sulaimani, leader of the Quds Force* and strategist of the Iranian military presence in Syria, sends a letter to the Supreme Leader of the Islamic Republic, Ayatollah Khamenei. In the letter Soleimani announces that the war in Syria against "Daesh" has been won thanks to the collective action of "the popular forces of Iraq, of Syria and of the Holy Shrine Defenders*."

December 2017
By the end of the year, the regime controls 55 percent of the territory, the Syrian Democratic Forces* 28 percent, the rebels 12 percent, and the Islamic State 5 percent.

20 January 2018
The Turkish army and the Free Syrian Army* attack the Syrian Democratic Forces* in the town of 'Afrin in northwest Syria, 30 km from the Turkish border. The town comes under Turkish control on 18 March. This offensive triggers the displacement of a large share of the region's population, which is mostly Kurdish.

29 January 2018
Peace talks organized by Russia and backed by Turkey and Iran take place in Sochi. The talks are boycotted by the Syrian National Council* and the Kurds.

4 February 2018
Start of the offensive on western Ghouta, east of Damascus, held by rebels since 2012 and under siege since 2013.

7 April 2018
Chemical attack at Duma, in western Ghouta, causing nearly seventy deaths. This triggers a limited counterattack by the United States, France, and the United Kingdom which bomb several sites in Damascus and near Homs on the night of 13 April, as part of Syria's chemical weapons program.

14 April 2018
Evacuation of the last rebel fighters from Duma to Idlib.

16 May 2018
Retaking of the last remaining rebel holdouts in the Homs and Hama regions.

19 June 2018
Offensive in the governorates of Daraa and Quneitra in southern Syria, carried out by the Syrian army, Syrian paramilitary units, Hezbollah, and Iraqi, Iranian, and Afghan Shiite militias (under the command of the Islamic Revolutionary Guard Corps*), backed by Russian aviation. This leads to a "reconciliation agreement" with the rebel forces of the Southern Front, affiliated with the Free Syrian Army*.

25 July 2018
The Islamic State attacks al-Suwayda and surrounding villages, causing around 250 deaths.

17 September 2018
Turkish-Russian agreement to set up a demilitarized zone in Idlib.

11 January 2019
The International Coalition* announces its withdrawal from Syria.

23 March 2019
End of the Caliphate* with the capture of the final Islamic State* pocket by the Syrian Democratic Forces* at Baghuz, in Deir al-Zur province. The IS

still maintains some underground cells. 8,500 fighters and their families are made prisoners, and around 60,000 women and children (including 9,000 foreigners) are detained at the al-Hul camp in the al-Hasaka governorate in northeastern Syria.

6 May 2019
Start of the Khan Shaykhun offensive in Idlib province, led by the Syrian army and backed by Syrian paramilitary groups and Russian mercenaries affiliated with private security companies. The Islamic Revolutionary Guard Corps* and Shiite militias from Iraq, Lebanon, and Afghanistan do not take part in this fighting. After three months of clashes, Khan Shaykhun is once again under regime control.

8 June 2019
Death of 'Abd al-Basit al-Sarut.

9 October 2019
The Turkish army launches an offensive against two border towns in the governorates of Raqqa and al-Hasaka. Abandoned by the United States, the Syrian Democratic Forces* reach an agreement with the Syrian army which redeploys on the Turkish border. The Syrian loyalist forces and the Russians take up positions in several cities controlled by the Syrian Democratic Forces: Kobani, Manbij, Tabqa, 'Ayn 'Issa, and al-Hasaka.

22 October 2019
Turkey and Russia reach an agreement that provides for the complete withdrawal of YPG* fighters to 30km from the Turkish border, and the deployment of Russian-Turkish patrols along the border.

27 October 2019
Death of Abu Bakr al-Baghdadi, head of the Islamic State, during an American raid in northern Idlib governorate.

19 December 2019
Fresh offensive by the Syrian army in southeast Idlib province. In two months, the bombings compel nearly one million civilians to flee toward the Turkish border—an unprecedented population displacement since the start of the conflict.

3 January 2020
The Iranian general Qasim Sulaimani is assassinated in Iraq by American forces.

5 March 2020

After eleven months of fighting, Turkey and Russia implement a ceasefire in Idlib.

March 2020

Since March 2011, the estimated death toll is set between 384,000 and 586,000 according to Syrian Human Rights Watch. 226,247 were documented by the Syrian Network for Human Rights as being civilians. Among these, 14,391 died in detention under torture. Another 129,989 are still in detention or have disappeared. As for the rebel forces, Syrian Human Rights Watch counts over 54,000 deaths. As for forces affiliated with the regime (Syrian army and paramilitary factions), casualties amount to over 119,000. Casualties among the major jihadist groups (Organization for the Liberation of the Levant* and the Islamic State*) are estimated at over 67,000.

Since 2011 (at which point Syria's population was just over 21 million), 15.2 million people have been forcibly displaced: 9 million within Syria and 6.2 million outside the country.

Bashar al-Assad's regime maintains control over 70 percent of a fragmented territory thanks to backing from Russia and Iran.

7–15 June 2020

Demonstrations in al-Suwayda denounce economic stagnation and call for regime change.

PART TWO
COMBAT

7

NATIONAL ARMED STRUGGLE AND GLOBAL JIHAD IN THE PUBLIC IMAGINATION

THE ACTORS, GEOGRAPHIES, AND TEMPORALITIES OF THE WAR

Cécile Boëx

Since 2011, armed resistance in Syria has undergone countless mutations. Stemming initially from the revolt and its repression, it has gradually internationalized in two principal directions: the increasing involvement of third-party countries that selectively supply logistical or financial support to certain factions of the Free Syrian Army* (FSA), and the emergence of jihadist groups that took advantage of the prevailing chaos.[1] Thus, other agendas clustered with the struggle against the regime of Bashar al-Assad—agendas that exceeded and diverted the political scope and national context of the revolt. Within this particularly complex and ever-shifting scene of conflict, our point here is to review how various visions of combat were constructed, while singling out the elements that characterize the two major poles at work: the groups included in a national perspective and those claiming a more transnational jihadist ideology. What images and narratives do they deploy to account for their existence and actions? Which geographies, temporalities, and ideologies are they working within? In order to understand both the grammar and audiovisual devices used to make these visions manifest, this contribution proposes to plot a diachronic course through the two divergent—or even rival[2]—spaces of combat. This movement through the chronology accounts for how different practices and cultures of image-making have evolved over time and highlights their power struggles. The FSA, for instance, started from scratch. Where their early images from the field of combat are practically illegible, we see a gradual formatting of the ways that weapons, men, and scenes of combat are displayed. And yet, despite this standardization, the videos coming out of groups affiliated with the FSA are strikingly eclectic. Conversely, the jihadist videos indicate audiovisual cultures purposefully designed within highly defined communication strategies, but which still need to be distinct from one another, as is the case for the Nusra Front* and the Islamic State (IS)*—two directly competing entities.[3] The videos analyzed here showcase various relationships to image-making, ranging from documentation, to bargaining tools (in exchange for weapons), to marketing communication strategies. Particular attention is given to how the combatants and battlegrounds are represented—whether that is those most local, as with videos from groups affiliated with the FSA, or the most global, as with the IS, which individualizes certain foreign fighters to a great extent.

The Disparate Worlds of Armed Rebellion Spawned by the Revolt

While the videos of defections and declarations of a coordinated armed struggle at the national level were emerging by May 2011,[4] the first combat events involving what was to become the Free Syrian Army in July 2011 were rarely caught on camera. It was not until 2012 that they started appearing on YouTube, around the time when certain factions were taking control of portions of streets and neighborhoods—notably around Damascus and in the old quarter of Homs.[5] The FSA, which numbered roughly 50,000 men at the height of its activity in 2013, is not a military institution, but rather a cluster of brigades (*liwa'* pl. *alwiya*) and battalions (*katiba* pl. *kata'ib*) that vary widely in longevity and manpower. With mainly defensive weaponry, some of it locally manufactured,[6] their actions were at first confined to protecting demonstrators, and later to attacking roadblocks or Syrian army positions. This piecemeal armed rebellion particularly came together at the local level: combat groups—made up of civilians or soldiers having defected—were organized and supplied. In effect, the FSA exerted little control over the many local groups deployed to defend a neighborhood or a village.[7] Moreover, many brigades broke apart or regrouped with others. This resistance army—motley and dispersed—which emerged in response to the regime's fierce repression, was devoid of any unified ideology. Although these factions were nationalist and pursuing the common goal of bringing down the regime, their Islamist or secular sensibilities diverged and evolved over time.[8]

Because of the combatants' close ties to the revolt and places of belonging (many fighters had taken part in the demonstrations), certain groups would assume the name of a martyr killed during the street protests, such as the Hamza al-Khatib Battalion which was named in memory of the son of Daraa tortured to death after attending a demonstration with his father, or al-Qashush Brigade, named for a popular singer who led demonstrations and who had his throat slit by the security forces. Thereafter, numerous factions took the name of the first martyred combatants from their group. Others used slogans and watchwords chanted during demonstrations, such as "freedom" (*hurriya*), chosen by groups in Jisr al-Shughur and Deir al-Zur in 2012, and "dignity" (*karama*), in Manbij. Names of neighborhoods, towns, villages, or regions also came to designate factions, foregrounding a territorial identity. These labels were mobilizing secular references, while others emphasized references to Islam, such as the Lions of Islam (Damascus and greater Aleppo), the Grandsons of the Prophet (Idlib), Salah al-Din (architect of the recapture of Jerusalem / Aleppo and Latakia), Ibn Taymiya (the traditionalist theologian who urged jihad* against the Mongols in the early fourteenth century / Daraa, Deir al-Zur, and al-Ghouta), and Khalid ibn al-Walid (a companion of the Prophet and a general renowned for his talents as a military strategist / Homs). This wide range of references is reflected in the combatant group logos (see a sample below) that draw from distinctly different graphic domains (the more local groups have none at all). Some affix an article of Muslim faith (There is but one God and Muhammad is His prophet), while others utilize versions of such traditional military symbols as the eagle and crossed swords. While between 2011 and 2012 the use of the flag of the revolution was practically ubiquitous, as the armed struggle was gradually Islamized, especially from 2013, this would no longer be the case.

7.1. Logo of the Free Syrian Army created in November 2011 highlighting the flag of the revolution—a revival of the one adopted in 1946 at independence and in use until the arrival to power of the Ba'ath Party in 1963.

7.2. From top to bottom, and left to right:
The Cavaliers of Justice Brigade (2012, Idlib)
The Mountain Falcons Brigade (2012-2016, Jabal al-Zawiya)
The Raqqa Revolutionaries Brigade (2012)
1st Coastal Division (2014-2018, Latakia)
The al-Faruq Battalions (2011-2013, Homs)
The Syrian Revolutionaries Front (2013, Daraa, Quneitra, Damascus)
The Sword of the Levant Brigades (2012, Rif Dimashq, Daraa)
The Followers of the Prophet Battalion (2012, old city of Homs)
The Rally of Brigades and Battalions of Syrian Martyrs (2011-2015, Idlib, Hama)
The Swords of Truth Battalion (2012, Kissweh)
The Freedom Brigade (2014, Raqqa, al-Hasaka)
The Army of Victory (2015, Idlib)
The Northern Sun Battalions (2014, Raqqa, Aleppo)
The Salah al-Din Ayubi Brigade (2012-2015, Aleppo)
The Authenticity and Development Front (2012, Aleppo, Homs, Hama)
Sources: Facebook, Twitter ("X"), Wikipedia.

Between 2012 and 2013, the FSA combat videos were often produced in conjunction with the media teams of the Local Coordinating Committees*—themselves a product of peaceful civilian organizations—which filmed and posted their videos of combat or declarations on their YouTube channels. What emerges from these early images is the fighters' lack of professional training, identifiable by their mismatched and at times inappropriate attire (some were wearing sandals), their body language, and their equipment. The inexperience and recklessness of those filming is also conspicuous. Completely involved in what they were filming, they affirm their presence and participate in the fighting with their exclamations, advice to the fighters to protect themselves, or locating of a sniper's position. Though images shot in the heat of battle are, by definition, chaotic and incomplete, many videos posted online by these groups are totally illegible, particularly those shot at night. Nevertheless, the videographers never fail to announce the date and place of the shoot to authenticate the films. Even if some groups are better trained and equipped than others, the asymmetry in the balance of power is plain to see, as in a video[9] shot by an activist during a battle in August 2013 in the historic, decommissioned train station of Qadam, near Damascus. To understand what is happening here, one must look for other videos of the clashes that took place there.[10] No armed faction claims to have produced this video. Only the logo of the Coordinating Committee of Tadamun, the Damascus neighborhood where the fighting took place, is affixed (Figure 7.3). The video, shot in one long take, shows men firing from assault rifles amidst the old rails and train cars. The young woman behind the camera indicates the location and date, but her voice is drowned out by gunfire and the fighters' shouts. Highly mobile, she is caught between her wish to film and the need to self-protect. Her movements are those of a threatened body in the midst of combat. The images that emerge from this particularly perilous situation are opaque, closer to traces than pictures.

7.3. Clashes between FSA fighters and the Syrian army in the al-Qadam train station, YouTube, 2013.

Over time, the combat videos, like the resistance army, turned more professional. To produce and disseminate their films, they no longer needed the help of the Local Coordinating Committees, whose power was weakening by 2014 as the conflict grew increasingly militarized and internationalized—notably with the heightened presence of jihadist factions. Some groups developed communication strategies to promote their activity and created their own YouTube channels that contained communiqués and tributes to martyrs fallen for the cause. At this point, it was about asserting an identity and a fighting force by displaying men, weaponry, and controlled zones. The videos produced by the Martyrs of Islam Brigade* give clear evidence of this trend. Founded in March 2013 by the merger of eight FSA groups active in Darayya (in the southern outskirts of Damascus), it was the largest combat formation of this city, which was under siege from 2012 to 2016. At its inception, it acquired its own YouTube channel ("Shuhada al-Islam Brigade," 35 videos posted until July 2016, 318,276 views on the channel), a Twitter (now "X") account (1,215 tweets until 2018), and a Facebook account (now deactivated). This channel documented the most important operations, such as the video posted on 7 June 2014 entitled in Arabic "Operation promotion: our salvation is in our jihad."[11] Part ad, part action film, the clip looks professional. With a soundtrack that recalls the theme music of broadcast news, the snappy editing gives a timeline of the operation and emphasizes control over the locale: men plot out an attack using a map, maneuver on top of buildings, move through a tunnel, then break through a wall between two housing units to carve out a passage. Different shots take stock of the weapons used: a grenade, a T72 tank (recovered from the Syrian army?), assault rifles, a sniper rifle, and various kinds of automatic weapons. At the end, a sidebar indicates the outcome of the operation: destruction of three tunnels used by regime forces, taking control of all buildings that served as the regime forces' strategic base, and control of part of al-'Abbas Mosque (Figure 7.4). Next to the logo of the Martyrs of Darayya Brigade (right) is affixed that of the Southern Front, which also participated in the action.

7.4. Final shot of the video "Our salvation is in our jihad," YouTube, 2014.

This display of strength goes beyond mere documentary or promotional aims: it is about the leveraging of the audiovisual medium, most probably meant for supporters of the group. Stefan Tarnowski has shown how certain videos fit into a wartime exchange economy, where video work can be traded for arms, such as BGM TOW 71 anti-tank missiles.[12] He references the creation of the YouTube channel RFS [Revolutionary Forces Syria] Media Office, created on 29 November 2013 (2,763,450 views to date, active through March 2017) and financed by the British government to coordinate and support the media production of groups identified as moderate. In each video, the logo of the fighting groups is clearly visible. This channel makes it possible to monitor who is using the weapons and ordnance for which actions. The channel hosts videos of the Darayya Martyrs Brigade. Production of this sort of video conditions the existence and firepower of certain groups, and it is crucial that it highlights a combat identity distinct from jihadist groups. In this respect, the sound design (the absence of *nashid**, an a cappella religious warrior chant) and the presence of the flag of the revolution stand as warranties. Nonetheless, the audiovisual production of rebel combat factions cannot be reduced to this economic function. The tribute videos to those martyred in combat reflect a multitude of memorial acts that have given rise to an unprecedented martyr culture in the Middle East, which is freed from official representations of warriors and heroism.[13] These practices challenge the silencing and erasure imposed by the Syrian regime on these fallen fighters, considered as traitors or terrorists. For the rebel combatants, it is thus imperative that they leave a trace, however fragile, of their involvement. Most of these tributes, produced by family members or media activists in Syria or in exile, are individualized, blending family photos with films of military feats. They conjure up places of origin and personal trajectories. The wounded bodies and the sadness of family, friends, and fellow fighters are fully a part of this vernacular memory. When available, extracts of videos of the funerals or the tombs of combatants are reused. This importance of birthplace, of the dead, and of their singular stories as told autonomously by those close to the fallen fighter is completely absent in the jihadist audiovisual culture.

Syria as Choice Terrain for Global Jihad
Combat De-realized, Warriors Exoticized

Unlike the audiovisual production of the Syrian armed resistance affiliated with the FSA, videos from the main jihadist groups fit into a previously established image-making culture,[14] even if the Islamic State (IS) updated its codes. Jihadist filmmaking is strictly supervised and centralized by production bodies such as *al-Manara al-Bayda'* (The White Minaret) for the Nusra Front, and the various media branches of the IS. All include in their soundtrack the *nashid*— part of the traditional jihadist repertoire—or a newer composition. Another common feature is that they do not contextualize the material during the editing process. Their images frequently lack any indication as to the date or location, and not necessarily for security purposes. This illustrates that authentication is not considered important, but also, and most importantly, that their relation to place is both de-territorialized and ahistorical: the fighters' actions (especially with IS) are not undertaken within the national Syrian framework but in the mythical lands of Sham*, which the Islamic Caliphate* is to encompass, refuting the regional political boundaries imposed by the Franco-British Sykes-Picot agreement of 1916. Finally, an overarching feature of the audiovisual production of jihadist combat scenes is the disembodiment of the images from whoever is capturing them, as is the absence of any scenes of dead or wounded bodies, mourning, or commemoration of individual fighters. The videographers never comment on what they are filming, and we never hear them panting or interacting with the fighters as we do in the videos produced by FSA groups: their role is purely technical. This sanitized version of violent experience contrasts sharply with the choreographed violence of execution videos, and with the even rawer images of the body parts of civilians regularly shown (especially by IS) to legitimize their commitment to jihad. Likewise, while certain fighters film testaments prior to their suicide operations (as is the case with the Nusra Front), we know nothing of their funerals, nor the place of their burial. The tribute videos, made by official production units, are rare and involve only the exemplary combatants.

This is the case for a Nusra Front video posted on 5 October 2013, which also provides insight into several basic elements of jihadist audiovisual culture. The fifth episode in a series entitled "The Beginning of the End"[15] which compiles the group's successful operations, it starts out, as do all jihadist videos, with the opening phrase of the Shahada or profession of faith written in white on a black background. The theme song, accompanied by a *nashid*, opens the video. The film consists of several images of explosions (indicated as having taken place in Hama, Aleppo, and Damascus) embedded into a borderless map of Syria and Iraq on which armed, hooded men advance in a column. Then comes a four-minute sequence showing a man during a gunfire exchange. The image has been darkened and the fighter is surrounded by a brighter halo of light (Figure 7.5). The visual erasure of location, which is never specified, or any hint as to the circumstances of the fighting, reinforces this idea of de-territorialization. This spotlighting also seeks to emphasize the figure's corporeal and psychic performance.[16] Effectively, his skillful maneuvering under fire reveals a certain mastery. In the moment he is hit, the voiceover that pays tribute to him specifies that the man is Abu Aisha, a Special Forces trainer for the Nusra Front in Aleppo. This tribute is centered on his agility and uncommon courage, highlighted by repetitions of the same sequence—a device that, alongside the poetic-sounding text read in the voiceover and the *nashid*, evokes a certain lyricism. This aestheticizing of combat prowess with help from eye-catching visuals and sound effects constitutes a recurrent motif in jihadist videos. Here, as in all Nusra Front videos, the identity of the fighter is concealed. While we most often see him from the back, when he does face the camera, his face is blurred out. In this way, the Nusra Front fighters are not individualized: they are represented as figures embodying the exemplary qualities and principles of the organization.

7.5. "The Beginning of the End," episode 5, The White Minaret, 2013.

While we do find certain recurring motifs, such as the diffraction of territorial space and the aestheticizing of combat, in all IS productions, this organization marks a paradigm shift in the use of images by jihadist groups—especially in 2014 with the advent of the Caliphate. This territorial conquest, unprecedented in the history of jihadism, orients a part of its video production toward recruitment. The videos focus on the way institutions are set up and run (schools, religious tribunals, hospitals, law and order, etc.) and how well the economy functions.[17] It is also about promoting the *hijra**, emigration into territories occupied by the Caliphate, by representing jihad as an adventure—a total but accessible experience.[18] From this perspective of "democratizing" jihad (formerly reserved for a religious warrior elite, notably within the ranks of al-Qaeda), jihad came to be seen as trivialized by a tendency to sublimate combat and violence. This is the case of a video posted online in 2014 entitled, after a hadith[19] attributed to the Prophet: "The Tourism of my Ummah is Jihad in the Path of Allah."[20] An audiovisual translation of this hadith which locates hijra at the heart of jihad, this video consists of several sequences shot unprofessionally with cell phones and assembled in a rudimentary montage. Still, this poor-quality video is stamped with the logo of the production unit al-I'tisam, an offshoot of the main office of the highly hierarchical and complex media organization of the IS.[21] Here, the amateur register is based on a communication strategy that places emphasis on the sense of togetherness among fighters during moments of relaxation, and on the delights of experiencing far-off lands and jihad. The production of IS combat videos was more closely monitored after the first bombings by the International Coalition* in August 2014,[22] for security reasons.

This video, less than six minutes long, is conceived as a compilation of the joys of the IS mujahid and is built around exotic experience, exaltation, and camaraderie. In a hybrid register somewhere between vacation footage and war film, it casts the jihad experience in Syria as both cozy and exotic. The various Arabic accents among the fighters, as well as the English title, contribute to the sense of internationalist jihadist utopia. The war, whose signs are nevertheless ubiquitous, almost fades into the background. In the first sequence, a fighter is cutting a pomegranate with his impressive military-grade knife and shares it with his brothers in arms. In the background, a man has just raised the black IS flag and shouts *"Allahu akbar"* (God is great), brandishing his Kalashnikov. The following sequence shows fighters in tee-shirts and rolled-up pants diving into the Euphrates (Figure 7.6). The camera sweeps over the landscape as the men intone a *nashid* that speaks of paradise and its houris. The person behind the camera comments: "Our brothers in the land of Sham." Another *nashid* is heard on the voiceover. With no transition, three fighters raise an IS flag and delight at the sunset over this mountainous terrain. The cameraman, whose shots are carefully studied, resumes the hadith that is the video's title between two exclamations. Wonderment and contemplation are at the core of this montage. Where this part is devoted to the fighters' esprit de corps, the second, more institutional, stages their training by IS. Against another *nashid*, this one to the glory of the organization, we see a rapid succession of shots showing groups of fighters in different situations: during training, receiving instructions from a commander, marching in formation in the forest, and riding in a line of pick-up trucks along a desert road, or again, surrounded by admiring children and teens. A brief insert also shows the soothed face of a martyr bathed in light. Death and sacrifice appear furtively in this slick image of divine reward.

7.6. "The Tourism of my Umma is Jihad in the Path of Allah," Al I'tisam, YouTube, 2014.

The blurring of warfare and entertainment euphemizes the violence and death of combat. At times, combat is presented in an almost playful manner, as in the video *The Sniper of the Province of Goodness* (2015), produced by the media bureau of Deir al-Zur province, and which draws directly from the visual universe of first-person shooter games (FPS). The gun features (category, weight, caliber, and range) are presented at the beginning and the "viewer" adopts the vantage point of the player/killer (Figure 7.7). The immersive character of this point of view is also rendered by a physical proximity to the shooter (Figure 7.8), whose heartbeat we can hear as he takes aim, then his shouts of joy as the target falls dead. The increasingly intense sonic modulation of the *nashid*, which urges the believer to defeat the infidels, reinforces this immersive feeling and contributes to producing a fictional universe. Zooms, freeze-frames, repetitions, and rewinds all contribute to decoupling the target and the act of killing from reality, turning the matter into a sanitized, distanced war game with sophisticated weaponry. In this process of de-realized violence, the fighter becomes an accessible heroic figure with whom it is easy to identify.

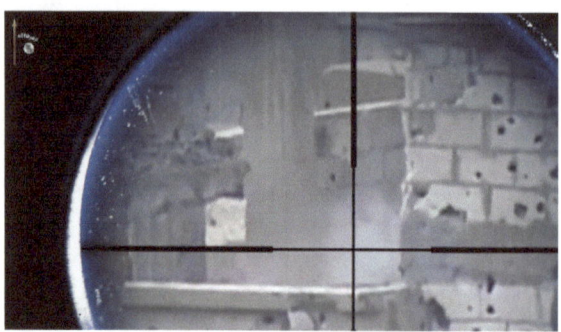

7.7. "The Sniper of the Province of Goodness, Media Bureau of Deir al-Zur province, 2015.

7.8. Mujatweet, episode 7 (al-Hayat, 2014).

This is how we come to observe a hyper-individualization of the fighter fig-ure—an innovation in the jihadist audiovisual production—with particular attention paid to foreigners who have performed the hijra. These outside recruits have an especially high profile in "Mujatweets," a campaign of eight short-format videos launched on Twitter in 2014 by al-Hayat Media Cen-ter (aimed particularly at a non-Arabic-speaking public) purporting to give an "inside look" at the daily life in the Caliphate. These videos are especially well-crafted: the image is sharp, playing with high contrast and depth of field. Many scenes are shot from a subjective viewpoint to immerse the viewer in the world of a travelogue, full of bright colors, welcoming locals, and abun-dant terroir foods and produce (Figure 7.9). We see combatants doing their shopping at the crowded Raqqa market amidst a joyful cacophony (Figure 7.10), eating tasty dishes at a canteen, and buying shawarma sandwiches as the vendor praises the renewed stability and security thanks to the presence of the IS "brothers," while another hands out cotton candy and ice cream to a crowd of children in a park. The point is to stage scenes of normalness while keeping the war, with its shortages and trauma, well out of sight.

7.9. Mujatweet, episode 7 (al-Hayat, 2014).

7.10. Mujatweet, episode 7 (al Hayat, 2014).

Paradoxically, the combatants are presented as guarantors of this return to a peaceful existence, as Abu Tamima[23] asserted when he launched an appeal to his "brothers and sisters to leave the lands of *tawaghit*"[24] (Figure 7.11). The combatants who make statements do so in their mother tongues, sprinkled with Arabic expressions belonging to the Islamist lexicon. This peculiar newspeak fits neatly into IS's internationalist utopia, highlighting its power to attract and assimilate young Westerners. These fighters were clearly chosen for their physique, as ambassadors of sorts, to represent IS. Once again, the hazards of combat are left off-camera, as in this Mujatweet where a young German man guides a visit to a modern clinic and asks after one of the wounded combatants (an Arab) who is recovering (Figure 7.12). Here, he invites brothers and sisters in Islam to come to "the land of honor" in search of the Shahada, and specifies that according to a hadith, the wounds of those who fight in the path of God will smell of musk on the Day of Judgment. The death of fighters is euphemized and sublimated in a war presented as a grand adventure, mingling the search for God and self-discovery.

7.11 Mujatweet, episode 6 (al-Hayat, 2014).

7.12 Mujatweet, episode 4 (al-Hayat, 2014).

Conclusion: Images at the Core of a Warrior Economy

This overview of various audiovisual grammars of groups affiliated with the Free Syrian Army, the Nusra Front, and the Islamic State reveals the broad outlines of distinct audiovisual practices and cultures that evolve with shifts in power dynamics, and the ways combatant life was being fantasized. This collective imagination conveys symbols, figures, and discourses grounded in the bodies and actions of the fighters. The ways of representing the fighting, their locations, their men, and their traumas are essential markers in these groups' self-imagining, whether they were invested in a national struggle, like the FSA, or a utopia, like the jihadist groups. These combat geographies, anchored in political struggles (to bring down the Assad regime) or religious crusades (to establish divine law), are very present in the images analyzed here. They also define the degree of concern for authentication of the images—prevalent in the FSA camp, whether for documenting and tracking an action or, in certain cases, for purposes of accountability to a sponsor, but considered by the jihadist camp as incidental. The Islamic State's audiovisual production even tended toward a fictionalization of combat and a communication strategy seeking to market the jihadist lifestyle. Thus, the audiovisual production of these different combat groups shows how crucial visuals are for representing the combat in action, but also for waging war. The progression of these three groups' image-making skills over time shows how the armed struggle that grew out of the initial revolt was "de-localized" and increasingly shifted onto jihad terrain—more specifically into the domain of the Islamic State, which greatly outpaced its adversaries in terms of visibility and media savvy thanks to a particularly sophisticated and attractive communication strategy, based on an immediately identifiable symbolic universe. Conversely, the sheer number of FSA references and the fragmented communication among its factions spread over so many media entities, often very local, all contributed to its gradual marginalization.

NOTES

1. Notably Turkey, starting in 2011, followed by Qatar, Great Britain, France, the United States, and Saudi Arabia.
2. Which has not prevented a certain permeability at various times and in particular combat zones.
3. See Chapter 8: "The Nusra Front's Audiovisual Jihad and its Break with the Islamic State in Iraq (2012- 2017)."
4. See Chapter 4: "Revolt With and Through Images."
5. Holliday, "Syria's Armed Opposition" (2012). This report is based mainly on videos posted online by different rebel groups.
6. A considerable number of videos are devoted to manufacturing and testing rocket launchers, handguns, automatic weapons, armored vehicles, etc. Furthermore, a sizable share of the rebel factions' weaponry comes from Syrian military personnel who have defected, from weapons seized during operations, and from contraband smuggled in from Lebanon, Iraq, and Turkey. Makeshift factories for producing weapons and ordnance were also started up in 2012.
7. Pierret, "La révolution syrienne" (2012), 75–82.
8. While a broad range of tendencies emerged as soon as the armed struggle took hold in 2011, starting in 2012, as violent repression escalated, the trend toward an Islamization of armed factions was noticeable. This can be partially explained by the need to appeal to financial backers in Qatar, Saudi Arabia, and the United Arab Emirates.
9. Posted on 19 August 2013 by the channel ShaamNetwork S.N.N. under the title: "Damascus, Qadam train station, violent clashes between the free army and regime forces," [translated from the Arabic]. https://www. youtube.com/watch?v=mrMxjb_wNr4&t=17s. With 23,080 views on 11 June 2024.
10. After doing a search in Arabic for "battle of the Qadam station" on YouTube, some twenty videos made it possible to draw up a timeline and uncover certain contextual elements. It played out in several acts from September 2012 until February 2013 and involved several brigades affiliated with the FSA, including the Division for the Liberation of Sham and the Lions of Islam Brigade. The objective was to take control of this zone which was home to a general headquarters of the Syrian army and pro-Assad militias responsible for numerous arrests in the neighborhood, and which represents the southern gateway into the heart of the capital. Shortly after the news that it had been taken on 28 January 2013, the Syrian army responded with an airstrike.
11. Cf. https://www.youtube.com/watch?v=LEUj-Q60D2E. With 5,280 views by 11 June 2024.

12. Tarnowski, "What have we been watching?" (2017).
13. Boëx, "Figures remixées des martyrs" (2018), 95–118.
14. El Difraoui, *Al-Qaida par l'image* (2013).
15. This video has disappeared, along with the rest of the series. On YouTube, it is indicated that the account which broadcast it has been closed. However, as is the case with many jihadist videos deleted from common broadcast platforms, certain episodes were saved on the Archive.org site by supporters.
16. I am grateful to Stéphane Audouin-Rouzeau, who brought this aspect to my attention.
17. On this type of institutional video, see: Rekik, *La fabrique audiovisuelle* (2018), 59–90.
18. In 2015, 30,000 combatants from 100 different countries are believed to have gone to Syria and Iraq, mainly to join the ranks of Islamic State. Cf. The Soufan Group, "An Updated Assessment of the Flow of Foreign Fighters into Syria and Iraq," 2015 (online) p. 6. The rest of the contingent is made up of Syrians and Iraqis. Most of the foreign fighters were sent to Syria.
19. A record of the statements and actions of the Prophet and his companions, transmitted through a chain of narrators ranked according to their degree of trustworthiness. These texts constitute references for behaviors and justifications. The hadith in question here is hadith 2481 taken from book 14 of the al-Sunan of Abou Dawoud collection (817–889).
20. "The Tourism of my Umma is Jihad in the Path of Allah." The link to this video, like those to be mentioned further on, was deleted, most likely during the drive to censure jihadist content on the Internet undertaken in 2015 by platforms such as YouTube.
21. In 2014, this main office, Diwan al-I'lam, equivalent to a Ministry of Information centralizing all media production (audio, radio, digital), is made up of 4 production units: al-Furqan (which has existed since 2006, founded by the Islamic State in Iraq); al-Hayat, intended for Western audiences and which also produces the online magazines Rumiyah and Dabiq; al-I'tisam, aimed at an Arab readership (ceased publication in 2016); and the Ajnad Foundation for the production of audio content and religious hymns. Under the supervision of this office, we find thirty-three regional branches that correspond to the provinces of the Caliphate and the territories in which IS was carrying out operations. In 2015, Syria counted eight media branches (Aleppo, Raqqa, al-Baraka, al-Sahel Hama, Homs, al-Khayr, and Damascus). Cf. Daniel Milton, "Communication Breakdown: Unraveling the Islamic State's Media Efforts," Combatting Terrorism Center at West Point, United States Military Academy, 2016.

22. Prior to this date, certain foreign fighters would post numerous photos and videos to their Facebook or Twitter accounts [now known as "X"], proudly displaying weapons, insignia, material comfort, and war trophies.

23. A Jihadist originally from Grenoble, whose real name was Abdallah Gitone, he garnered a certain notoriety thanks to Facebook, where he would depict his day-to-day life. He was killed in 2014 in Raqqa, shortly after posting this "mujatweet."

24. A theological term, this word refers to idolizing or slavishly obeying a group, an individual, or a thing that is not God, and which transgresses His will. Here it refers to countries that do not adhere to Islamic law.

8

THE NUSRA FRONT'S AUDIOVISUAL JIHAD AND ITS BREAK WITH THE ISLAMIC STATE IN IRAQ (2012-2017)

Giulia Galluccio

The audiovisual productions of jihadist groups gradually emerged in Syria from 2012,[1] against a highly complex background of militarization and fragmentation of the armed struggle. These groups existed in a temporal and territorial space that extended beyond Syria's borders. They consisted of Syrian fighters who participated in the war against the American invasion of Iraq in 2003, former Syrian prisoners (members of the political opposition or the Muslim Brothers*), and foreigners from far and wide. They all shared the same political agenda in Syria: the fall of Bashar al-Assad and the establishment of a transnational Islamic state. They did not acknowledge the Syrian opposition in exile abroad (the Syrian National Council*). On the ground, apart from the occasional tactical collaboration, they were distinct from the Free Syrian Army* (FSA) which they also sometimes engaged in battle, and at times resorted to suicide bombings. However, this common agenda did not result in any coherence, or a merging of jihadist fighter groups. Quite the opposite: they alternated between alliance schemes and breakups throughout the entire conflict. Among the more militarily organized was the Nusra Front*, which gained visibility during the series of car bomb attacks in the downtown areas of Damascus and Aleppo in December 2011.[2] During its creation phase, officially announced in a video posted online on 24 January 2012, this group was a direct offshoot of the Islamic State (IS) in Iraq, also known as al-Qaeda in Iraq*. However, relations between these two branches, al-Qaeda in Iraq and the Nusra Front, were contentious.[3]

By analyzing two Nusra Front videos, this chapter takes a close look at the alliance schemes, the deal-making, and the breakups between the two jihadist groups. These audiovisual productions help frame their political evolution chronologically, and show how their communication strategy evolved, as witnessed in the imagery of combat and jihadist fighters that each of their videos carefully portrayed. I will first study the group's earliest video, posted on 24 January 2012. This video launches a call to jihad* in Syria and is broadly based on the imagery and aesthetic of al Qaeda productions—even though the Nusra Front would not declare its allegiance until a year later, on 10 April 2013. I will then examine the transition period in representations of global jihad, as witnessed in a clip broadcast during the summer of 2013. This video was produced shortly before the official break between the two branches and the appearance of the spectacular and macabre videos of the Islamic State in Iraq and the Levant, proclaimed on 4 July 2014, thereby becoming the official rival of the Nusra Front and al-Qaeda among jihadist movements.[4] This second video, then, is evidence of a compromise between two different visual cultures compelled, at that point in time, to cohabit in a wartime media space. The final section of this chapter analyzes the videos that the Nusra Front produced between 2014 and 2017, which shed light on how a new audiovisual communication process came to rival that of the IS. These new productions indicate a political and strategic evolution expressed through novel formats and content.

The Influence of al-Qaeda in the Visual Language of the Nusra Front

The first video distributed by the Nusra Front made the group's creation official.[5] With a length of 16 minutes and 48 seconds, the video was posted on 24 January 2012 on its production and broadcast channel, The White Minaret (*al-Manara al-Bayda'*). As it was posted online to several social networks and forums that sometimes changed its title, the video is called either "*Kata'ib Ahrar al-Sham*" (The Free Men of the Levant Brigades) or "*Sham al-Jihad*" (The Syria of Jihad),[6] and is structured in four segments of varying lengths, each opening with the text: "The Syria of Jihad" ("*Sham al-Jihad*"). After the opening credits, there is text quoting a sura from the Quran to justify the name "Nusra Front" and its combat in Syria.[7] The fighters, filmed in desert settings, declare their commitment to overthrow Bashar al-Assad. The second part consists of photos of Damascus projected between screens bearing Quranic verses highlighting the importance of *Sham** and of that city in the history of Islam (Figure 8.1). The next segment, the longest, is devoted to the speech by the leader of the Nusra Front, Abu Muhammad al-Julani, who announces off-screen the group's main objectives,[8] and lists the countries considered as enemies. Images of heads of state and politicians clipped from Syrian TV channels (e.g. Addounia TV) accompany his speech. Finally, the last segment concludes on the same images and fighter testimonials as in the first part of the video.

The first noteworthy element is the importance of calligraphy and text, which are given prominence over human representations (Figures 8.1, 8.2, 8.3, and 8.4). Before the opening credits, we see a still shot with three textual elements, each in a different font against a light blue background with a few clouds, suggestive of the paradise that the martyrs of jihad are promised (Figure 8.2). A particular calligraphic style (*riq'a*) is used for the opening Quranic verse ("In the name of God, the Most Gracious, the Most Merciful"), and a standard font is used for the name of the production company. Finally, the month and year of the video are specified according to the Muslim Hijri calendar in a third font.

The logo of the production company appears next, overlaid on the Dome of the Rock in Jerusalem (Figure 8.3), the emblematic site of jihad representing the Muslim struggle against Jews and the State of Israel, which is an essential feature of the grand jihadist narrative. The Nusra Front flag is set next to the dome, as well as at the center bottom of the screen on a world globe, which appears very often in the credits of al-Qaeda productions and symbolizes the global dimension of jihad. The other black banners, set below the Nusra Front flag, do not bear the name of the brigades but simply display the first sura of the Quran and the profession of faith (Shahada). They confirm the Nusra Front's claim to federate the various jihadist groups in Syria. The white minaret of the Umayyad Mosque of Damascus, to the left of the Dome of the Rock, doubles the symbolic value of the image and the struggle: Syria has become a jihad cause of the same caliber as the Palestinian cause. The soundtrack over this opening sequence is a series of laser-like sounds, as the Nusra Front flag rises on the right-hand side of the screen.

8.1. "The Free Men of the Levant Brigades," The White Minaret, 2012.

8.2. "The Free Men of the Levant Brigades," The White Minaret, 2012. Translation of text: "In the Name of God, the most Gracious, the most Merciful. The White Minaret Information Foundation. Year 1433 (Hijri)."

8.3. "The Free Men of the Levant Brigades." The White Minaret, 2012. Final image of the introductory credits.

After the introductory sura, we encounter one of the typical devices of al-Qaeda videos: the use of pictures-in-pictures, often oblique fly-ins. These screens, embedded in the background, are always moving and stand out against a white backdrop with downward mirrored reflections (Figure 8.4 and 8.5). At the top of each screen is a caption indicating the territories where the Nusra Front fighters are deployed (Idlib, Daraa, al-Ghouta, Deir al-Zur, and al-Bukamal). No other contextualizing feature is present. The shots show desert areas with no anchoring reference, or simply masked faces of the fighters brandishing, all together, the Nusra Front banner. These images return time and again, most likely indicating a dearth of material and visual resources, a gap filled by images taken from Syrian TV channels. The English subtitles demonstrate the determination to reach an international public. Sound effects punctuate the transition from one sequence to another, accompanied by a *nashid*. The final sound shot consists of a speech by Nusra Front leader Abu Muhammad al-Julani, over which is superimposed, at the very end of the video, faraway voices of combatants declaring their allegiance to the group. Al-Julani's speech, in classical Arabic, makes selective use of historical and geopolitical facts (such as the 2001 war in Afghanistan, the Palestinian cause, etc.), and of Quranic verses. It manifests propaganda techniques involving varying degrees of manipulation, selection, and shading of the truth, as well as theological knowledge typical of Sunni ulemas who are aiming for a high-profile position in the international arena.[9] Even though the official allegiance to al-Qaeda did not take place until 10 April 2013, this video already reveals "a visual allegiance" by virtue of resemblances in format, symbolism, and iconography used by al-Qaeda for the past twenty years.[10]

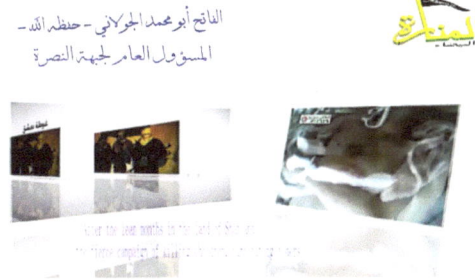

الفاتح أبو محمد الجولاني - حفظه الله -
المسؤول العام لجبهة النصرة

8.4. "The Free Men of
the Levant Brigades,"
The White Minaret,
2012. Translation of text:
"The conqueror Abu
Muhammad al-Julani,
Allah protect him, head of
the Nusra Front."

8.5. "The Free Men of
the Levant Brigades." The
White Minaret, 2012. "The
Pride of Idlib."

Compromise Between the Visual Cultures of the Nusra Front and the Islamic State

The video titled "Mu'askar" ("A Camp") reflects the growing tension between the Nusra Front and the Islamic State in Iraq.[11] It aims to recruit new fighters by staging the atmosphere and activity of the fighters under the command of warlords belonging to either the Nusra Front or the Islamic State in Iraq. Posted online on 1 August 2013, it was likely produced a few months earlier.[12] It sets the scene for the first signs of a turning point in jihadist audiovisual communication. Rather short for Nusra Front videos (just over three minutes), there is evidence of a greater financial commitment and significant post-production work. A formal change appears right from the opening credits—this time without the habitual first sura of the Quran as an introduction (Figure 8.6).

8.6. "A Camp," The White Minaret, 2013. Image at the end of the opening credits.

The celestial backdrop of the first video is traded for a black backdrop overlaid with several images. Al-Qaeda's trademark visuals (pictures-in-pictures, the globe in the background, and the Kalashnikov) remain, but are diluted in a wash of special effects. The soundtrack is clearly improved: a filter cuts the bass frequencies to better accentuate the *nashid*. Mixed into this warrior hymn are sound effects that completely drown out the speech, and the sound of a helicopter grows louder and closes out the opening. Calligraphy is completely absent, except for the initial title shown only once at the end of the opening credits, losing its prominence. Images shot outdoors in a training camp open the video. A ray of sunshine and a dark halo overlaid in post-production surround the images of this video that show fighters—mostly masked—in a military training camp.

The colors are filtered to match a certain palette, and the video presents all the features of an alluring jihad: weapons, motorcycles, computers, and high-tech watches. These representations of the camp alternate with instruction sequences where new recruits, notebook in hand, are taking courses in weapons handling or watching war scenes projected onto a wall. A masked leader, armed with a Kalashnikov, leads the training sessions. Here, the valuation of collective effort also leaves latitude for individual personality development. The soldiers are filmed as a group as well as individuals, with certain shots focused on a charismatic personality or an action performed by a particular recruit, who deploys his weapon while riding a motorcycle, or makes a perilous jump while keeping hold of his weapon (Figures 7 and 9). The editing is paced by slow-motion effects and shots that emphasize camaraderie and focus on weaponry or the Nusra Front banner.

8.7. "A Camp," The White Minaret, 2013.

8.8. "A Camp," The White Minaret, 2013.

This latter video is exceptional in comparison not only to the Nusra Front's previous videos, but also to its future audiovisual productions. It approximates the Hollywood aesthetic to be ushered in a year later by the IS in some of its productions. Because the Nusra Front was administered by the Iraqi wing of al-Qaeda,[13] it is likely that recruits from al-Qaeda in Iraq had a hand in making this video, at a time of political flux where the two visual cultures were working side by side. The first subordinates form to content, the second is almost blasphemous regarding a certain Sunni orthodoxy: by valorizing an appealing jihad, it fails to invoke historic or religious causes in favor of material resources.

The Audiovisual Languages of the Nusra Front

The analysis of these two videos sheds light on the audiovisual practices that, in an extremely competitive context, interact through imitation or by seeking to set themselves apart. Starting in July 2013, the group introduced a new channel named Himam News Agency. The Nusra Front distanced itself from Islamic State productions that, by 2014, included videos of beheadings, public hangings, and stonings, adopting a much more Westernized staging and aesthetic of deadly action scenes. Unlike those images that play on voyeurism and the star power of certain fighters, the Nusra Front would go on to focus on the local dimension of its jihad in Syria.[14] Taking the form of TV reportage, these videos set aside the al-Qaeda visual rhetoric, opting instead for interviews with local personalities which emphasize the services provided by the Nusra Front in a range of locales (Aleppo, Daraa, Homs, and Idlib), as demonstrated in an untitled clip from 24 August 2014 broadcast by the channel Himam News Agency of Latakia. It shows food distribution and clean-up activities carried out under the direction of Nusra Front fighters, as the townspeople look on approvingly. However, this channel soon ceased its activities. Between August and December 2014, Nusra Front communication officials decided to maintain The White Minaret as their only production channel, incorporating the Himam News Agency videos. The logo was modified in December 2014 (Figure 8.9), adopting a more neutral graphic, closer to that of mainstream news channels (the black flag, for instance, was eliminated).

8.9. Nusra Front's new logo which reads "Correspondent of The White Minaret in Aleppo," 2014.

All these videos open with the first sura of the Quran, a nod to the group's Muslim character,[15] and run between one and three minutes. Reports and opinion polls conducted with the local population aim to show that the group garners support among the locals, and how the Nusra Front comes to their aid. The subjects vary: clean-up efforts and the upgrading of the sewer system in Idlib under the supervision of Nusra Front fighters,[16] or street interviews with young shopkeepers or village elders to ask what they think about the Russian and Iranian attacks of November 2015[17] (Figure 8.10). This demonstrates the group's determination to break with the al-Qaeda templates and refresh its communication strategy, aiming to consolidate its legitimacy and usefulness in Syria. These videos occasionally alternate with former templates at certain moments of the conflict or combat (*nashids* in the background, images of outdoor camps, fighters with blurred faces shooting into the woods, or bodies, filmed at a distance or close-up, of Syrian army soldiers killed by the Nusra Front).

8.10. "What is your impression of the fierce Russian and Iranian attacks against the Syrian people?" The White Minaret, correspondent in Idlib, 2015. Channel Shabakat Murasel al-Manara al-Bayda' – Murasel Idlib, jihadology. net, https://jihadology.net/2015/11/ page/4/, accessed on 20 June 2019.

The "long" formats (over ten minutes) remain, especially when it comes to tribute videos to martyrs fallen in combat, videos shot with drones, or those filmed with GoPro by the mujahidin at the front. These videos fit into the relentless flow of productions from late 2015, representing the Nusra Front's victory against Iranian forces, with the purpose of demonstrating the group's military effectiveness. The aesthetic choices hark back to the previous al-Qaeda visual culture but also appeal to newer visual features. The quality of Nusra Front videos differs depending on the context and the availability of technology at a given moment (such as the use of drone cameras starting in 2015,[18] or GoPro cameras between 2016 and 2017). While video production was becoming an increasingly competitive issue among all groups, jihadist or otherwise, the Nusra Front's communication was evolving. By summer 2014, the Front was opting for shorter formats (three minutes or less) than their previous ones modeled on al-Qaeda productions, thus moving closer to the more appealing "mujatweets" invented by IS.[19] Video production was also evolving as a consequence of the presence (confirmed by the summer of 2012) of foreign combatants in Syria coming from Europe, among other places, and whose expertise may well have played a role.[20] Since 2012, the audiovisual strategy of the Nusra Front gave signs of permeability to influences from other fighting groups, while maintaining distinctive features in accordance with its own values, the context, and its basic objectives (to recruit, to pay tribute to martyrs, and to legitimize its military and political role in Syria). This flexibility proved effective, for despite its change of name on 29 July 2016[21] and its merger on 28 January 2017 with the Organization for the Liberation of the Levant (Hay'at Tahrir al-Sham*), this group remained, until January 2020 at least, a major jihad player in the provinces of Hama and Idlib (northwestern Syria) and in the struggle to overthrow the Assad regime.

NOTES

1. The main jihadist-Salafist fighting groups in Syria were the Free Men of the Levant Brigades (Kata'ib Ahrar al-Sham*), The Levant Falcons Division (Liwa' Suqur al-Sham), and the Umma Division (Liwa' al-Umma, the world community of Muslims). They emerged as the key local actors operating in the country, especially in the north. These conservative Salafist rebel groups broke from the Free Syrian Army, contributing to the fragmenting of the armed struggle. Cf. "Tentative jihad: Syria's Fundamentalism," International Crisis Group, *Middle East Report* no. 131, October 2012.
2. Between December 2011 and May 2012, a series of attacks struck Damascus and Aleppo. The Nusra Front claimed responsibility, asserting they were aimed at the Syrian authorities. Cf. "Un obscur groupuscule revendique l'attentat sanglant de Damas," *Le Monde*, 05/12/2012; and Leverrier, "Syrie. Bachar al Assad, le Front de Soutien, l'État islamique et le peuple syrien (2/4)," and "Un œil sur la Syrie," *Le Monde*, 04/03/2014.
3. In a communiqué dated 21 March 2012, the Syrian leader of the Nusra Front, Abu Muhammad al-Julani, asserted that he condemned "Iraqi-style" extremism and declared that their objective was neither to start a sectarian war nor to kill civilians. Cf. "Opération contre la direction de la sécurité aérienne et le département de la justice pénale," djihadology.net, accessed on 25 July 2013.
4. In an audio recording from 29 June 2014, Abu Muhammad al-'Adnani, spokesman for the Islamic State in Iraq, announces the group's new name "Islamic State in Iraq and the Levant" and acknowledges Abu Bakr al-Baghdadi as caliph. Al-Baghdadi officially proclaims the restoration of the Caliphate on 4 July 2014 in the Great Mosque of al-Nuri in Mosul. In the video, al-Baghdadi declares himself caliph of the Islamic State and calls on all Muslims of the world to support him. Cf. "Abu Bakr al-Baghdadi Appears in Video, Delivers Sermon in Mosul," *Site Intelligence Group*, 07/05/2014. The Nusra Front does not acknowledge this Caliphate.
5. Video "Kata'ib Ahrar al-Sham" [The Free Men of the Levant Brigades], posted on 24 January 2012, jihadology.net, https://bit.ly/2XnlpXO, accessed October 2019.
6. At that time (until late 2013) the Nusra Front had a Facebook page and a Twitter [now "X"] account. Its videos were also available on other platforms (especially YouTube), as well as several jihadist forums such as Ansar al-Mujahidin (supporters of the mudjahidin).
7. After the opening credits comes a still image lasting one minute, of verse 75 of the sura "al-Nisa'" (The Women). A voiceover recites: "Why, then, should you not fight in the cause of God and of the oppressed, helpless

men, women, and children, who cry out: 'O Lord! Bring us out of this land whose people are oppressors, and appoint for us from Your Presence a protector, and appoint for us from Your Presence a helper!" [helper in Arabic is nasiran, the same root in Arabic as an-nusra, "help, support"].

8. The fall of Bashar al-Assad, the return of an Islamic state in Syria, the restoration of the Caliphate, and the application of Sharia law.

9. Al-Julani denounces the rebels who accept aid from Western countries to overthrow the regime of Bashar al-Assad. He accuses the Turkish government of being a pawn in the hands of the Americans and strongly opposes the Arab League and its role as mediator in the conflict, as well as the Iranian forces "who seek to revive the times of the Persian Empire."

10. For an in-depth look at al-Qaeda's visual culture and its evolution, cf. El Difraoui, *Al-Qaida par l'image* (2013).

11. Tension gradually increased after the declaration by Abu Bakr al-Baghdadi—leader of al-Qaeda in Iraq at that time—of a merger between the two organizations and the birth of the Islamic State in Iraq and the Levant (ISIL). The next day (April 10, 2013), the leader of the Nusra Front, Abu Muhammad al-Julani, denied this declaration through an Oath of Allegiance (bay'a) to al-Qaeda in order not to submit to the Iraqi branch of al-Baghdadi. The leader of al-Qaeda, Ayman al-Zawahiri, then tried to resolve these tensions by appointing in June 2013 an emissary, Abu Khalid al-Suri, to supervise the collaboration between the two branches and cancel their merger. This decision was contested by al-Baghdadi, and the two groups went through a phase of tension which lasted until the official split in June 2014.

12. "A Camp," posted 1 August 2013, archive.org, accessed 24 May 2020.

13. Burgat and Paoli, *Pas de Printemps pour la Syrie* (2013).

14. Since 2005, al-Qaeda chiefs had banned the broadcast of videos depicting the decapitation of foreign hostages and Shiite Muslims, especially among its Iraqi branch headed by al-Zarqawi, after the American invasion in 2003. However, the Nusra Front broadcast videos of the mass execution of soldiers from the Syrian army on 26 July 2016 via its official channel, without stage-directing the deadly action.

15. Though not used systematically, a Quranic sura can serve as introduction to the video.

16. Video of 31 December 2015, lasting 1 minute 24 seconds, entitled "Supervision of the municipality of Darush: clean-up and refurbishment of the sewer system." *Shabakat murasel al Manara al-Bayda'* – Murasel Idlib, jihadology.net, accessed on 10 June 2019.

17. Video of 30 November 2015, "What is your opinion of the ferocious attacks by Russia and Iran against the Syrian people?" *Shabakat murasel al-Manara al-Bayda'* – Idlib, jihadology.net, accessed on 10 June 2019.

18. As in two videos devoted to their victory against the Iranian forces in the mountains of al-Turkman, near Latakiya. "Report on the removal of Iranian forces on the hills of al-Hawiz and al-Qarasi and on the imprisonment of Iranian fighters," posted on 27 November 2015; and "Breaking the Iranian defense forces that flee before the Mujahidin assault vehicles," posted on 28 November 2015, jihadology.net, accessed on 15 June 2019.

19. See Chapter 7: "National Armed Struggle and Global Jihad in the Public Imagination."

20. Awan, "The Impact of Jihadist Evolving Narratives on Radicalization in the West," in Staffell and Awan (2017): 183–254.

21. Leader al-Julani declares the end of his allegiance to al-Qaeda, thanking al-Zawahiri for his support, and announces "the cancelation of all operations taking place under the name of Jabhat al-Nusra" which will become Jabhat Fath al-Sham. Video available at Al-Jazeera.com: "Al-Nusra Leader al-Julani announces split from al-Qaeda," Al-Jazeera, 07/29/2016.

9

THE AFFAIR OF THE SISTERS OF SAINT THECLA

THE CHRISTIAN COMMUNITY IN SYRIA AT THE CENTER OF COMPETING IMAGES AND NARRATIVES

Anna Poujeau

In the autumn of 2013, the Syrian army and different rebel factions clashed over the renowned Christian village of Maaloula located to the north of Damascus, in the Qalamun. Home to numerous churches and two ancient monasteries, the village has been touted by the regime since the 1980s as a national symbol of Christianity, serving at times as a "showcase" of Christians in Syria for the authorities who take official Western delegations to visit there. Starting on 4 September 2013—the first day of fighting—the thirteen nuns of the Greek Orthodox monastery of Saint Thecla found themselves in the thick of the war and the battle of images that opposed the Syrian regime and the rebel fighters, particularly those of Islamist and jihadist persuasion. The nuns were called upon to testify before the cameras of this or that group about the deeds attributed at times to those called "terrorists" by the regime, and at other times to the regime by the rebels. Their monastery, which houses the tomb of Saint Thecla, is a place reputed for visitations and miracles. Dedicated to the saint and sheltered from the outside world while remaining close to thousands of the faithful, the nuns rarely leave the monastery. They occupy a special place in the country's Christian community.[1]

This chapter examines "the affair of the Sisters of Saint Thecla"[2] based on some forty videos shot by different warring actors who were disputing the narrative. Backed by my on-the-ground knowledge acquired between 2003 and 2010 when I was researching this community, I analyze the religious and political issues behind these images broadcast mainly by Lebanese media. The Lebanese media occupy an important place in this affair for two reasons: the clampdown on Syrian media and the involvement of Lebanese actors in the conflict. Syrian media broadcast only the official national narrative and censured images from opposition parties, while Lebanese actors were involved at the military, political, and media levels: Hezbollah fighting alongside the regime, the head of Lebanese security intervening in negotiations, and Lebanese experts debating on TV talk shows about how the affair was developing. I will analyze these images based on three crucial moments of the affair: the taking of the village by the rebels, the departure of the nuns for the town of Yabrud under rebel control in early December 2013, and the return of the nuns to Damascus on 9 March 2014. In each case, the videos shot by the different parties narrate the event, testifying to or contradicting the allegations of the opposing party. A real battle was waged in this circulation of images that also determined the way the regime and the rebel factions related to the country's Christian minority, and how they manipulated the affair to their own ends. Indeed, certain crucial aspects of the war were swirling around the issue of sectarianism, ranging from private reasons touched upon by individuals to justify their involvement or non-involvement in the protest, all the way to regional and inter-state alliances that extend far beyond any personal concerns.[3] Scrutiny of the images produced by this affair discloses the various narratives and counter-narratives of the revolution and the war, and sheds light on the place of interfaith relations in all these stories.

4 September 2013: Videos of the Capture of Maaloula by Rebel Factions

At dawn on 4 September 2013, the village was attacked by fighters of three opposition factions: the Nusra Front*, the Islamic Movement (Harakat Ahrar al-Sham al-Islamiyah)*, and the Brigade for the Liberation of Qalamun* (Liwa' Tahrir al-Qalamun)—a group affiliated with the Free Syrian Army* (FSA). One jihadist, Abu Haytham al-Harduni, Jordanian and member of the Nusra Front, committed a suicide attack with a pick-up truck loaded with explosives at an army post located near the entrance to the village. That same day, his video testament was posted to YouTube by the Coalition of Battalions and Brigades of the Martyrs of Syria (Tajammu' Kata'ib wa-Alwiyat Shuhada' Surya*) and the Voice of Truth Brigade (Liwa' Sawt al-Haqq*). These images of the attack were filmed in static camera from a remote position: they show the interactions between the fighter and those filming, then the explosion in a huge roar amidst shouts of joy. Eight minimally armed conscripts were killed in the explosion, their bodies covertly visible in another video shot and posted by the Qalamun Media Center (QMC) shortly after the attack. Then, the fighters took Maaloula. A few villagers of the People's Defense Committee (against the rebels) were either killed or kidnapped.

The same day, a second video posted to social networks was picked up by some Lebanese media. Filmed by the rebels, it shows one of them ordering the others not to target churches or civilians (Figure 9.1).[4] It seeks to demonstrate that they did not wish to attack Christians, as claimed by the regime that presented its own position as protector of religious minorities against the rebels whom it called "terrorists."[5] This communication was coming at a particularly sensitive time that year: the Islamic State* (IS) had taken control of Raqqa over the summer and several Christian clergy members had been kidnapped. But in Maaloula, the IS was not present, and native to this majority Sunni region, with its sizable Christian minority, were numerous rebel fighters struggling together within different factions. In the Qalamun, as in southern Syria where radical Islamist groups had not managed to gain a foothold, there had so far never been major clashes between Sunnis and Christians—unlike what had been happening in the north and northeast of the country.

9.1. Al Jadeed News, 09/04/2013.

The villagers holed up at home took advantage of a counterattack by the army a few days later to flee. At this point in the war, the rebels' goal was to capture the string of villages that stretched from the foothills of the Qalamun mountain range to the highway connecting Damascus and Homs. Capitalizing on this counterattack, Lebanese and Syrian media covered the story. The only remaining occupants of the monastery were the thirteen nuns and the three postulants who, as required by their vocation, kept vigil over Saint Thecla. In fact, this monastery was not at all withdrawn from the world, but rather was engaged in the ongoing challenge to prevailing politics by the power of the saint, in opposition to the prelates who were caught up in its relations of patronage with the State authorities. The Sisters, who related to the saint through daily apparitions and dream-like visions, thus adopted a dissident stance toward male power, be it religious or political. This unusual position comes through in the narrative of the village attack that they address to the media.

The Superior, Mother Bélajia, was questioned on several occasions by journalists trying to find out whether the fighters mistreated them, committed massacres, forced the locals to convert to Islam, or ransacked the churches. Rumors circulated as to likely abuses, especially since videos of the funerals in Damascus of the men from the People's Defense Committee were circulating on social media at that time. Mother Bélajia's declarations and those by the families of the victims came together to establish the narrative of how the village was captured. In a video running a little under two minutes posted to the site Elnashra,[6] Mother Bélajia describes their interactions with the fighters who came to the monastery (Figure 9.2).[7] She expresses herself in a somewhat surprising register which, in hindsight, sheds light on the resolute positions the nuns would take a few months later once they had left the monastery and been taken away to Yabrud by the rebels. Far from denouncing the attack on the village, she declares that there are no abuses to report, while remaining neutral in her demeanor regarding the parties in conflict.

9.2. Elnashra, 09/07/2013.

The interview takes place in the monastery's reception room, with sporadic gunfire audible in the background. The Superior does not stick to a mundane narrative, instead beginning by evoking the many miracles of Saint Thecla. Thus, by painting a picture of life at the monastery, she seeks to remove herself from the contingencies and issues of the war before announcing that, throughout the fighting, the saint appeared to help the nuns. She goes on to explain at length how the motor that pumps water up to the monastery stopped miraculously, after working for eight hours in a row, once the cistern was full. This reference to miracles allows the Superior to show the outside world that the monastery and the community are protected from the war by the power of the saint. At the end of the interview, she declares that they feel safe with the Syrian army back in the village, even though they hold nothing against the rebels. When an insistent journalist seems to want her to come out in favor of the army, the Superior replies: "The army is the head of the State and the security of the country. All armies must protect the State, be it the Syrian army, the Lebanese army, or any other army in the world."[8] Thus, the Superior manages not to take sides and never mentions the name of Bashar al-Assad. Still, in a context where this name is automatically invoked by everyone to guard against accusations of treason, this silence implies a refutation of the kind of allegiance to the regime that most ecclesiastic authorities feel compelled to embrace. In other television interviews, she unequivocally contradicts the rumors concerning the destruction of churches by the rebels. And to the journalists' queries as to her opinion about the events in general, she responds with prayers.

5 February 2014: The Sisters of Saint Thecla in Yabrud Filmed by the Rebel Fighters

In late September, the rebels succeeded in retaking their position. For several months, the fighting was relentless, with the different factions allied with the regime taking part, including the Syrian National Socialist Party, Lebanese Hezbollah, and the People's Committee for the Defense of Saidnaya.[9] In early December, news that the nuns had left their monastery for an undisclosed location was circulating on the Facebook pages of people from Maaloula and Saidnaya. On 5 February 2014, the LBC channel, in a scoop, broadcast a four-minute-and-fifteen-second video produced by the rebels that tells the story of the Sisters. A previous video had been broadcast on Al Jazeera, then on Al Jadeed News 6 December, only five days after their departure from the monastery.[10] In the video they announce that, trapped by artillery fire for two months, they had felt obliged to flee. Sheltered at first in a less exposed house in the village, they were then escorted by the rebels to Yabrud, to the house where the first video was shot. Later, they would be housed in the luxurious villa of a wealthy Christian of the town, where the second video was then shot (Figure 9.3). Multiple commentators were speculating about the nuns' possible kidnapping by the rebels. The images broadcast by the LBC served to quash that rumor and announce that negotiations were underway, involving an exchange between the Sisters and prisoners of the regime.

9.3. LBC, 02/05/2014.

In a meticulously staged shoot, the Sisters answer questions posed by a man whose voice is disguised. The Superior intervenes occasionally to add a detail or clarify, and to encourage them to reassure their families. The videographer shows them all, clearly as proof that they are alive and in good health. The Sisters repeat that the fighters did indeed help them flee, that they have been treated with respect, and that they hope to return to their monastery. The repetition suggests that their speech is being strictly controlled, with little room for improvisation. While one of them is speaking, footage shot outdoors shows them laughing and throwing snowballs with two men whose faces have been blurred. This insert is meant to highlight the good relationship between the nuns and the rebels, as well as their freedom of movement. Still, their stating that the monastery is where they hope to return, emphasizing that they cannot live elsewhere, is a way of once again withdrawing from the reality of the conflict in which they have become unwillingly involved. Their world cannot be affected by the war.

At the end of the video, the Superior assumes the role of spokeswoman and directs her words to the adversary. At this point, it is no longer a matter of reassuring either side but of speaking on their position in the upcoming transaction. Without mentioning the regime or the rebels, she speaks of "all the detainees and all the prisoners arrested with or without cause" who must be released during this operation, for which the Sisters are "the victims or the reward." This double self-designation sounds like a cautious attempt at self-preservation, at appearing as neutral as possible toward all parties. In effect, the Sisters are consenting hostages and the situation could backfire once they are back home and the regime gets its revenge. The Superior still makes no mention of Bashar al-Assad but appeals to God and thanks "people all over the world who still take interest in us; we ask that they continue to do so, and that we might meet someday, wherever we may be."[11] This is how she ends, as if she were asking for guarantees about what might happen to them next. At the head of the monastery for some twenty years and accustomed to dealing with clerical or political authorities, she knows all about the political stakes of speaking out and the paramount importance of caution. And yet, this phrasing and word choice, however cautious, do not fit into the boundaries of authorized speech in Syria. By not condemning the rebels, the Sisters have crossed a red line.

The video then takes a more formal turn. Two sisters hold a sheet of paper with the day's date to authenticate the time of filming, and a male voice then speaks in classical Arabic:

> *Communication still remains open with a few professional institutions outside Syria to facilitate the removal of the Sisters to a secure place as soon as possible. But the outlaw al-Assad is still trying to thwart these attempts, and what's more, he is trying to put the Sisters in harm's way so as to accuse the mujahidin [fighters]. We appeal to God for help.*

This video prompted a flood of commentary over the credibility of the nuns' declarations and their consent. On Lebanese channels, a parade of experts weighed in: Are they genuine victims of a kidnapping, or are they complicit with the rebels to obtain the release of prisoners detained by the regime? Were they compelled to remove their crosses? Don't their habits and veils suggest a conservatism akin to that of the rebels? Mother Bélajia's personality was also subject to debate. Some claimed that she allowed the fighters to hide in the monastery in exchange for a sum of money for the partisans of Samir Geagea.[12] Other videos disclaim the kidnapping scenario with testimony by the combatants and footage from the field that attests to both the scope of destruction caused by the regime and the control of the village by the rebels. The opposition channel Orient News, as early as 3 December 2013, aired a brief on-the-scene report.[13]

The reporter announces the liberation of the village while commenting on the scope of destruction, and then arrives in front of the monastery to explain that artillery fire rained down on the buildings even while the Sisters were still present. He adds that official media announced that they had died. Next, we see a member of a combat faction clearly affiliated to the FSA posted at the entrance to the house of worship. He explains to the reporter that the Sisters are safe, having sought shelter in the village. According to him, the fighters decided to get them out of harm's way because of the fighting. He explains that the villagers were long gone, and no one remains in the village except regime forces and rebel combatants who eventually took back control (Figure 9.4).[14] While he is speaking, the camera films two armed men entering the partially destroyed monastery. At the end of the interview, we see once again the façade riddled with bullet marks before returning to the reporter who announces upcoming reports on Maaloula and its liberation, and relief provided to the Sisters.

9.4. Orient TV, 12/03/2013.

9 March 2014: Handing over the Sisters
On the night of 9 March, a new video[15] was posted to YouTube by Hadi al-Abdallah.[16] Running a little over six minutes, it shows the exchange of the Sisters and the regime's political prisoners. The video was rebroadcast by various Lebanese media outlets. The montage is built around three sequences:

the Sisters exiting their house in Yabrud surrounded by fighters; the vehicles driving, by night, along a steep road to the site of the exchange operation on the border with Lebanon near the locality of Wadi 'Ata and finally, the hand-over. The camera captures the moments that testify to the good faith between the Sisters and the fighters. For instance, in the first sequence, the cameraman recalls (with the Mother Superior shot in close-up) how well the fighters behaved with the Sisters, having conducted themselves "as Muslims." Both the cameraman and the Mother Superior call upon God in nearly every utterance. Though Syrians tend to do this in general in their everyday speech, in this context, this religiously inflected way of speaking takes on special significance and allows their faith differences to fade into the background. Their shared piety creates a certain complicity between them, each evoking his or her duty accomplished before God in a long ceremonious exchange in which Mother Bélajia succeeds in subtly slipping in remarks as to how long their captivity lasted—"it's been four months!"—and the disproportionate value the Sisters represent in the exchange compared to 152 released prisoners.

We next see a hooded, armed man carrying one of the Sisters (Figure 9.5). Here again, these images testify to the respect these men have for the women, some of whom are elderly. An insert shot shows a man who calls out to the cameraman: "Al-Hajj Abu Qatham, the commander of the al-Furqan* brigade, sends his warm greetings." This shot allows this brigade to claim its participation in the exchange, and the spectator understands that numerous fighting factions are allied in this affair. This is why the video, like the two previous ones of the Sisters broadcast on 6 December and 5 February, does not bear the signature of any one group. The camera then captures the farewell moments: everyone expressing a wish to stay alive and invoking God's protection for the other. As the vehicles leave the scene, in the cameraman's car we see the driver in a balaclava waving the black Nusra Front flag out the window. On the flag is written in white lettering the Shahada, the Islamic profession of faith. As was the case in the previous shot, which made a point of attesting to the participation of the al-Furqan brigades in the operation, this one pointedly shows the involvement of the Nusra Front. In the second part of the video, shot from inside the vehicle, the camera films the smiling nuns and purposely shows their confidence even as they are being driven in the middle of the night by a masked and heavily armed man.

9.5. YouTube channel of Hadi
al-Abdallah, 03/09/2014.

These final images of an intensely emotional sequence chronicle a risky night-time operation on a narrow mountain road. The armed rebels, jihadists among them, are on the Lebanese border meeting up with men from Lebanese General Security led by 'Abbas Ibrahim, who took part in the handover negotiations. A final statement by the Mother Superior attests to the bond forged between the nuns and the combatants: "We are very grateful for your kindness and your conduct with us, and may God protect you and protect everyone." She even asks the hooded Nusra Front driver to send greetings to a certain Om 'Azem and to tell an Abu Malik that he is a man of honor.[17] As the nuns finally join up with the men from General Security, the fighters shout out, as a sign of victory and defiance: "*Allahu akbar! Allahu akbar!*" On the Lebanese side, the armed personnel—extremely tense—are poised to intervene, which contrasts with the relaxed atmosphere among the Syrian fighters who have just won a political victory and scored a media coup against the regime. Clearly giving lie to the regime's narrative that presents them as terrorists, they allied themselves with the Sisters and, thanks to this personal bond, were able to win the release of many detainees and their children. The Sisters come upon a woman and her four children (probably the family of an al-Qaeda leader) being carried by men from Lebanese General Security. The handover takes place: an armed man in a balaclava grasps a little girl and starts to cry while victory shouts rise from the fighters: "*Allahu akbar! Allahu akbar!*" (Figure 9.6).

9.6. YouTube channel of Hadi
al-Abdallah, 03/10/2014.

The cameraman then questions the hooded driver: "So, brother Azzam, we have just witnessed the exchange operation where the Sisters were handed over, and the 152 prisoners, among them a mother and four children, were released. What do you have to say about that?" The fighter speaks quickly, a sign his emotions are running high: "We thank God [. . .] and we ask God to have all the prisoners released. By God [. . .] we shall not rest until we have obtained the release of all female prisoners from the dictator's jails." The next shot shows him at the wheel reciting a line of poetry about the smile of a little boy sitting on his knee: "*Ibtisam fi jabin al-'izi shama*" (a smile on the forehead of glory is like a mole). Then, it was the little boy's turn to be questioned: "Where have you been?" The smiling child answers: "Us? In Syria." The images show the children seated in the car looking into the camera one last time. As for the Sisters, they are on their way back into Syria where a number of Syrian and Lebanese TV reporters await them for a live press conference. Beneath a huge portrait of Bashar al-Assad, the Sisters are hounded with questions about their living conditions with the fighters. The reporters are trying to get them to say they were mistreated, but none of them changes her version of the facts. Confusion reigns as the live broadcast contradicts the Syrian regime's official narrative.

The Impossible Return of the Sisters

The affair of the Sisters of Saint Thecla was far from over. Their declarations and positions represented a genuine challenge to the Syrian regime. The few images analyzed here are part of a much more extensive body of material issuing from various parties to the conflict. Numerous narratives and versions collided, and several camps clashed. Taken together, they make it possible to follow the thread of a story that still arouses controversy in Syria today, particularly among Christians and the people of Maaloula. At the time of writing, the Sisters have still not returned to their monastery, though it was entirely rebuilt and inaugurated with much fanfare in 2018. These reprisals for their stances compelled them to live henceforward in another monastery, where they have not been permitted to leave, nor may they receive visitors. The Saint Thecla monastery is now occupied by a cleric. What the Sisters had for many years feared might happen—as I learned in the 2000s when I was doing my ethnographic field work among their community—finally came to pass: the men of the Patriarchate took over the monastery and wrested the Sisters from their saint.

NOTES

1. See Poujeau, *Des monastères en partage* (2014).
2. Taken in the sociological sense, an "affair" gives rise to numerous—and often contradictory—discourses and narratives and mobilizes a multitude of actors. On this subject, see: Boltanski et al., *Affaires, scandales et grandes causes* (2007).
3. On the subject of interreligious and inter-state alliances, see: Salloukh, "The Sectarianization of Geopolitics" (2017), 35–52.
4. https://www.youtube.com/watch?v=MhNfxL-YEDo. Accessed on 5 September 2013.
5. For an analysis of how the regime framed the conflict along sectarian lines, see: Pinto, *The Shattered Nation* (2017), 123–142.
6. Online Lebanese media outlet with links to the Shiite party, Amal, led by Nabih Berri and more generally, to the 8th of March Movement that, in 2005, came out in opposition to the Cedar Revolution which called for an end to Syrian oversight in Lebanon.
7. Accessed on 8 September 2013. This video is no longer available.
8. All translations of the videos are the author's.
9. Another majority Christian village in Qalamun.
10. https://www.youtube.com/watch?v=G7DpwOZCBqw. Accessed on 5 February 2014.
11. The affair did in fact attract international media attention.
12. Head of Lebanese Forces, he is historically opposed to the regime in Damascus.
13. Founded in 2009 by a Syrian businessman opposed to the regime, Orient News participated extensively in covering the war in zones under the control of the opposition.
14. https://www.youtube.com/watch?v=QjS6LMvKs5Y. Accessed on 4 December 2013.
15. https://www.youtube.com/watch?app=desktop&v=oLqG7UD6vfQ. Accessed on 10 March 2014.
16. Journalist and activist from the town of Qusayr*, he is known for his coverage of the conflict since 2011 on several fronts: Homs, Qusayr, Qalamun, Aleppo, etc. He was seriously injured by an explosive device in an assassination attempt at his home in Aleppo, an attack that killed his cameraman Khalid 'Issa. He received an award in 2016 from Reporters without Borders and is currently based in Idlib where he continues to report via social media.
17. Probably the Nusra Front commander in Qalamun, Abu Malik al-Talli.

10

THE "YPG PRESS OFFICE" YOUTUBE CHANNEL

MILITARY COMMUNICATION OF A KURDISH PARTY IN SYRIA

Lucile Irigoyen

Faced with the revolution that touched off in 2011, the Bashar al-Assad regime made the choice of violent escalation. Starting in 2012, the conflict militarized and internationalized. In July, greatly weakened by the political situation, central authority withdrew from the greater part of the Rojava* region, made up of three majority Kurdish cantons. Provided that they refrain from attacking the Syrian regime and its armed forces, the Kurdish political party PYD (*Partiya Yekîtiya Demokrat* – Democratic Union Party) was granted latitude to administer the region. Its political agenda did not fall in line with the Syrian Revolution, nor did it conform to the Assad regime. Its armed forces, the YPG* (*Yekîneyên Parastina Gel* – Units for the Protection of the People) were officially created in 2011.[1] It consisted mostly of Kurds belonging to the Rojava area. In November 2012, Serêkaniyê was the first city of Rojava to come under attack by Islamist troops.[2] Accordingly, the YPG asserted itself locally and became the main opposition force in northeastern Syria. The military capacity of this combat group was sufficient to defend the region, and its ranks grew with every new combat situation. Thanks to their victories, the PYD asserted its legitimacy locally and internationally. By 2013, the YPG was elaborating a whole communications universe on the Internet: a YouTube channel,[3] Twitter ("X") account,[4] Facebook page,[5] and a website.[6] In a war where each fighting force was developing its own media tools, visibility was a strategic imperative that allowed non-state actors to garner the material and financial backing of foreign donors. The sustainability of the PYD's political project and its territorial grounding also played out on the field of image-making. A military propaganda tool, the YouTube channel called the YPG Press Office was largely devoted to the visual depiction of this armed organization's military advances.

In 2014, PYD forces became allied with the International Coalition[7] in the fight against the Islamic State*. Concomitantly, the PYD was introducing a political project for the liberated regions based on the theories of Abdullah Öcalan, the PKK leader (*Partiyan Karkeren Kurdistan* – Kurdistan Workers' Party*). It wanted to reorganize society into multiple "Communes" (*Komîn* in Kurdish), which would bring together the inhabitants of a given territory at various scales (neighborhood, town, canton, etc.) in order to tap into the people's wishes at the local level and compile them into a broader program for society. In this system that decentralizes a portion of power heretofore concentrated in Damascus, acknowledgment of the people's cultures and, above all, their Kurdish-ness, was essential. In this context, the propaganda of the Kurdish forces of Rojava was aiming for a more widespread recognition, both militarily and politically. The official narrative on their YouTube channel is structured around recurring figures and motifs: fighters, martyrs, light weaponry, crossfire, speeches by military commanders, Kurdish dancing, and singing.[8] These short videos (mostly one to four minutes) correspond to the political and media expectations of a Western audience that had become aware of the notion of a Kurdish resistance prepared to make the ultimate sacrifice to counter the barbaric acts of radical Islamism. Brought together on a YouTube channel and spread throughout social media, these easily accessible representations helped to shape an imagery that the Western media both exploited and influenced. In this war that also played out in images, their role was more important than it might seem. This chapter explores how an alliance with the International Coalition influenced the evolution of YPG YouTube productions. Through these communications choices, it is the material and political conditions in which the YPG was operating that come to the fore. Out of the 1,207 videos to date posted to their YouTube channel, only a few dozen have been viewed. My first sampling is based on one video seen for each month of posting, or about one out of twelve videos posted. In addition, the postings by the Syrian Democratic Forces (SDF)* and Women's Protection Units (YPJ)* also fueled my research. The cumulative effect of these disparate postings narrates the ongoing political evolutions of the time. An interview conducted by Mervan Qamishlo, member and spokesperson of the YPG communications team, helped me narrow down my sample to five videos. These speak to the close ties that formed over time between the political strategies of the PYD and the communication approaches of the YPG armed forces. For the former, it was about sustaining its influence, and for the others, about broadening their audience.

From "Dissimulation"[9] to 31 Million Views

Prior to 2011 and the start of the Syrian revolution, the Kurds had been rendered invisible in Syria. In a country where the central Baathist power had instrumentalized Arab nationalism, this ethnic group was subjected to numerous restrictions—or even prohibitions—both politically and culturally.[10] Mervan Qamishlo explains that amidst the political upheaval that Syria was experiencing, "a tiny opportunity opened up."[11] By lending media support to the military combat, the YPG YouTube channel and its camera operators were part of the overall political struggle being waged in Rojava. These military propaganda videos are thus stakeholders in a larger and much older struggle for political and cultural acknowledgment of the Kurds. The role of those behind the cameras was just as important and dangerous as that of the combatants. In one tribute video, YPG member Xerîb Welat is presented as a "warrior for truth [in the sense of a just struggle]."[12] With slow, rhythmic music in the background, a voiceover reads through his biography with emphasis on his engagement in the Rojava resistance. Most pictures and videos show Xerîb holding his camera. These views highlight his early role as camera operator. Halfway through the video, his military combat and his media combat are mirrored. To the left of the frame, Xerîb, is taking aim with his sniper rifle to the right. Next comes an image with opposite vanishing lines. From the right-hand part of the frame, he looks into the eye of the camera pointed left. Between the two shots, a crossfade makes the transition, thereby connecting the two military functions. Held by the same man, the rifle and the camera are the weapons of a single combat.

Members of the YPG, the camera operators are also combatants. Depending on the urgency of a situation, they would head to the front in camera crews composed of four to six people. Always staying near the place where the images were shot, they would often edit their images the same night and then, on foot or by car, go out in search of an Internet connection to post them online. Starting in 2013, this intensive and repetitive labor led to the posting of 1,207 videos to the YPG Press Office YouTube Channel. By February 2020, 45,700 people had subscribed to the channel and the account had generated 31,220,227 views.[13] The first armed group founded by the PYD, the YPG fighters have been the main showcase of this political party.[14]

10.1. The two weapons of the same struggle. Video posted on 04/23/2017.

Editorial Evolution under the Influence?

During our interview, Mervan Qamishlo felt it important to point out that the group at the root of YPG communications learned the job on the fly.[15] "At first, there were no media tools. [. . .] It was people who had no prior skills in the area who decided to get involved. A few people who were native to the region and were familiar with camera work participated, and folks from outside also contributed to the evolution of our messaging work."[16] Although the YPG videos feature a diverse range of technical and narrative quality, their mastery of communication coding markedly evolved over the six years of posting on YouTube. On 7 November 2013, "Azadkirina Tilkoçer" [Liberation of Tilkoçer][17] was the first post, titled in Kurdish and Arabic. In a deserted village, it shows men outfitted with military equipment as well as perceptible traces of combat, such as bullet holes on the sides of buildings. The format resembles the style of the video clip. The black frame-within-frame accentuates the shakiness of the low-definition camera. Shot from a moving vehicle driving through Tilkoçer, the first shots purposely zoom in on the evidence of recent battles. The framing also foregrounds the strategic buildings, such as grain silos and official facilities where the YPG flag has been raised. Photographs of these same locations intercut the low-definition video shots in an attempt to compensate for their relative illegibility.

This poor definition overall is indicative of how little technical material was available and how hard it was to come across as professional. At the same time, the repetition of enhancement effects presents the group as strivers, seeking to convince viewers of this unit's military capacity.[18] In the final shot, an overtly staged scene deploys a storybook lexicon of conquest that contrasts with the video as a whole. With a mix of registers and media, this first production is extremely amateur. It does testify, however, to the construction of a visual discourse which, by emphasizing military victory, announced the implementation of a new combat organization that was now taking charge of its communication. By comparison, its last video, posted on 20 December 2020 from the same YouTube channel, is more formatted and looks like a television feature story. "Bîranînên Berxedana Serêkaniyê" [Commemoration of Resistance in Serêkaniyê][19] evokes recent battles that took place in the city. High-definition images combine with precise framing, and the narrative itself is more polished. An introduction contextualizes, with image and text, the site of the action. By opening with two explosions, the first shot anchors what will follow in the midst of the war. Next, a text insert specifies the place, and the camera closes in on armed personnel inside the city. Here is where the first interview begins. Whereas the previous posting featured anonymous soldiers, here two testimonies give voice to the fighters. At the same time, they are recounting what has happened in Serêkaniyê; other shots are intercut to illustrate what they are saying. This video is an occasion to pay tribute to two people killed at the front. By providing the viewer with a fair amount of specific information, this video represents considerable progress in editorial skill.

Since its founding, the YPG communication agency has sought to collaborate with foreign media, notably to provide them with images from the field. Over the years, exchanges grew more frequent. The YPG team would send its shots directly or would respond to specific requests. The media channels that the cameramen worked with were Arab, Kurdish, American, and European. Concurrently, journalists were welcomed on site—an important point that

Mervan Qamishlo revisits. He refers to their benefitting from "Kurdish hospitality" via various structures that offer to help them.[20] For these missions that fluctuate between acting as fixer and subcontracting film work, the YPG press agency "decided not to take a single euro."[21] These activities were not seen as a commodified service, but rather focused on an enhanced recognition of combat carried out at and around the war front. In Rojava, the members of media-related, political, cultural, and military bureaus created since the arrival of the PYD defined themselves above all as revolutionaries. These differences in status and motivation between most foreign media outlets and the local media imply all sorts of unfairness. Let us also note that relations and differences in treatment would vary depending on whether they involved international media channels, independent reporters, or militant journalists. It is also worth mentioning that the greatest number of deaths occurred among local media crews. "Since our founding, we have lost fifteen members in combat. On more than one occasion, we shot footage for international channels without their mentioning our names at the time of broadcast—even though people got hurt while doing these shoots."[22] Though it cost these channels nothing, those who shot the images paid with their blood.

Between Qamishlo and Washington, an Asymmetrical Balance of Power

In March 2019, the YPG's "Parade for the victory over ISIS in Qamishli Stadium" was posted on YouTube.[23] Battalion members fill a grass-covered sports field; a marching band is in the forefront; and vehicles circle the racetrack that surrounds the playing field. The protocols that govern the annual State military parades seem to have inspired this staging. Yet, despite the number of combatants present, everything points to the YPGs' precariousness. While these parades are also a chance to display the military equipment they possess, here the vehicles are mostly simple pick-up trucks topped with machine guns. The very texture of the images inspires doubt as to how long this armed group is likely to last. Framed in close-up, wide shot, or from an overhead drone, this parade yields images of uneven quality. Certain videos are shot in high definition with professional cameras, while others are filmed on small, low-definition devices. Major differences in calibration accentuate this impression of unevenness. Though official allies of the International Coalition, the YPGs ultimately appear poorly backed.

In addition to revealing an evolving mastery of audiovisual techniques, the first and the last videos posted to the channel (referred to earlier) give differing presentations of the YPG forces. In the first, "Liberation of Tilkoçer" (2013), the images seek to favorably compare the combatants to a standing army. The unit's flag and military material are highlighted. The uniformed combatants are anonymized. Conversely, the last video on the "Commemoration of the Serêkaniyê Resistance" (2019) introduces two ordinary members of the armed forces. Though their discourse is identical, each opens his story by introducing himself with the name of his native town. It is important here to also define them as members of the local population, since they are in civilian dress when these interviews are filmed. Six years apart, these two videos were also produced in widely differing circumstances. In 2013, the YPGs had won their first battles. But by late 2019, the situation was no longer in their favor. The second video, for the first time, articulates a defeat. On 9 October, as the International Coalition looked on and allowed it to happen, Turkey invaded part of Rojava.[24] Between ground forces and the people's militia, the whole complexity of the YPG's status itself emerges at the core of these two videos. Indirectly, the different imaging choices reveal how shaky these fighting forces had become, as they strain to define themselves. Allied with state powers, most YPG combatants are not soldiers by profession. And because of their PYD affiliation, they are in fact criticized by regional and international states for their links to the PKK. At the same time, it was undoubtedly their experience with the PKK, created some forty years ago, that allowed the YPGs to acquire their military skills.[25] Militant and military, depending on the situation, the YPGs are compelled to perform both sides of their identity.

10.2. A highly precarious military parade. Video posted on 03/31/2019.

At the core of their YouTube channel aesthetic, this political affiliation is discernable; it was even foregrounded during the first two years of posts. The YPG logo, which repurposes the red star and colors of the PKK flag, is in fact displayed on each of the videos until 2015. In addition, tributes to martyrs also derive from PKK practices and adopt their formal codes. While the leader Öcalan is not ubiquitous in the videos, his portrait does appear regularly in the productions that celebrate victories. At the same time, however, an implicit threshold, dictated by a certain decorum imposed by the alliances with the Coalition, prohibits any overly conspicuous display of this political affiliation. In 2017, the images produced of the liberation of Raqqa, until then the capital of the Islamic State, set off a diplomatic crisis. On 19 October, Nesrin Abdullah, spokesperson for the YPJs (Women's Protection Units), was first to speak publicly at the time of the liberation of the city. Looking into the cameras, she was standing in front of a huge portrait of Abdullah Öcalan as she spoke.[26] On social media, the PYD's intentions were sharply vilified, notably by activists in the Syrian revolution. Two days later, the video "YPG and YPJ fighters speak out about Abdullah Öcalan's struggle"[27] brings together seven testimonials from Kurdish, American, and Arab women and men who take turns speaking before the camera. They express how important Abdullah Öcalan's ideas were in their ability to liberate Raqqa. In order to reach a broad audience, they were chosen for their different backgrounds. The post, titled and subtitled in English, has garnered 48,522 views at the time of writing. The choice to fully assume this diplomatic faux-pas was clear, as was the choice to reassert the ideological grounding of the Kurdish movement of Rojava.[28] Waged at the behest of the International Coalition, the battles at Raqqa were widely covered in the media. Historic as they may have been, the victories of the PYD armed forces were not enough to ensure its sustainability. The party's political agenda means that it remained a cumbersome partner for the members of the International Coalition.

The Turkish invasions of January 2018 and October 2019 further accentuated the PYD's instability, its perennial problem. In April 2019, hundreds of portraits of martyrs were brought together in a single video for the first time. The camera focuses in on their eyes to highlight their individuality, then pulls back to emphasize the scope of the losses. Traditionally, photographs of martyrs adhere to standard codes that emphasize the collective over the individual. A front-facing bust portrait gets pasted onto a uniform background that highlights membership to a specific unit (mainly the YPGs, the YPJs, and the Syrian Democratic Forces, (SDF)*). In this video, the first portraits do not directly associate the fighters with a specific brigade. Trees and concrete walls replace the classic uniform backdrops here, and they root the faces in the natural environment where the photo was taken, thereby immortalizing their choice to enlist—for those backdrops are subtle reminders that these armed women and men are also civilians. The textual inserts account for the death of 9,490 fighters since the start of the struggle against the Islamic State. Titled in English and Kurdish, this tribute to martyrs obliquely points to the debt of the International Coalition member states, which had no boots on the ground.

10.3. Imaging debt through a tribute. Video posted on 02/04/2019.

Alliances Break Down, Statements Sound Uneasy

While the YPGs had been posting dozens of videos per month since 2013, this chapter was written in February 2020, after the YPG account was blocked. Their last post, dated 20 December 2019, came from the coalition channel formed by the Syrian Democratic Forces (SDF). For its part, SDF Press[29] continued to post at a sustained pace. In our interview, Mervan Qamishlo points out that certain members of the YPG press are also involved in SDF communication. Now, in early 2020, the film crews of the YPG are probably prioritizing work for the SDF. Until now, the YPG press agency was deploying visual strategies aimed at promoting the group's military capacities and the merits of its local involvement. Since 2013, the victories in the fight against the Islamic State underpinned all of the YPG's videos. In 2019, the last territories controlled by that enemy were taken back—a feat that paradoxically failed to mark the end of the conflicts and compelled the YPG forces to redefine themselves. The Turkish invasion of October, central to the final YouTube videos of the YPG Press Office channel, redrew the contours of the war. Even as Turkey was absorbing the Islamist troops defeated by the Kurds into its army, it was with the consent of the United States, principal member of the International Coalition, that Turkey entered Syria. In this defeat, which undermined the alliance framework and the joint objectives as stated up to this point, the YPG press agency seemed to be having trouble finding fresh perspectives for maintaining its video-based communication. The interruption of their YouTube channel ushered in an unprecedented phase in which, perhaps, the YPGs would no longer be the PYD party's main showcase.

NOTES

1. On their website, https://www.ypgrojava.org/, the YPGs refer to an underground formation that dates to 2004. This site is no longer accessible.
2. In 2012, the town of Serêkaniyê, then controlled by the Syrian army, was attacked by brigades allied with Jabhat al-Nusra and Ghuraba' al-Sham. Made up in part by locals from Serêkaniyê, they entered the town through the Turkish border and took hold of majority Arab neighborhoods. In majority Kurdish neighborhoods, the citizens took up arms to fight back. The Syrian army withdrew. In summer 2013, with the backing of the YPGs, the town managed to fend off the Islamist brigades.
3. https://www.youtube.com/user/YPGmedia/videos. Accessed 11 June 2024.
4. https://twitter.com/defenseunits. Accessed in January 2020. This account no longer exists in 2024.
5. https://www.facebook.com/YPG/. Accessed in January 2020. This account is no longer accessible in 2024.
6. https://www.ypgrojava.org/. Accessed in May 2020. This site is no longer accessible in 2024.
7. In 2014, the International Coalition was created by the United States to fight against the Islamic State in Iraq and Syria, and was then composed of some twenty members. By February 2020, eighty-two nations were taking part. They were involved militarily in "Operation Inherent Resolve" which also included a humanitarian component aimed at combating the ideology channeled by the Islamic State.
8. The enemy was almost never shown in the first years of posting. When it was, the image was one of a lifeless body displayed like a trophy among the military equipment plundered at the time of victory.
9. This term is used by Jordi Tejel Gorgas in an article that summarizes the identity strategies of Syrian Kurds since the 1920s: Gorgas, "Les Kurdes de Syrie" (2006), 117–133.
10. Ibid.
11. Interview conducted on WhatsApp, 17 February 2020, with live translation from Kurdish into French by Reşo Altin.
12. "Şoreşgerê Nemir, Şcrvanê Heqîqetê Xerîb Welat [Immortal revolutionary, fighter for the truth, Xerîb Welat] (04/20/2017)": https://www.youtube.com/watch?v=mJ8kBatAtIQ, accessed on 12 December 2019. This video is no longer accessible in 2024.
13. Between February and May 2020, the channel recorded an increase of 2,565,168 views.
14. Note that women fighters are regularly filmed for this YouTube channel, and that the YPJs, the non-mixed counterparts of the YPG, are by far the most represented in Western media.

15. For security reasons, Mervan Qamishlo preferred not to divulge the number of persons working for YPG communications. Work is organized into sectors. Qamishlo mentions a section specialized in translation, as distinct from the film teams.

16. Mervan Qamishlo, op. cit.

17. "Azadkirina Tilkocer": https://www.youtube.com/watch?v=GFRX4bX-EhdM&t=18s, accessed on 22 September 2019. This video is no longer available.

18. Subsequently, showcasing the locals' witness reports, videos of the Tilkoçer battles adhered more closely to the communication codes of official armies that sought to present factual material the audience would accept as accurate, while also legitimizing their actions as welcomed by the liberated populations.

19. "Bîranînên Berxedana Serêkaniyê": https://www.youtube.com/watch?v=FqmGP6VMwP0&t=1s. Accessed on 12 December 2019, with 9,774 views on 11 June 2024.

20. Within the YPGs and YPJs there are people in charge of welcoming foreign journalists. Since 2018, the Rojava Information Center (RIC) has worked hard to facilitate their research. They write reports, connect interested parties with fixers, send out translated videos, etc. In one WhatsApp group, RIC members disseminate regular reports on the situation and answer inquiries. This information center has become the chief contact for such channels as the BBC or CNN, as well as for independent journalists.

21. Mervan Qamishlo, op. cit.

22. Ibid.

23. https://www.youtube.com/watch?v=zmW_GUsFvkI&t=17s. Accessed on 23 October 2024.

24. Turkey, for which the PKK is the nation's number one enemy, defines the PYD as a stakeholder in this "terrorist" organization. In January 2018, with the backing of Islamist troops, it invaded the Kurdish canton of 'Afrin, to the west of Rojava. In October 2019, it launched operation "Source of Peace" with the aim of annexing a strip of land running along its entire border, therefore including Rojava. Each of these interventions took place in full view of the International Coalition. In January 2018, Russian forces left the targeted region shortly before the attack. In October 2019, it was the United States that withdrew two days before the start of the Turkish operation.

25. In Rojava, the PKK's experience did not benefit the military sector only. Cultural centers and art academies, born after 2013, were part of the Tev Çand, the cultural network linked to the PKK. Its influence in media matters was also most certainly beneficial. Starting in 2012, this field was taken over by the PYD which launched Ronahî TV, the first Kurdish channel in

Syria. In 1995, the PKK itself inaugurated the first Kurdish satellite channel, Med-TV.

26. This speech was not posted to the YPG YouTube channel, but the same day, on stage, Nesrine Abdallah gave an interview to this press agency. It has been posted under the title "Nesrîn Ebdulah: Felsefeya rêber Apo yekîtiya gelan ava dike" (Nesrine Abdallah: Apo's [Abdullah Öcalan] philosophy is to unite the people): https://www.youtube.com/watch?v=bsg29NOPKw-c&t=60s, accessed on 10 January 2020. This video is no longer available.

27. "YPG and YPJ fighters speak up of Abdullah Öcalan's struggle": https://www.youtube.com/watch?v=zVx7nktKCNM&t=3s, accessed on 10 January 2020. This video is no longer available.

28. Taking a position on this media crisis was tricky. Some of the martyr portraits were taken down, particularly in the towns of Rojava—a decision that did not have unanimous support among supporters and allies of the PYD.

29. "Lights of our path – *Şehîd rêberên têkoşina me ne* [The martyrs are the leaders of our struggle]" https://www.youtube.com/watch?v=9HugQS0jIPI, accessed on 12 December 2019. This video is no longer available.

11

THE CIRCULATION OF IMAGES FROM THE FRONT

OBSERVATIONS FROM THE "IRANIAN CAMP"

Agnès Devictor & Shahriar Khonsari

This chapter looks at the ways videos and photographs circulate between the battle zones and the home front, and between enemy camps. It is based on a corpus of images shot by the Holy Shrine Defenders (*modafehan-e haram**) operating in Syria since 2012, which bring together various combat forces under the command of the Iranian Quds Force*, a foreign branch of the Islamic Revolutionary Guard Corps (IRGC)*. The first part addresses the shooting and circulating of images within the Fatemiyoun* division, created in 2012 and which would later fall under IRGC command. It was made up of exiled Shiite Afghans residing in Iran and Syria and, starting in 2013, of ethnic Hazara[1] Afghans coming directly from Afghanistan, and more unusually, of Iranians who had managed to join this group. The analysis will then focus on the circulation of images of enemy camps into the "Iranian camp." It is based on a corpus of some 400 photographs and 300 videos taken by the Holy Shrine Defenders (Iranians and Afghans) and posted on an online sharing platform (Aparat), social media (mainly Telegram and Instagram), and on the cell phones of the fighters and their families.[2] The analysis is also based on data gathered in some thirty interviews conducted in Iran between 2017 and 2019 in the suburbs of Tehran (Varamin) and Mashhad (Golshahr), as well as three interviews conducted in Afghanistan (Kabul) with Fatemiyoun and/or members of their families.

The Circulation of Photos and Videos among Fatemiyoun Fighters
A Relative Invisibility
Until July 2015, when Iran was reinstated into the international community after signing the nuclear framework agreement in Vienna,[3] very few images or information concerning the military presence under the command of the Quds Force in Syria appeared in the international and Iranian media. After 2015, the Holy Shrine Defenders gained visibility inside Iran, but remained obscure internationally, especially on YouTube. This platform, jammed by the Iranian regime, remained at that time relatively underused in Iran despite the

use of VPNs. In fact, some refused to use it on ideological grounds, since at that point it was being used by the Islamic State (IS)* and the Nusra Front*, and was mainly intended for entertainment.[4] This lack of interest in YouTube can also be ascribed to the fact that the Quds Force, and especially the Fatemiyoun, were not speaking to a world audience: their videos were confined to Persian speakers. If a statement of any sort can be detected in these films, it concerns the sense of engagement among the Fatemiyoun as compared to those—in Iran as well as Afghanistan—who explain theirs only in reference to the monthly $500 they were receiving.[5] In response, the fighters emphasize their role as bulwark against the IS and the religious dimension of their engagement, relating back to their belonging to the family of 'Ali, whose name is constantly evoked during battle.[6] This tentative media visibility also stems from security concerns for the Fatemiyoun of Afghanistan, for their engagement was liable to land them in prison upon return to their country. More generally, up to 2015, the Iranian media confined themselves to mentioning an intervention that amounted only to "assistance" in "training" as well as "aid to civilians" in Syria. The tombs of martyrs, both Iranian and Afghan, bear no indication as to the place of their death. Sasan Fallahfar, Iranian filmmaker of documentaries about the Fatemiyoun, notes that Seyyed Ebrahim was one of the first tribute films to a martyr to be broadcast on Iranian television in 2016, on the Ofoq channel (very conservative and close to the IRGC). Prior to that, it had been strictly forbidden to even mention the deaths in Syria on the national media.[7]

The turning point that took place in 2015 is also identifiable by the creation of the Resaneh Fatemiyoun communications agency, whose purpose was to produce professionally made, official films about the Fatemiyoun. Equipped with high-resolution handheld cameras, a dozen operators (former Fatemiyoun fighters trained by two Iranian filmmakers) shot images at the front that gave rise to two types of films. The first concerned productions mostly broadcast on official social media (such as the Resaneh Fatemiyoun channel on Telegram) or at commemorative events. These films, with their great fanfare and flag-waving, scenes of heavy artillery against a blazing sunset, and symphonic soundtrack, glorify the heroic action of this combat group. The other way these images have served is in montages for documentaries on the war in Syria and especially on the Fatemiyoun by Iranian filmmakers such as Sasan Fallahfar. These documentaries, distributed in DVD or VOD format, or screened at cultural centers linked to the conservative wing of the regime, could also be seen on programs at festivals devoted to war films. This gradual, relative visibility brought with it a process of oversight of images produced among the Fatemiyoun. Confronted with videos freely circulating through less conventional circuits—on social media and notably on the Dam-e 'eshq Dameshq channel, as we will see—these official productions sought to give a more classic and glorious representation of the war, but also a more standardized one.

The Fighters, Their Cell Phones, and the Internet

One member of the Fatemiyoun, a very active cameraman in Syria, puts the number of fighters equipped with cell phones that have cameras at 70 percent between 2015 and 2019.[8] There were no clear official guidelines when it came to using smartphones to shoot and distribute images from the war zone,[9] except for one prohibition period between November 2014 and March 2015.[10] According to the interviewees, this decision to suspend use for a few months is especially revealing when it comes to the hierarchy's reluctance when confronted with a device that had become so ubiquitous in civilian life that it proved difficult to monitor, as witnessed by the number of images—all accessible on social media—taken during this period of prohibition. More broadly, the consecutive filtering due to political monitoring of society in Iran, though it never fully interrupted the circulation of images, resulted in their constant shifting to other networks.[11] This also applied to the Holy Shrine Defenders and their families.[12] Meanwhile, even if limited sharing among groups of friends went mostly unmonitored, each platform set its own rules: from using stickers or blurring the faces of living commanders (Figure 11.1), to limiting the number of daily postings by any one fighter[13]—though these rules were never strictly adhered to.

11.1. A martyr, Seyyed Ebrahim, and two living combatants blurred.

Once commanders were able to be identified and hunted down, the internal monitoring grew tighter. Images posted were sometimes deleted by other fighters more worried about security measures.[14] Thus, the interaction between security and dissemination of images remained a complex one, with the majority of fighters continuing to post their videos despite the risks—as if this digital mode of existence had become vital for them. In the war zone, the Fatemiyoun, mostly based in the outskirts of Damascus, Hama, and Aleppo, seemed to have relatively easy access to the Internet: taking turns, one fighter at a time would go purchase phone cards,[15] or the military section of communications (which included the Fatemiyoun) would share the network with little difficulty.[16] Still, given the cost, the low speed, and power outages, the output was mainly low-resolution photographs sent to family and friends. Except for images of martyrs, many Fatemiyoun say they did not immediately share their images, instead waiting to arrive back home.[17] But given low storage capacities, many photos and videos were deleted.[18] Some fighters went into exile, bringing their images with them, while others got newer phones or lost their backup drives—not to mention cell phones that were destroyed during operations. Thus, when they were not immediately shared among friends or posted on social media, a large portion of these images were lost.

The photos we were able to access on cell phones, or those we saw in people's homes, belong to the broad category of non-professional war pictures where the fighter stands proudly, holding his weapon, and making the V-for-victory sign with his friends while perched triumphantly atop a tank. They testify to the presence of the Fatemiyoun at the front, and their skilled handling of weapons that give a certain power to those who in civilian life are often demeaned in their own countries or in exile. The photos and videos taken in front of the Sayyida Zaynab* shrine, alongside other fighters in civilian dress, attest particularly to the religious dimension of their military engagement. There are also videos that show fighters relaxing as they enjoy their downtime, not unlike the images that were widespread among troops during the First World War.[19] Some of them elicit the success stories, like those migrants in exile send to their families via smartphone. At the front, no videos reveal doubts, fears, or regrets, though there are many testamentary selfies and videos shot during battle that look as if they might be the subject's last.

Two Videophile Commanders

Known by the names Abu ʿAli and Seyyed Ebrahim,[20] these two commanders were among the rare Iranians to join the Fatemiyoun group posing as Afghans, at a time when it was impossible for Iranians to enlist as volunteers in Syria.[21] They rapidly emerged as charismatic figures, claiming membership in this division, which is far from trivial for an Iranian since Afghan refugees were despised in Iran.[22] Alongside his military functions, Abu ʿAli and, to a lesser degree, Seyyed Ebrahim, made intensive use of their cell phones to cover the field of operations with no official mandate to do so. They shared these videos among an ever-widening group that eventually resulted, in 2015, in the creation of a highly popular channel among the Fatemiyoun, Dam-e ʿeshq Dameshq[23] managed by Abu ʿAli on the Telegram app. Rallying some 7,000 subscribers when Abu ʿAli was still alive,[24] this channel includes over 1,000 videos, some shot by him or close associates, others downloaded from other groups or channels. His widow points out that Abu ʿAli also would record sound during the operations.[25] After her husband's death (11 September 2016), videos continued to feed this channel, which she went on to administer. In 2020, the channel was still active. Often poorly framed and with sudden shifts of perspective, of poor quality, and extremely brief (ranging from a few seconds up to just under three minutes), these videos translate, by the very nature of their texture, the intention of Abu 'Ali and those working alongside him: record as much as possible,[26] with no editing—from combat to changing a truck tire, to lunches at the canteen, fatigue after an offensive, hospital care, prayers at Sayyida Zaynab, testaments (especially the commanders'), distribution of water, and so on. These situations are shared without any context clues, as a security measure, because these moments were filmed for the present or the future of a martyr, and because the audience knows the situations—and not for information purposes, or as archival material.

In these videos, focused more on people than on places (except when they include religious shrines), the person filming (usually a commander) is asking a fighter some questions. In one of them, shot in a dormitory, fifteen Fatemiyoun are questioned about their native provinces in Iran and Afghanistan and the reasons they enlisted, as the person filming makes jokes about their accents. This video reveals the various backgrounds of these enlistees and hints at the asymmetrical relationship between filmmaker and subject: the commander can make fun of a simple fighter, who goes along with the joke or prefers to lower his gaze (Figure 11.2). Other videos show "fighters at work," such as when Abu 'Ali films some Fatemiyoun terracing the ground before an offensive, again using gibes at their expense (Figure 11.3). These are reminiscent of films shot during the Iran–Iraq war by Morteza Avini's team of operators who filmed the engineering work implemented ahead of offensives, building floating bridges or berms. But back then, the actions were recorded over time and the simple volunteer fighters were viewed through the lens with deep respect, like holy people.[27]

11.2. From a cell phone.

11.3. From a cell phone. Dam-e 'eshq Damishq videos posted on Telegram.

These videos showcase the two commanders and their closest brothers in arms, often Iranian, rather than the simple Afghan fighters. Although recording with a cell phone elicits a more trivial behavior than with a professional camera, the filmmaker–subject relationship remains unequal. By resorting to a comic register, the videos stamped Dam-e 'eshq Dameshq shot by the commanders indirectly reveal how this division fell short of professional military standards. Take for example a selfie video by Seyyed Ebrahim, which would be incorporated into the tribute documentary *Seyyed Ebrahim* after his death on 23 October 2015. The commander speaks derisively as he films himself, then shows the Fatemiyoun he is training and mocks their lack of professionalism: "If these are the soldiers of the Hidden Imam[28] . . ." implying that they're off to a bad start. These recordings, where the leaders crack tasteless jokes, situate the war in Syria in a register more akin to summer camp than a conventional army. In early 2016, a wounded Abu 'Ali is said to have been suspended from missions in Syria for six months because of his filming and subsequent disseminating of images on his Dam-e 'eshq Dameshq channel.[29]

Countering the Image Flow: the Archive

To eschew this all too trivial representation of the war, another commander, this time an Afghan called Muhammad Reza Khavari or Hojjat, favored the creation of a press agency Resaneh Fatemiyoun, for which he would train while remaining a fighter. He advocated for more professional camera operators at the front, for a more worthy and professional representation of Fatemiyoun participation in the war. Keen to conserve the memory of their involvement in the conflict, he and a few of his close collaborators pooled their resources to purchase a professional camera (8 megapixel) as soon as they arrived in

Damascus in 2012, despite a ban by the Iranian military chain of command. Their carefully conserved images were intended only for archival purposes and never circulated on the Internet.[30] If the Islamic Revolutionary Guard Corps (IRGC) banned cameras and camcorders but authorized smartphones at the Syrian front, it was undoubtedly because they knew that these devices did not serve the same function when it came to how they would be used down the line. Depending on which device was in use, the camera operator's gaze upon the men and the unfolding events was not the same. Hojjat chose a professional camera to film events according to his own insights, to leave a record for posterity, and because he was mindful of working for the long term and producing quality images. From the very first frames, he was committing a transgression, for his films were designed as vectors of combat remembrance, independent of the official Iranian discourse, to remain as a trace resistant to the marginalization of the Fatemiyoun in the writing of the history of this conflict. Even though these images were confiscated after his death and are inaccessible today,[31] the act alone remains incredibly significant: it is, in and of itself, the archive of a conception of images from the battlefront.

Short Circuits

The extremely fast data flow, via social media, from the battlefront to all points behind the lines, has meant that a family would often learn of the death of a loved one before the official announcement by the IRGC or the Martyrs Foundation, which have been entrusted with this role since 1980. Without the solemnity and rituals that should accompany such announcements, they cause great emotional distress. During our interviews, some Fatemiyoun—among them a few who were close to Hojjat—denounced these practices, notably those of the Dam-e 'eshq Dameshq channel.[32] Starting in 2017, social media sites had to wait for the official announcement before posting images and information about martyrs. Moreover, it would happen in Iran that spouses would connect in secret to accounts and groups that their partner was subscribed to, thereby gaining access to his communications. In a war zone, such practices led to the circulation of data and images that escaped the control of the military high command. The wife of martyr Mohsen Hojjaji (see below) explains very candidly in an interview that she learned of her husband's abduction from IS even before the military authorities, by tuning in live to exchanges among his friends and witnesses to the abduction, who were exchanging messages on their Telegram group to which she had (indiscreetly) gained access. Likewise for the beheading that was to follow.[33] She then initiated her own communication around this event, sparking repercussions at a national level.

From One Camp to Another
Getting Data

One of the jobs of an army command during wartime is to intercept intelligence from the enemy. But with the Internet, an ordinary fighter has access—practically in real time—to images posted by the enemy, images liable to supply data about ongoing combat. For instance, one fighter of the Fatemiyoun recalls watching, along with his fellow fighters, videos shot by those they call "Daeshi"[34] south of Aleppo, in the Khantuman operation (5–6 May 2016)—a particularly deadly one for their camp—while they themselves were stationed in the Damascus suburb. Enemy drones were filming one camp as well as the other, making it possible to observe the losses, the advances of one side, and the retreat of the other (Figure 11.4 and 11.5). At that point, the Iranian authorities were unable to hide their massive defeat and their strategic mistakes, which rendered chain-of-command relations between the IRGC and the Fatemiyoun even more brittle. Afghan fighters would also occasionally consult images posted by the enemies on YouTube (easily accessible in Syria), to glean data concerning Fatemiyoun that had been taken prisoner.[35]

11.4. Drone footage of the Khantuman operation.

11.5. Drone footage of the Khantuman operation.

Enlisting Enemy Images in the Mobilization

Obtaining data was not the only way the enemy's social media was being used. According to testimonies by Fatemiyoun combatants,[36] pictures of Shiites being beheaded that were taken by Jihadist forces and posted to the Internet are thought to have had a decisive influence on their engagement. This is also what Seyyed Ebrahim says in a long interview where he looks straight into the camera,[37] as does the mother of two Fatemiyoun fighters who explains that she accepted the departure of her sons for Syria after seeing these photographs.[38] Other testimonies corroborate this mobilizing effect sparked by the enemy and not by internal propaganda, though the latter would go on to exploit it at a second stage. The choice of these images in the mobilization effort attests to a singularity in the history of propaganda: whereas, in the West, decapitation and any explicit representation of dismemberment are particularly reviled during wartime, belonging to one of the strongest taboos in cinema and war narratives in the twentieth century,[39] these representations are received far more ambivalently in certain countries of Shiite culture—particularly in Iran and to a lesser extent Afghanistan—since they can signal the victim's status as a chosen one, while still sometimes carrying the same taboo. For instance, the picture of the head of a young commander Reza Esmaili (killed in February 2015) of the Fatemiyoun, posted by the Nusra Front*, showed up shortly thereafter on Fatemiyoun social media. It is in fact this photograph that is often cited in our interviews to explain why a fighter enlisted. The numerous stories we were told say that right before the decapitation, members of the Nusra Front gave Reza Esmaili a walkie-talkie so that he could scream in terror and paralyze the Fatemiyoun with fear. But instead, he just shouted *"Ya 'Ali,"* the rallying cry of all Shiites. In the documentary film devoted to him, *The Teacher* [*Mo'alem*, Mohsen Ardestani Rostami, 2014], one of Reza Esmaili's friends tells: "He took the mark of Hussein. It is an honor to offer up one's blood, to offer up one's head."[40]

For Shiites who connect it to the beheading of Imam Hussein at the Battle of Karbala*, Esmaili's tragic death became the supreme sign of his having been chosen. This picture is thus interpreted both as a revolting barbarian act and a sign of being favored. It is highly unlikely that the jihadists assessed the ambivalent effect—among their Shiite enemies—of these images, especially since the images demonstrated everywhere else their effectiveness in unanimously provoking stunned terror. This ambivalence toward beheading, an attitude that did not exist in other combat factions,[41] had as an unexpected effect the reuse of photos and videos made by the jihadist enemy in Fatemiyoun propaganda. As Jacques Ellul has effectively demonstrated, propaganda creates nothing ex nihilo but is based on myths, myths that offer "a driving image infused with emotion,"[42] triggering commitment without reflection. If, during the Iran–Iraq war, the appeal to two myths, one religiously inspired (Karbala) and the other more secular (the grand destiny of Iran), fit into this same framework, the use of the Karbala battle narrative proved particularly effective and appeared once again operable among the Holy Shrine Defenders. This picture of Reza Esmaili had a "driving" effect among the Fatemiyoun and their fellows, reinforcing the correspondence between this conflict and the founding event of Shiism, and contributing to the relative backgrounding of other motives for engagement that nevertheless did also exist—more specifically, the more purely military ones, as with the three interviews we did in Mashhad with furloughed Fatemiyoun.[43]

Another "driving image infused with emotion" produced by the enemies had similar effects, becoming the "driver" of an unprecedented mobilization in Iran since the start of the war in Syria. Mohsen Hojjaji, an Iranian member of the IRGC, captured on 7 August 2017, was decapitated the next day by members of the IS. His death was officially announced on 9 August with the posting of a video on Al Furat, one of the media branches of the IS. The video then went viral in Iran, especially on Telegram and on all major media outlets, including national Iranian TV (the martyr's wife was notified ahead of time, amplifying the circulation and increasing the number of interviews). Based on this IS propaganda video, Hojjaji's capture changes into the "Karbala ambush," and the myth is reactivated in the eyes of Shiite Iranian viewers and is replayed nearly in full. Already, Hojjaji's brothers in arms had circulated images of his beheading on their Telegram group with the caption: "The headless martyr is the blessed martyr" (shahid bi sar shohadat mobarak). The video would trigger an unprecedented mobilization around the Defense of the Holy Shrines, a conflict that until then had had relatively little resonance in Iran. In a desert landscape, we see men firing automatic weapons at seven or eight soldiers who are attempting to retreat behind a berm. We hear nashids exalting the combat. A pickup truck arrives on the scene, driving over the head of a man lying on the ground. An IS fighter recites verses from the Quran and explains that God has prepared a painful punishment for the renegades. A tent is set on fire, and in the thick, black smoke a fighter brandishes a weapon as a sign of victory. An Iranian soldier in IRGC uniform is taken away as captive by this same fighter armed with a knife. Placed in the back of the pickup, the Iranian prisoner looks exhausted. In the next shot, he is bare-chested and lying on the ground, a combatant's foot on his belly. Here stops the video that circulated on social media and national television, while the original, seen in Iran but censored two days after its broadcast, shows the man being decapitated with a knife.[44]

As with the historical–mythological episode of Karbala, the Iranians are surrounded, outmanned, and outgunned; tents burn, the camp is ravaged and littered with corpses, a Shiite is decapitated. This scenario directly resonates with commemorations that replay this drama every year, in a collective emotional outpouring, a theatrical religious pageant, the *Ta'zieh*. But in the case of this video, the scenario is in the here and now, a real decapitation, caught on film. The myth is performed. In short order, a screen capture of Hojjaji as prisoner became an "icon" (Figure 11.6). From this point, the original video, which was still circulating rapidly on social media, was also modified. On 10 August, the graphic artist Hassan Roholamin signed a painting directly inspired by it, where Hojjaji is being held by the IS fighter disguised as soldier of Yazid, as, on the left-hand side of the picture, Shemr (Yazid's general) gazes away, not seeing the decapitated Imam Hussein, depicted from the back, alongside his sister Zaynab, who takes Hojjaji into her arms. On the right-hand side of the picture, a corpse lies on the ground (the one seen in the video). Hojjaji is the only one wearing a uniform, the others are staged in costumes suggesting the Karbala era (Figure 11.7). This picture went on to be shared thousands of times on social media, where it would morph once again. A short subject was immediately shot by Mojtabah Ellamoradi and produced by the Fars News Agency, whose "making of" film is swiftly posted to social media. "This film aims to replay the scenario of the Daesh video and the episode of the taking of Karbala," explains the filmmaker, who does not shy away from turning this IS video into a costume drama (Figure 11.8).

11.6. Hojjaji taken prisoner, Al Furat video.

11.7. Roholamin painting based on video.

11.8. Ellamoradi's "making of" film.

Enemy propaganda was thus reappropriated according to an emotionally charged mythological reading. Faced with what had seemed until then to be national disregard for the Defense of Holy Shrines, the authorities exploited Hojjaji's death, turning it into a cause that galvanized Iranian society. For instance, between August and September 2017, from the beheading to the burial of Hojjaji, a whole range of merchandise, from wedding cards to school backpacks (Figure 11.9) and even postage stamps (Figure 11.10) began flooding public spaces, based either on the iconic image derived from the IS video or on a portrait of Hojjaji depicting him as a volunteer in the Iran–Iraq war (Figure 11.11).

11.9. Schoolboy backpack.

11.10. Iranian postage stamp based on the Roholamin design.

11.11. Based on his dress, haircut, and beard, Hojjaji looks like a volunteer in the Iran–Iraq war.

These examples show how, at the instigation of the State, social actors seized this figure and turned the Defense of the Holy Shrine into a collective issue.[45] Two elements contributed to this process: first, the fact that the returning of the body coincided with the previous days of the Shiite mourning celebration of 'Ashura (the 10th of Muharram), thus this martyr being associated with the martyrdom of Imam Hussein at Karbala; and second, his resemblance with a "body" from the Iran–Iraq war (very thin, dressed in much the same uniform, wearing his beard in the same fashion . . .), a war that continues to be intensively celebrated in public space in Iran. Organized by the authorities in power, a national funeral cortege followed the remains throughout the country, bringing together millions of Iranians between 27 and 29 September, with ceremonies in Tehran, Mashhad, and Isfahan until the burial in his native town Najafabad on the eve of 'Ashura (the day commemorating the martyrdom of Hussein at Karbala). The Moharram days turned into a celebration of Hojjaji in an intense emotional outpouring where both events were mapped onto one another (Figure 11.12 and 11.13). A series of video clips that were going viral at this time, such as Saeed Hamzehmusavi's

"After You," celebrated this martyr come to "purify the Iranian nation" with computer-generated imagery.

11.12. Imam Hussein prays over the remains of Hojjaji.

11.13. The decapitated head of Imam Hussein hails that of Hojjaji.

This symbiotic event would appear to be the ultimate stage in a deliberate process of national appropriation of the "Defense of the Holy Shrine" cause by exploiting the Karbala drama. This story is the most apt at rallying the Iranian population to effusive displays of emotion. But although the figure of

Hojjaji did garner a broad consensus, the conflict in Syria did not necessarily attract a mass following. It was this single figure, a young Iranian decapitated just like Imam Hussein, and who resembled a volunteer in the Iran–Iraq war, who engendered cohesiveness more than the conflict itself. Until at least 2020, Hojjaji would continue to be celebrated: painted murals bear his likeness, and during graduation ceremonies at the Imam Hussein University on 13 October 2019, a collective choreography transformed Hojjaji's face into that of Ayatollah Khomeini, the regime's most sacred figure. This equivalency testifies to how supremely valorized Hojjaji had become, sanctified thanks to the viral spread of the IS video.

Conclusion: The Political Impact of Disseminating Images

The various modes of propagating images among the forces under IRGC command show that the use of cell phones as a filming tool remains active and loosely monitored. It gave rise to a more trivialized representation of the war, and a new way of "being in combat," with the fighter now equipped with a weapon and a smartphone, both of which seem almost equally essential to the war effort. Moreover, access to images generated by the enemy, on the battlefield and disseminated in real time, has changed the immediate understanding of combat and the relations between the chain of command and foot soldiers. This access has also led, particularly in the case of decapitation images, to the assimilation of enemy propaganda into the mobilization apparatus in Iran and among the Fatemiyoun, even without any explicit misappropriation that might shift the message—as is so often the case in wartime. This literal integration, seemingly paradoxical, in fact validates the adage that the same image shifts meaning depending on the reception, even in such an extreme case as a beheading.

A culture of war, incomparably less powerful than that edified during the Iran–Iraq war, emerged after three years of hiding Iran's military involvement in Syria. This culture is largely composed of visual symbols (the photo of Sayyida Zaynab's tomb placed on commemorative posters and graves), musical video clips,[46] flags, and images taken and shared by the fighters themselves. Images that became icons are few, such as those of Reza Esmaili, undoubtedly the most widely shared among the Fatemiyoun, and that of Mohsen Hojjaji, which physically rallied millions of Iranians. Although produced by the enemy, these "driving images infused with emotion" supplied material for the most effective propaganda, whereby the Syrian war became not only a metaphor for the Battle of Karbala but an actual reenactment of it. This bridging of the war in Syria with the famous battle removes any political or historical dimension from the conflict, in a way comparable to jihadist groups when they justify their combat by framing it in terms that harken back to the founding of Islam.

Even if the fighters themselves embrace this grand narrative, employing terminology referring to the Battle of Karbala and to the family of ʿAli to describe this war—as evidenced in their videos (particularly those shot at the Sayyida Zaynab sanctuary)—this does not prevent them from also having a political interpretation of the conflict, often expressed only implicitly. Certain Fatemiyoun that we met in Mashhad did not hesitate to say that Iran was reluctant to welcome them when we asked them, in April 2019, what they would do once the war in Syria was over. Lowering their voices, and with a certain bitterness, they added: "They'll just find another conflict to send us to, sprinkling it with some religious excuse."

NOTES

1. The Hazaras belong to a majority Shiite ethnic minority. They are the main target of attacks by the Taliban and the Islamic State in Afghanistan. See: Monsutti, Homo itinerans (2018).
2. Most of the persons interviewed prefer to remain anonymous.
3. Signed on 14 July 2015, by the United States, Russia, China, France, the United Kingdom, Germany, the European Union, and Iran, this framework agreement aimed to monitor Iran's nuclear program and to lift the economic sanctions that were affecting Iran. On 8 May 2018, Donald Trump announced he was withdrawing the U.S. from this agreement and was stepping up economic sanctions against the Islamic Republic of Iran.
4. Interview with Mohammad Mehdi Kaleghi, maker of several documentary films about the Fatemiyoun, including My Son [Pesaram 2016], 04/04/2019, Mashhad.
5. Interview with one of the Fatemiyoun fighters, 04/04/2018, Varamin.
6. In addition to videos shot by fighters, see also the documentary The Men of Life [Mardom-e zendegi, Yahya Rezai, 2018], where Fatemiyoun fighters, even on the verge of death, never cease to implore Sayyida Zaynab* or Imam Hussein.
7. Interview with Sasan Fallahfar, 12/12/2017, Tehran.
8. Interview with a member of the Fatemiyoun (encountered in March 2019 in Mashhad), by e-mail on 10/31/2019.
9. On the other hand, all communication during training in Iran was strictly prohibited.
10. Interview with a member of the Fatemiyoun, 12/15/2017, Varamin.
11. For example, from Orkut to Viber, Telegram, and WhatsApp.
12. It is not uncommon to see women in Iran—mothers of Fatemiyoun with little or no technological know-how—who skillfully navigate social media in order to stay in touch with their sons, and who equip themselves with VPN to get around the State's blocking of certain apps.
13. Email interview with a member of the Fatemiyoun, 11/03/2019.
14. Ibid.
15. Costs remained high: 5,000 Syrian pounds—about 15 euros for 1 gigabyte per month.
16. Interview 04/05/2019, Mashhad.
17. Interview 12/19/2017, Varamin.
18. Interview 04/18/2019, Varamin.
19. Véray, Avènement d'une culture visuelle de guerre (2019). On the representation of war in films shot by the combatants themselves and that resemble home movies of summer vacations, see: Bertin-Maghit, Lettres filmées d'Algérie (2015).

20. Their real names, respectively: Morteza Atahi (enlisted in January 2015) and Mostafa Sadrzadeh (enlisted in 2013).

21. It is hard to situate the exact date when volunteer Iranian combatants officially started coming, but until 2016 at the very least, it was impossible for them to leave for Syria.

22. Sasan Fallahfar recalls the evolution of her judgment of Afghans, whom she looked upon negatively as a "community imposed on Iran, but after witnessing their courage and commitment in Syria, and after making this film [Seyyed Ebrahim], [her] feelings toward them completely changed." Interview 12/31/2017, Tehran.

23. One translation might be "The breath of love, Damascus." The term Dam suggests a mystical dimension in Persian. If some users of this channel define it as an initiation to the "spirit" of this Defense of the Holy Shrine, for others, it's just a channel like any other.

24. Interview with a member of the Fatemiyoun, 11/03/2019.

25. http://shahraraonline.ir/news/69353, accessed on 09/15/2019. This video is no longer available.

26. He has several portable, external batteries that make up for the lack of electricity at the front.

27. Devictor, Images, combattants et martyrs (2015), 362–63. Abou 'Ali was familiar with these films, and was often compared, in fact, to Morteza Avini for his intensive filming of warfare.

28. In Twelver Shiism, it is the Twelfth Imam who announces the Parousia.

29. Interview, 11/03/2019, Tehran.

30. Interviews with one of the Fatemiyoun close to Hojjat, 04/04/2019, Mashhad.

31. It is possible to see extracts of this corpus edited into the documentary My Son [Pesaram, Mehdi Kaleghi, 2016] which is dedicated to Hojjat. But it was during an interview with the filmmaker, and with some of his close friends, on 4 April 2019 in Mashhad, that we discovered the exceptional trajectory of this combatant in his relation to images and the archive.

32. Interview with three Fatemiyoun fighters, 04/04/2019, Mashhad.

33. See the Monthly magazine Shahed Javan, No. 145, Shahrivar 1396 (September 2017).

34. The terms "Daeshi" (members of IS), often a catch-all designation of the enemy, and "Takfiri" are used by the Fatemiyoun in our interviews to define what Westerners ordinarily call "jihadists." The second is less common in spoken discourse, however.

35. When rebels kill their enemies, some disseminate images, for example: https://www.youtube.com/watch?v=UQ1MrinMCsk, accessed on 05/18/2024.

36. Interviews in April 2019 in Mashhad.
37. Interview inserted into the documentary devoted to him, Seyyed Ebrahim [Sasan Fallahfar, 2015].
38. Interview 12/15/2017, Varamin.
39. Stéphane Audoin-Rouzeau recalls how today's public has refused to watch extreme forms of wartime violence, in particular violence inflicted upon bodies. Audoin-Rouzeau, Combattre (2008), 41–42.
40. Authors' translation.
41. We should note that this ambivalence does not seem to exist among the Shiite fighters of Hezbollah.
42. Ellul, *Propagandes* (1962).
43. Several testify to their record as fighters, not only in Afghanistan and in Syria, but also in Bosnia, Chechnya, or Lebanon, without any explicit mention of the Shiite dimension of their experience.
44. Note that during the Iran–Iraq war, feature films showed the decapitated heads of Iranian soldiers—something unheard of in the cinema during wartime—though such images were still censored in the press. Devictor, "Du cadavre au martyr" (2011), 19–48.
45. Devictor, "De la 'Défense sacrée'" (2018), 115–144.
46. Interview with the singer Seyyed Mosafer, 12/12/2018, Rey. See his clip: https://www.youtube.com/watch?v=n5zPRllkH94, accessed on 05/18/2024.

12

LEBANESE HEZBOLLAH'S AUDIOVISUAL PRODUCTION THROUGH THE PRISM OF THE SYRIAN CONFLICT

Erminia Chiara Calabrese

On 25 May 2013, in the middle of the al-Qusayr offensive*, Hassan Nasral-lah, general secretary of Hezbollah in Lebanon, officially admitted to the pres-ence of his fighters on the Syrian front. From that point on, cameras would accompany weaponry. Hezbollah's audiovisual coverage of the conflict started to appear. Previously, between 2011 and spring 2013, the party denied that its fighters were present on Syrian soil, even though troops had been there unofficially since 2011.[1] Ever since its emergence in the 1980s as a force in the struggle against the Israeli occupation of Lebanese territory (1978–2000), Hezbollah had been using images to "influence public opinion, spread its mes-sage, and advance its military objectives."[2] Starting in the 1990s, this armed politico-religious party, the only one granted permission to bear arms on behalf of the struggle against the occupation of the country,[3] designed its audiovisual communications with the goal of creating "a common memory [. . .] based on the narrative of resistance against the Israeli other."[4] The audiovisual pro-ductions that emerged from the Syrian conflict marked a major turning point in the symbolic and semantic grammars traditionally mobilized by Hezbollah. There was now a need to come up with visual responses to ideological reconfig-urations and especially their military action. For the first time, in fact, Hezbol-lah was engaging in cross-border combat in Syria, a country with which Leba-non has a long and tense history.[5] Furthermore, the enemy was not the Israeli occupier, and the cause no longer that of liberating Lebanon. The key symbols of the struggle against Israeli troops, whose representation had hitherto been recurrent in its audiovisual productions, were yielding to others who would gradually come to dominate Hezbollah's media landscape and impose their reading of the Syrian conflict.[6] This audiovisual production, evolving even as the war was underway, was heavily influenced by military and political trends on both Syrian and Lebanese terrain,[7] and continued to develop through-out the conflict. Drawing on both religious and patriotic reserves, depend-ing on the political context, Hezbollah first mobilized between 2012[8] and 2014 around the protection of Shiite holy sites (such as the Sayyida Zaynah* mausoleum in Damascus) threatened with destruction or already destroyed by certain armed groups opposed to the regime of Bashar al-Assad, and then around the protection of Syrian villages inhabited by a majority Shiite Lebanese population. For instance, between 2013 and 2014, we note recurrent motifs for paying tribute to fighters killed in Syria, such as the dome of the Sayyida Zaynab sanctuary in Damascus, red banners inscribed with "At your command, O Zaynab" (*"Labbayki ya Zaynab"*) (Figure 12.1), or a woman with a blurred face welcoming fighters with open arms. Prior to 2011, it was the dome of the al-Aqsa Mosque in Jerusalem that was traditionally associated with tributes to martyrs fallen in combat against Israel. The symbolic register surrounding Zaynab, a sacred female figure, introduced a new feature into audiovisual representations of combat, and would prove a major distinctive sign of this armed cross-border engagement (Figure 12.2).

12.1. "At your command O Zaynab." Video tribute to fighter Muhammad al-Juni, who died on 26 June 2014.

12.2. Video tribute to fighter Mustafa Hawli, who died in Syria on 27 July 2015.

By the summer of 2014 Hezbollah was adopting a security agenda of national protection against the infiltration of Lebanese territory by members of jihadist groups like the Nusra Front* and the Islamic State*. These images were meant to mobilize, legitimize combat, and recruit fighters. But it was not until 13 September 2014, as part of a tribute video shot by Hezbollah's War Media Unit (the party's media agency, active since 1986[9]) honoring commander Hamza Ibrahim Haydar (killed in Homs on 29 June 2013), that combat scenes from inside Syria were broadcast for the first time by Al-Manar, the party's television channel. Fall of 2014 coincided with the gradual legitimizing of Hezbollah's military involvement in the fight against the Islamic State. This was not surprising, since by 2014 several armed combat groups, notably the Nusra Front and the Islamic State, had taken up positions on the high ground of 'Arsal, al-Qa', and Ras Baalbeck[10] This chapter analyzes the audiovisual grammars of that cross-border armed engagement by comparing official productions with videos shot by fighters at the front. It examines three aspects: representations of the fighter's status, the enemy, and Syrian territory. It is based on viewings of videos disseminated[11] from a variety of sources: official videos broadcast on the al-Manar[12] television channel, on Hezbollah's War Media Unit site, on the Al-Ahed News site, or via videos that circulated on Facebook and YouTube. This body of visual material also consists of videos shot by fighters who showed them to me on their cell phones during field work,[13] never circulated beyond close family and acquaintances. This recording practice was in fact officially forbidden by Hezbollah, which made a point of confiscating cell phones whenever such videos were discovered.

Making a Hero of a Fighter at the Syrian Front

The video of Commander Hamza Ibrahim Haydar[14] clearly belongs in the category of tribute videos to Hezbollah martyrs, intended by the party to "publicize the martyr's memory and tell his story."[15] This video, nearly seven minutes long, broadcast on 13 September 2014 on the al-Manar channel and rebroadcast the same day by all the major Lebanese TV channels (Future TV, Al Jadeed News, OTV, MTV Lebanon, and NBN), opens with images of destruction in the Khalidiya neighborhood in the city of Homs, the first neighborhood to rise up on 25 March 2011 in support of the city of Daraa. The city was laid siege to by the troops of Bashar al-Assad. Amidst abandoned, ruined houses, Commander Hamza Ibrahim Haydar is seen from the back, performing various military actions (firing missiles, loading munitions, defining military objectives, and coordinating combat).

12.3. Tribute video to Commander Hamza Ibrahim Haydar, killed in Syria on 29 June 2013.

The soundtrack of the opening credits is borrowed from the popular series *The Victors* (*al-Ghalibun*), broadcast by al-Manar in 2011.[16] The fighter is immediately recognizable as belonging to Hezbollah by his yellow armband. Unlike fighters who are still alive,[17] his face is not blurred. The video alternates images from the front, filmed by the War Media Unit—whose objective had always been to archive combat footage—with others, representing moments from the combatant's civilian life, edited by the Association for the Revival of Resistance Legacy. Note that images from the front are grittier, filmed in low resolution to remind viewers "that we are witnessing reality."[18] The credits are intercut with excerpts of speeches by Nasrallah, an element often found in Hezbollah's audiovisual productions, as well as in certain of its *nashids**. Other elements indicate the commander status of this fighter: we see him giving orders, coordinating operations, and delegating combat tasks.

12.4. Tribute video to Commander Hamza Ibrahim Haydar, killed in Syria on 29 June 2013.

At minute two, the opening theme gives way to *nashids* combined with excerpts from Nasrallah's speeches. This sequence stages the fighter's heroism constructed around two registers: that of sacrifice—made explicit by the words of Hassan Nasrallah—and that of courage, underscored by shots where he is always seen on the front lines. From this point forward, photos of the personal and family life of Hamza Ibrahim Haydar are inserted into the montage. We see him playing in the park with his little daughter or having a picnic together with her and his wife. This slideshow is accompanied by phrases extracted from his official testament[19] and gentle background music.

12.5. Tribute video to Commander Hamza Ibrahim Haydar, killed in Syria on 29 June 2013.

This side-by-side, between the battlefront and the home, shows both the fighter and the father, a man like any other—a "son of the people" as Nasrallah calls him. This choice of depiction, classic in its war imagery, fits into a mobilization strategy, as it allows for strong identification. Various visual elements appear here, ones found in other official videos. They signify the semantic and symbolic evolution of Hezbollah audiovisual production which, until then, had been centered on the struggle against Israel. This evolution is marked by several notable features. The first concerns geography: from the mountains of southern Lebanon, the scene moves to an urban setting with houses destroyed by bombings and abandoned, empty streets where the sole human presence is that of Hezbollah combatants, or desert zones with military encampments.

12.6. Tribute video to Commander Hamza Ibrahim Haydar, killed in Syria on 29 June 2013.

The second feature has to do with how the fighter relates to the territory. Previously, the fighter's strong sense of belonging to Lebanese territory was the prime theme in representations of combat against the Israeli occupier, illustrated at times literally with images of combatants bleeding into the ground from their wounds, symbolizing their sacrifice for the sake of its liberation.[20] Combat in Syria, however, was taking place on "foreign" soil, an indeterminate place that is never really named, with which the fighter does not necessarily have a connection. The videos make no attempt to contextualize. A third feature is the use of weapons: several shots show Kalashnikovs or tanks belonging to the Syrian army—cluing the viewer to the cooperation between Hezbollah and the regime of Bashar al-Assad (while Syrian soldiers are almost never present in the image)—and different types of missiles. Although the fighter is filmed handling these weapons, we never see their target, nor the destruction they wreak, while in the fighting against Israel, images showing the destruction of Israeli tanks or attacks on Israeli outposts were recurrent features.

12.7. Tribute video to Commander Hamza Ibrahim Haydar, killed in Syria on 29 June 2013.

The Experience of Combat Filmed by Ordinary Combatants

Ali H., a native of southern Lebanon but living in the south suburbs of Beirut, enlisted with Hezbollah in 2011. Married and father to two children, he left for Syria in 2013. He was killed in an Islamic State ambush in the region of Idlib on 25 February 2015, at the age of 35. His mother told me of the death: "The same day he was supposed to come home to Beirut, members of Islamic State set an ambush for his group. When he saw his friends surrounded, Ali sought to break through the encirclement to save them. And that's how he died."[21] His mother was still waiting for the body to "have the stone where I can weep."[22] These videos were given to me by Ali when he was still alive, then by his sister Zaynab after his death in combat. Zaynab, very emotional, tells me that these images are the final memory of her brother and a "testimony to his courage for his children." The content of these videos is wide-ranging: messages sent to his family (mostly to his mother and his children), military operations filmed by other fighters so that he could be seen in action, and social time where the fighters are having a meal or making coffee. This eclectic series is representative of videos seen on the cell phones of other fighters and is typical of images sent back home from the front.[23] Here, again, the enemy is never represented: we see Ali firing a missile and handling a Kalashnikov, but we never see his target. We see no corpses, neither of the enemy nor the fighters, nor any wounded. Syrian civilians, Syrian army soldiers, and fighters from various rebel factions, are all systematically left off-screen.

This invisibility of the enemy, also a feature of official productions, differentiates these videos from representations of combat against Israel. In the latter—particularly the videos of the 2006 war[24] with the wounded Israeli soldier who tearfully abandons the battlefield—combat scenes where the Hezbollah fighter and the Israeli soldier were present in the same frame, as was the arsenal of the Israeli army, constitute recurrent motifs that depict the enemy's vulnerability despite the asymmetrical power dynamic. In the editing phase of these videos, certain images were sampled by Hezbollah from Israeli film sources, the point being to deflect the enemy's discourse. But in the audiovisual production on the war in Syria, the fighters from different armies opposing the

Syrian regime are never represented. The encompassing word, *takfiri*,[25] used by Hezbollah to designate the enemy, allows for a unilateral enemy where, in reality, there is a plethora of armed opposition factions against the Bashar al-Assad regime.[26] The use of this term also signifies an attempt by Hezbollah to place its groups outside Sunni Islam and Islam in general: "They are not Sunnis; they are criminals," declared Hassan Nasrallah after a car bombing in the southern suburbs of Beirut,[27] against the backdrop of increased sectarian tension.

Filming themselves at the front and sending these videos to their families represented for these young fighters an attempt to stay in touch with their people back home. It also allowed them to leave traces of their combat. Viewing and analyzing this content produced by the fighters themselves undoubtedly provides a different image to that generated by official Hezbollah media. These videos depict the men's private experience of combat as well as their state of mind: after the thrill of combat often follows exhaustion, affective distress, and the fear they will never make it back home. For these ordinary fighters, so often posted to forward positions, every filmed challenge may well be their last. For instance, before returning to Syria, Ali showed me a video in which he had filmed all the places at the front where he had inscribed his four-year-old daughter's name. "It's for my daughter," he said, visibly emotional, "for when I'm not here anymore; she has to know that I never stopped thinking of her."[28]

Conclusion: Documenting Combat, Staging Victory
The analysis of these videos sheds light on Hezbollah's new audiovisual representations, both official and vernacular, since 2011. Though they bring out a range of memories of this conflict and the different subjective experiences involved, both nevertheless document and archive the event, while targeting different audiences. From the standpoint of content, these productions dovetail in several ways: invisibility of the enemy, the relation to territory, and the concealment of pain and damaged bodies. This absence of the enemy does not preclude the inclusion of a semantic register around victory. Although the enemy's defeat is never visible, victory is staged by the fighter's exaltation, or a radio communication where the fighter announces the success of a military operation, and the congratulations of other fighters once the mission is accomplished. Unlike the conflict with Israel, this "victorious self"[29] does not seem in this context to need the other/another to assert itself. Rather, it seems to express itself all alone and leave it up to the viewer to imagine who appears in the counter-shot.

NOTES

1. See Calabrese, "'La cause c'est nous'" (2016), 103–114.
2. El-Houri, *The Meaning of Resistance* (2012), 123.
3. At the end of the Lebanese civil war (1975–1990), all the other militias were dissolved.
4. El-Houri, op. cit., 124.
5. Picard, *Liban-Syrie, intimes étrangers* (2016).
6. The same is achieved through various written works and pamphlets published in 2012 onward by intellectuals of the party seeking to legitimize the combat in Syria.
7. The conflict in Syria once again shows the permeability of Syro–Lebanese space: Abiyaghi and Calabrese, "Penser le militantisme en contexte de guerre" (2018), 13–19.
8. In 2012—while Hezbollah's presence in Syria was not yet official—in the south suburbs of Beirut, one could see gigantic posters of the Sayyida Zaynab mausoleum in Damascus with the slogan "Zaynab shall not be captured a second time."
9. Although the first mission photographed by this group dates back to 1986, the War News Unit (or War Media Unit) site was institutionalized and took its name in 1994 while Hezbollah was fighting against Israeli troops in Lebanon. One of the photographers who worked in this organization explained to the Lebanese daily Al-Safir that at first this media outlet employed a dozen people, whereas today some 1,000 people are on the payroll. According to the same source, by 2016, at least 250 members of the organization were covering the fighting in Syria. See Al-Safir, 09/20/2016.
10. Calabrese, "Ruptures et continuités dans le militantisme" (2018).
11. The total set is based on my watching around 150 videos.
12. Launched on 3 June 1991 by "a group of friends and personalities not affiliated with Hezbollah, but deeply involved in supporting the Resistance," the channel was not controlled by the party until 1997. See Lamloum, "Le Hezbollah au miroir de ses médias" (2008), 35.
13. Some of these images could be used by the family and friends of a fighter in the editing of non-official tribute videos to the martyred combatant.
14. According to several sources, this commander was also in charge of al-Rida, Syrian auxiliary forces. See Smith, "Libanese Hezbollah's Islamic Resistance in Syria, The Washington Institute (2018).
15. Interview with the director of the Association for the Revival of Resistance Legacy, Beirut, 07/20/2015.

16. This TV series recounts the early years of the Islamic resistance (1982–1985) against the Israeli occupation of Lebanon. It was written by the Syro–Palestinian Fathallah Omar, and produced by al-Manar, the association al-Risalat, and the Lebanese Association for the Arts. See Calabrese, "Al-Ghâlibûn" (2013).
17. For security reasons, the fighters are not identifiable.
18. El-Houri, op. cit., 125.
19. Before leaving for the front for the first time, each fighter writes out his testament and submits it to the Martyrs Association. After his death, the association is responsible for transmitting the news to his family and close friends. This testament would also be used in the martyr's tribute video. Interview with the director of the Martyrs Association, Beirut, 01/20/2014.
20. See: Chaib, "Le Hezbollah libanais" (2007), 119.
21. Conversation 04/12/2015, southern suburbs of Beirut.
22. Ibid.
23. See Chapter 11: "The Circulation of Images from the Front."
24. On 12 July 2006, in reaction to a deadly ambush and the subsequent abduction of two of its soldiers on its western border with Lebanon, Israel launched a military operation against its neighbor, with the goal of "eradicating" Hezbollah. On 13 August 2006, Israel officially accepted a UN-sponsored ceasefire, which called for an end to Israeli military operations and to Hezbollah attacks. On 14 August at 08:00, when the ceasefire went into effect, Hezbollah proclaimed its "divine victory." For an analysis of the audiovisual production on this war, see El-Houri op. cit.
25. This designation includes a whole series of Islamist, jihadist, and nationalist actors opposed to the Bashar al-Assad regime, but especially the jihadist fighters of the Nusra Front and the Islamic State Organization. Within the Syrian context, Hassan Nasrallah used it for the first time in a speech on 30 April 2013, thereby justifying the presence of Hezbollah fighters in the vicinity of the Sayyida Zaynab sanctuary in Damascus: "Decent and righteous mujahidin [fighters for Islam] must rise up to prevent the fall of the village and the mausoleum of Sayyida Zaynab [. . .] There are people on the ground who are preventing the advance of the takfiriyyin." L'Orient le Jour, 04/30/2013.
26. Although the "takfiri" is never represented in these audiovisual productions, he is nevertheless very present in the fighters' narrative accounts of the war, in the party's literary production, and in Nasrallah's speeches.
27. In this same speech, Nasrallah declares: "The criminals would have you believe that the Sunnis are responsible. Don't fall into the trap[. . .] The takfiriyyin are targeting Muslims as they do Christians, mosques as well as churches." L'Orient le Jour, 08/16/2013.
28. Conversation 02/13/2014, southern suburbs of Beirut.
29. El-Houri op. cit., 126.

13
TERRORIZING AND KILLING WITH IMAGES

AMATEUR VIDEOS BY THE SYRIAN ARMY SOLDIERS AND EXE-
CUTION RITUALS OF THE ISLAMIC STATE ORGANIZATION[1]

Cécile Boëx

Torture, death, and horror are parts of political strategies that involve tormentors, victims, and an audience.[2] This audience, of variable size, is always carefully targeted. Based on two terror-practicing actors in the Syrian conflict, one a "state" actor, the other not, this chapter explores the role of video in the economy of extreme violence.[3] At different moments of the conflict, the Syrian army (between 2011 and 2013) and the Islamic State organization (IS)* (between 2014 and 2019), made particular use of video during sessions of torture and execution. The Syrian army did so (almost) clandestinely, while the IS took the public display of horror to the extreme. In what sense do these videos take part in terror and humiliation? To what extent are they intrinsic to a wartime strategy? Whom do they address? The images under study here belong to antithetical strategies of visibility. For those issuing from the Syrian army, they are semi-underground, meant to remain confined to the national community in order to bolster the supposed power and impunity of the Bashar al-Assad regime and quash any form of opposition.[4] The images produced for this "domestic" consumption, amateur footage shot by those participating in the violence, are often unclear due to their low resolution and erratic camerawork that gives them a raw, unfiltered look. Though little forethought is involved in the actual shooting of images, the presence of the camera contributes to an escalation of violence and its self-staging. In the case of IS execution videos, intended for a globalized viewership, the image is a highly scripted, slick production, leaving no room for improvisation. It is not the torturers who produce the images but teams of communications professionals, specialists in the exhibition of agony for the world's terrified gaze. Here, the maximizing of viewership relies upon the principle of ever-novel atrocities, different for each execution, and an exuberant staging, playing into various registers of mass entertainment culture and blurring the borders between fiction and reality. The shock effect proves particularly effective for maximum circulation and dissemination.

213

Annihilate the Inner Enemy

Unlike the IS execution videos broadly disseminated and discussed by the media, the videos of torture and execution filmed by soldiers in the regular Syrian army are little known, even though they are far greater in number.[5] They surfaced on YouTube around May 2011, a few months after the start of the revolution, and are labeled "leaked videos" (*musarrab*). The broadcast of them grew scarcer by late 2013, the phase where the revolt and armed struggle had evolved into a regional and international conflict. Filmed among soldiers in a military setting, these videos were not supposed to be released to the public. They were leaked to the Internet through several channels: they were picked up by opponents from military personnel who exchanged them for money, or directly from cell phones belonging to captured or slain Syrian soldiers. They were then posted online to denounce the violence and humiliation endured by civilians and incite them to revolt. Some, however, suggest that the regime encouraged this kind of leak, both to terrorize the population and to fan the flames of sectarian hatred,[6] since the soldiers, like the al-Assad clan, belong overwhelmingly to the Alawi minority, within a majority Sunni population. As it happened, no measure was ever put in place to check this practice. This semi-clandestine dissemination on the Internet, tolerated or even encouraged by the regime, was addressed, and remained confined to majority Syrian "public." The videos, untranslated and of poor quality, at times almost unintelligible, are intended for those who "already know" what they are about. Filmed on smartphones by soldiers or members of the security services, who often flip the phone around for a selfie, these images are of the most amateur type—with all the closeness and triviality that genre implies—which makes them even more unbearable. At the time of writing, many of these videos are still on YouTube with, for certain ones, a mandatory warning about violent content, as required by the platform. They are still "active," with comments left years after the date the videos have been posted, attesting to their continued potency. Some comments express indignation and anger, while others, before the fall of the regime, congratulate the killers.

The Syrian population obviously did not discover the brutality of the regime through these videos. Many had already experienced it in the early 1980s during the presidency of Hafez al-Assad, who was behind the bloody suppression of a protest movement—notably with the bombing and plundering of the city of Homs, killing over 30,000 people. In the aftermath of that traumatic event, the anticipation of massacre, detention, and torture became part of a veritable governing strategy.[7] This embedded violence, barely spoken of in the privacy of families, was completely stifled in public space. Only a few writers addressed it, especially in the 2000s.[8] Even though many were preparing for the worst, even though families were returned the mutilated bodies of their loved ones who had been in detention, seeing and hearing scenes of torture and murder was a genuine shock. These videos document, unwittingly, a vast array of abuses, insults, torture techniques, and executions. They also show the attitudes of the torturers—a curious mixture of casualness, hatred, and euphoria—as well as the extreme suffering and humiliation of the victims, for the most part civilians. These videos cannot be considered as one-offs or marginal. Their number is considerable (we estimate 1,000), produced over a three-year period, indicating that the practice was standard, institutionalized. They show the intensity, diversity, and scope of the violence perpetrated against the activist civilian population—or those suspected of activism—in the revolt movement denied by the regime, which considers its actors as terrorists or "undercover operatives." The cruelty and impunity lie in the words and in what the bodies had to endure. They lie, also, in the act of filming itself.

It is challenging to draw up an inventory of the acts of violence that appear in these videos, so broad is their scope. They could be practiced collectively or individually, in a torture room of a detention center, in a bus during the transfer of detainees, in a private apartment, or even outdoors. They range from humiliation (men stripped, shaved, insulted, and mocked) to murder. The extent and target of the violence are just as variable: wounded detainees beaten in their hospital beds,[9] insults (always accompanied by beatings and laughter), the rape of both women and men. In some videos, quite specific torture and interrogation techniques appear: a man, blindfolded, hands and feet bound to either end of a fork suspended over a pair of double doors; three Alawi officers, having defected, are stripped and placed in a metal barrel, their eyes taped closed; a man whose skin has been lacerated at knifepoint is smeared with salt; etc. In numerous videos, demonstrators are forced to kiss the portrait of Bashar al-Assad and say that he is their god (Figure 13.1). Even the dead do not escape infamy. "Games" with corpses or bones are frequent: two soldiers imitate a soccer match with a skull they say belonged to a "terrorist," others insult corpses of rebel fighters, beating or dancing on them. Through the flesh, it is identities, values, convictions, and beliefs that were being denied and desecrated.

13.1. During his interrogation by two men from the intelligence services, a detainee is beaten and forced, under threat with a weapon, to bow down before this portrait. Cf. https://www.youtube.com/watch?v=DfnK_KeJfQ, YouTube, 2012 [video no longer available].

Video thus takes full part in the "economy" of cruelty. Firstly, it confirms the actors' sense of superiority and impunity (real or imagined). The often "playful" character of the violence, in addition to being a kind of implicit retribution, allows them to trivialize it, to own it and even brag about it. We can easily imagine that these videos are viewed among soldiers and shared with friends and family, like trophies. They could also be shown to one's superiors, as proof of a mission accomplished with zeal. During the act of violence, video contributes to confirming the torturer in his role. With the familiar, almost friendly presence of the cell phone camera, the violence tends to escalate as the actors stage themselves in the scene. In a video posted online on 11 February 2012,[10] (Figure 13.2), three members of the security forces are joking around during the interrogation of a detainee, prostrate, blindfolded, and wearing nothing but a tank top (it is winter, judging from the jackets the others are wearing). They not only pummel and insult him, but they also set up a fake dialogue between themselves and the detainee. One of them, falsely emphatic, shouts out in Arabic: "You want a miracle? Well, have a look, I'm going to personally perform a miracle" (he repeats, clapping his hands). Another asks him to get up, to be proud of himself. When the detainee raises his head, he receives another blow. The tormentors seem to compete for the privilege of torturing. A third man, holding an iron rod, is acting impatient: "Bring him to me!" The first insists: "No, I want to show him how I perform a miracle!" The recording stops. Here we perceive the group effect on the mounting intensity of violence, boosted by the presence of the camera. There are those who see, those who film, and those who show, and the one deprived of seeing is cast before the gaze of others. With this video, we also understand that on a fundamental level, the filming proceeds from the same logic as the act of cruelty, in the sense that it is also a way of appropriating the body of the other by capturing his image, of maximizing the humiliation by granting oneself the right to show it to others, to replay it and to reassert, each time, the torturer's omnipotence. For the victim, it is a form of social and symbolic death, which prolongs and multiplies the indignity.

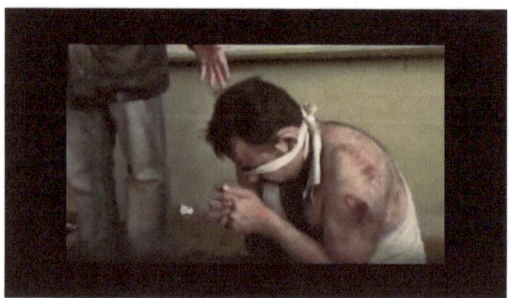

13.2. "Leaked video. Torture of detainees by security forces" [translated from the Arabic], YouTube, 2012.

The act of cruelty via image also plays out in the framing. On 4 October 2012, the Coordinating Committee* of al-Hajar al-Aswad, in the Damascus suburbs (as specified in the text that accompanies the post), published a video[11] where we see military personnel torturing young men, undoubtedly because they had been taking part in demonstrations. At the start of the sequence, one of the victims passes out after being struck multiple times. One of the soldiers pours water on his face to revive him. The lens then tracks to the right to film two other detainees who are sitting against a wall. It is clear they have been beaten. One of them is staring down at the floor, and the other is writing something on loose-leaf paper (Figure 13.3), most probably a false declaration stating that he had been incited to take part in the demonstrations by underground operatives and that he promised to never again demonstrate. The cell phone camera draws closer. The man filming orders in Arabic: "Raise your head." He brings the camera right up into the man's face to film him and turns to the side, as if to work the close-up (Figure 13.4). The young man stiffens, gazes dispiritedly, fearful. Filming this way, the torturer captures and appropriates this gaze enjoying the way it reflects his power over the victim; he sees only himself, abolishing any reciprocity. This act of image taking, uncommonly violent, isolates the head from the rest of the body, as if to decapitate it. It is a way to possess the body and the dignity of the one they consider as the enemy. Capturing the other by his demeaned image creates a void within him by dis-possessing his gaze, rendering him sightless.

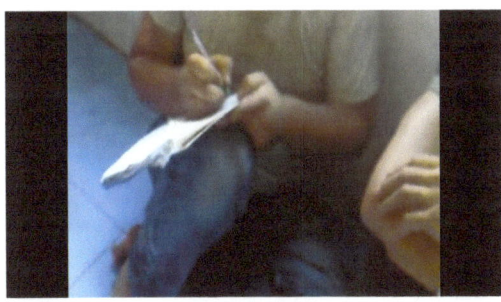

13.3. "Leaked video. Torture of civilians by the gang at the Nisrin Street barracks" [translated from the Arabic], YouTube, 2012. This screen capture leaves the young man's eyes outside the frame so as not to replay the torturer's act.

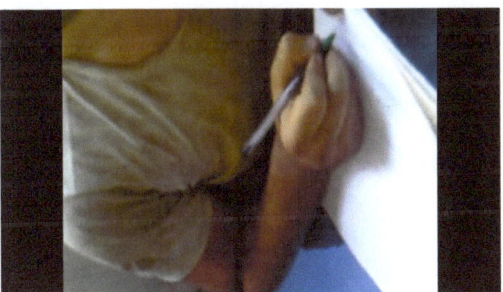

13.4. "Leaked video. Torture of civilians by the gang at the Nisrin Street barracks" [translated from the Arabic], YouTube, 2012. This screen capture leaves the young man's eyes outside the frame so as not to replay the torturer's act.

Horror, Enhanced and Globalized

The videos shot by the soldiers of the Syrian army are of limited availability, locally confined to those who inflict the violence or condone it or, when the videos are leaked, to opponents and their sympathizers. This relative confinement is reflected in the amateurish, extremely rudimentary quality of the films. At the other end of the spectrum, the audiovisual productions of the Islamic State (IS) targeted the broadest possible viewership based on a carefully elaborated communication agenda. While jihadist groups were not developing territorial settlement strategies, the IS had established itself as a proto-state, controlling a territory[12] with administrative and enforcement powers. Within this quasi-governmental framework, it created a communications agenda to broadcast its worldview and assert its status as new political actor. Between 2014 and 2015—a period of expansion and stabilization of the "Caliphate"[13]—the IS posted over a dozen videos per week, translated into several languages, thanks to a sizable media infrastructure.[14] Thoroughly developing the concept of media jihad* as conceived by al-Qaeda*,[15] the broadcasting of these videos—as with IS print propaganda—relied on a vast network of accounts created and updated daily on Facebook and Twitter ("X"), as well as online magazines, forums, and blogs.[16] Both a weapon of war and a legitimizing recruitment tool,[17] the audiovisual production of the IS was diverse up until its decline in 2016,[18] depicting not only combat scenes but also well-run administrations, hospitals, factories, and businesses, in a style akin to corporate promotional films. Their execution videos represent but a tiny share of their overall production. Although most are highly produced, not all receive the same elaborate treatment. Rather, the more politically important the target would prove, the more spectacular and scripted the video would be. For instance, when an execution involved Westerners or Arabs participating in the coalition against the IS, all the production values were greatly enhanced.

In order to maximize the impact of execution videos—a genuine source of communicational, political and military leverage—the IS plays on what is unprecedented and monstrous about the execution techniques (a bladed weapon, fire, water, crucifixion, interment, bleeding, throwing from a cliff, etc.), emphasizing the passage from life to death. The novelty of the cruelty itself must make big news. The ostentatiousness of the horror is played out in a macabre, hallucinatory dramaturgy, where the camera probes the hostage's every gesture, until his last breath and the degradation of his body. The ordeal lasts the full length of the video (between five and twenty-two minutes), without counting the length of the shoot. Since the execution can be shot only once, several cameras frame the shot from different angles so that no detail is lost. The filming takes days, even weeks of rehearsal, involving as many simulations of execution for the prisoners. This certainly explains why the victims always seem so calm. The murder and agony are not simply recorded on film but are designed as a show by virtue of the exorbitant artifice of their staging: camera movement, multiple POV angles, poses, gestures, speech, clothing, set, inserts of 3D images, and clips from other media. The soundtrack is also very sophisticated: sinister sound effects and throbbing warrior hymns (nashids*) instill shock and awe. Unlike the Syrian soldiers' far more amateur videos, in which the presence of the torturers is asserted (either because they appear in the frame or because they film in an identifiable way), the IS videos are disembodied, in the sense that their shots are rigorously still frames where the face of the torturer is practically never seen. The contrast between the spectral but massive presence of the torturers and the hyper-exposure of the victim is stark. This phenomenon of extreme violence as spectacle draws largely on the visual and narrative codes of the entertainment industry (movies, reality TV, and video games).

The video[19] entitled "A Message Signed with Blood to the Nation of the Cross" conjures up an execution ritual. Broadcast on 15 February 2015, it stages the beheading of twenty-one Coptic Christians abducted in Libya. Like all IS videos, it begins with a black screen on which is written in Arabic, in white: "In the name of God, the Most Gracious, the Most Merciful."[20] Next appears, in golden calligraphy, the production unit logo, in this case al-Hayat Media Center, which descends like a water droplet with a streaming sound in the background. The first sequence opens with a wide shot of hostages dressed in orange arriving on the seashore, like the Guantánamo[21] prisoners. They are accompanied by their executioners, who wear balaclavas and are dressed in black (Figure 13.5). Those at the head of the line are particularly tall, a very literal metaphor of their supposed superiority. This march is staged as an apparition, a nightmarish vision that appears and disappears repeatedly against a crackling sound. A low-angle shot followed by an aerial view accentuate the vanishing point to give the impression of uninterrupted scrolling. As in a feature film, the title of the video appears against a black background, subtitled (in Arabic): "A letter signed in the blood of Christian nations." At the end of this procession, executioners and victims line up against the horizon line of the sea in perfect synchrony. Two tracking shots follow to highlight the large number sentenced to death. When the hostages kneel, we observe a slight slow-motion effect. The different angles and modulations in the scale of shots and how fast the images scroll by all diffract time and space, constantly blurring the viewer's perception and destabilizing them before delivering the actual collective decapitation scene. One of the executioners, placed at the center and wearing military dress, pronounces a threatening speech in English, repeatedly pointing his knife at the camera. After this warning, the beheading is shot at actual speed, then a slow-motion tracking shot exhibits the heads set on the bodies. The final shot, accompanied by a *nashid*, shows rough sea tinted red.

13.5. "A Message Signed with Blood to the Nation of the Cross" [translated from the Arabic], al-Hayat Media Center, 2015.

The IS videos deal in a hypervisibility of horror[22] that transgresses the documentary representations of violent death in the contexts of warfare that had prevailed up until then. At times, the executions are so highly staged that they look unreal, like the video of the execution of a Jordanian pilot, burned alive in a cage, posted online in February 2015.[23] At twenty-two minutes long, "Healing the Believers' Breasts" (translated from the Arabic) produced by al-Furqan Media is conceived as an act of vengeance after coalition bombings against IS (of which Jordan was a partner). The first part of this video, particularly elaborate, suggests the omnipotence of the enemy by turning its own images against it, in a bid to justify the vengeful act. For instance, the "crusade" against "the land of Islam" is represented by a tightly edited montage of grand Hollywood productions of war scenes showing aircraft carriers, tanks, horses, and men. The incrimination of Jordan, the video's chief target, is substantiated by clips from TV news broadcasts and interviews with King Abdallah II. A voiceover speaking in newscaster style denounces the historic collaboration of Jordan with the "Crusaders." This introductory sequence ends with a 3D animation that shows a fighter aircraft taking off from the Jordanian flag, bursting into flames and breaking up in midair. The scattered debris then reassembles to form the title of the video, explicitly indicating that the video is a response to the bombings. The different sources of images used in this first part are standardized with a streaking effect and contribute, here again, to the blurring of borders between reality and fiction. The second sequence, still making use of image remix, starts by narrating the capture of the pilot by means of various Arab and Western news broadcasts. After this demonstration of media clout, the pilot appears in an orange jumpsuit, medium shot, facing the camera. Here starts a "performance" where the victim takes an active part in the staging of his own execution.[24]

Mu'adh al-Kasasba's face is bruised. After stating his identity and the salient facts of his professional trajectory, he goes into detail about how the bombing and his capture unfolded.[25] Like someone giving a full confession, he also gives information as to the material used by the different countries participating in the coalition, and their mode of coordinating and targeting. These statements are backed by 3D animations, figures, geolocation schemes, and sound effects (typing on a keyboard, beeping sounds when data appear onscreen) typical of an investigative report or a crime series. Through this sonic and graphic environment, the IS presents its claim to be in possession of confidential strategic information. At the end of this sequence, the pilot gives a message to the "Jordanian people" in the hands of a government, an "agent of Zionism," that should be directing its warplanes against the forces of Bashar al-Assad who "is killing millions of Muslims." He asks parents not to allow their children to participate in these operations, so that they do not "end up like him." Thus, a man sentenced to death is speaking, announcing his own impending execution, which is also reflected in the image processing. Indeed, as if to accentuate his strictly scripted text, his body is dematerialized; it vanishes, disintegrates (Figure 13.6). He is already no longer human, reduced to an IS propaganda avatar. After this sequence, a bombing scene is simulated by means of a plane flying amidst video clips showing civilian victims and devastation. The film then zaps through operative images of air strikes taken from aircraft. Next appear in 3D animation the different types of bombs deployed, each followed by a brief video excerpt showing the charred remains of a child's body. The transitions between these shots are rendered by flames, as if to announce (and justify) the burning to come. These videos, whose source remains unknown, are presented as incriminating evidence.

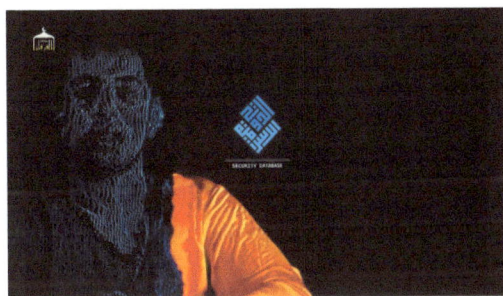

13.6. "Healing the Believers' Chests" [translated from the Arabic], al-Furqan Media, 2015.

The first image of Mu'adh al-Kasasba's arrival at the site of his execution follows this macabre path. Visibly a bombing target, the place is littered with rubble and fragments of concrete. A backhoe can be seen in the background. The particularly bright image makes it look as if dust is still floating in the air.

While he seems to be moving forward, looking around, a parallel montage gives POV shots of a search for victims in the wreckage, showing the reverse shot of the bombing in which he participated, reconstituted from his boarding the plane until the dropping of the bombs. He is thus compelled to take the full measure of his action and serve as an example, especially since he is a Sunni Muslim who, in their view, ought to have taken sides with the IS. He arrives amidst a row of hooded fighters in military dress. Others are posted, almost geometrically, on several floors of a bombed-out building. The camera focuses on the face of the executioners who are glaring at the pilot with looks full of hatred. Reverse shots stage this exchange of looks (or the impossibility of this exchange), to better emphasize the pilot's absolute solitude in this punishment ceremony. Like the shredded bodies embedded in the wreckage, he is trapped (Figure 13.7). This metaphor is extended through the use of the cage, the place that brings his wandering to a close. The absence of any acoustic accompaniment, erasing even the sound of footsteps on the rubble, adds to the unreal, nightmarish feel of this whole sequence. The immolation is extremely theatrical. Emphatically and in slow motion, one of the balaclava-wearing fighters kneels to light a tracer made with an inflammable product leading to the cage. Visually, nothing escapes the camera lens, but the victim is consumed in silence,[26] against the soundtrack of a religious hymn. This sonic sanitizing contrasts with the hypervisibility of cruelty, the performance of which is always augmented by slow-motion or special effects. Here, the flames appear to be pasted into the image. Once the body is completely burnt, it is "buried" in the rubble by the backhoe, which then bulldozes over the remains. The video ends with a call for a reward for the capture of Jordanian air force pilots whose names (and for some, photos and addresses) are displayed.

13.7. "Healing the Believers' Chests" [translated from the Arabic], al-Furqan Media, 2015.

Conclusion: New Audiovisual Forms of Extreme Violence

History is marked with examples of the strong connection that images have sustained with violence in all its forms, if we think of Italy's *pittura infamante* from the late Middle Ages,[27] intended to shame and banish convicts from the city, or, in a more contemporary context, the degrading photographs of Iraqi detainees taken by American soldiers at Abu Ghraib prison in 2004. Punishment by pictures thus takes multiple forms depending on the political, war-related, and technological context. It involves different gestures, words, objects, techniques, and dramaturgies. Whether intended for a broad audience or a closed circle of soldiers, its scales of visibility vary depending on the status and purpose of those who resort to it. Although the use of images in the practice of violence is hardly new, the antithetical regimes of visibility studied here give rise to unprecedented audiovisual forms, scales, and modes of circulation. They also show how much the forms and modes of dissemination are imbricated, defining whether an item remains contained or goes viral, which itself reveals the political and geo-strategic forces at work. However different their production and dissemination modes might be, these videos proceed from strategies of political survival that draw on one another in a kind of symbiosis. It is striking to observe the dwindling number of videos posted online by the Syrian army after 2013. This period represents a pivot point in the internationalization of the conflict that resulted in a proliferation of actors on the battlefield. The rise of jihadist groups in Syria starting in 2013, and particularly the hyper-publicized establishment of the "Caliphate" in June 2014, constituted the most effective argument in favor of keeping Bashar al-Assad in power. From that point forward, the fight against Islamist terrorism could serve as a front for the repression of political opposition. Thus legitimized, violence redeployed in broad daylight with the backing of foreign allies on the ground (mainly Iran via different militias) and in the air (Russia, by 2015), could more easily justify their intervention in the conflict. In response, this unabashedly repressive violence fed the mobilizing discourse of jihadist groups. The hyper-visibility of the jihadist phenomenon ended up completely eclipsing the actors in the revolt and the initial meaning of their struggle. It also contributed to obscuring and minimizing the crimes committed by the Syrian regime.

NOTES

1. This text is a reworked version of the chapter "Dramaturgies audiovisuelles de la terreur en Syrie. Les vidéos amateurs de soldats syriens et les vidéos-spectacle de l'Organisation de l'État islamique" from the collective volume *La transgression, de l'antiquité à nos jours*, edited by Pimouget-Pedarros and Barrondon, Presses Universitaires de Rennes, 2021.
2. See: Humphrey, *The Politics of Atrocity and Reconciliation* (2014).
3. I would like to emphasize here how hard it was to work with these exceedingly violent images emerging from a very recent past. To deal with this challenge, I developed filtering techniques, such as preliminary viewing of a video on the scrolling bar to crop it into sequences, cutting out the sound, or, for some of them, only listening to the audio. I also self-imposed a strict viewing time limit, choosing the moments when I was ready to watch. At seminars and conferences, I never show violent images and instead use stills.
4. As Yasser Munif has stressed, "The difference between IS and the Syrian State is not a matter of how cruel but rather of how visible. When regime militias executed over one hundred Aleppo civilians and threw their corpses into the river, knowing that the current would carry them to east Aleppo, controlled by the opposition, their objective was that the inhabitants of that zone would see the massacre. The violence of such an act is practically invisible outside Syria [. . .] but it is very visible inside. The issue of visibility is essential because it is used by the State to remind the population of the enormous cost of its opposition stance." See: Munif, *The Syrian Revolution* (2020), 36.
5. It is impossible to quantify them in any accurate way, as YouTube is not an archive site; some have probably disappeared since their being posted. Still, they do number well over one thousand.
6. Haj Saleh, "Tahdiq fi wajhi-l-fazi'" [Gaze at the horror] (2015).
7. See: Ismail, *The Rule of Violence* (2018).
8. One example being *L'éloge de la haine [In Praise of Hatred]* by Khaled Khalifa, published in 2006 in Lebanon, and *La coquille [The Shell]* by Mustafa Khalifa published in 2007, also in Lebanon, when the author was living in exile.
9. Many of the wounded were finished off in public hospitals with the complicity of medical personnel.
10. Posted by Nimr Suriya (pseudo) under the title (in Arabic) "Leaked video torture of detainees by security forces." https://www.youtube.com/watch?v=rkt-gt4QjUg, with 22,619 views on 11 June 2024.
11. "Leaked video. Torture of detainees by the gang at the Nisrin Street barracks" [translated from the Arabic]. https://www.youtube.com/watch?v=lWTTlkb0Ga0, with 14,932 views on 11 June 2024. This video is no longer available.

12. In 2015, IS controlled about 40 percent of Iraq (170,000 km2) and 33 percent of Syria (60,000 km2).
13. The Islamic State is not a new organization; rather, it emerged in Iraq in 2006 with Islamic State in Iraq, whose objective was to repel American forces present in the country since 2003 and create a zone of Sunni power in reaction to the monopolization of political power by the Shiites. The Islamic State in Iraq gradually evolved with the stated ambition of establishing an Islamic State, the Caliphate. Taking advantage of the context of violence in Syria, the group gained momentum and became "The Islamic State in Iraq and the Levant," then the "Islamic State Organization" in June 2014, when it achieved its expansionist aims by proclaiming the restoration of the Caliphate.
14. According to a report aired on the program *Envoyé Spécial* entitled "The Image Soldiers," broadcast on France 2 in 2016, the IS media department employed between 700 and 800 cameramen whose pay varied between 3,000 and 7,000 U.S. dollars per month.
15. See: El Difraoui, *Al-Qaida par l'image* (2013).
16. Since 2017, this content is difficult to access online due to increased surveillance by social media watchdogs.
17. See: Rekik, *La fabrique audiovisuelle de l'État Islamique* (2018).
18. Due to a series of territorial losses to offensives by the coalition created in 2015. On 23 March 2019 the end of the Caliphate was proclaimed and, on 27 October of the same year, Donald Trump announced the death of Abu Bakr al-Baghdadi following a raid. Nevertheless, the Islamic State continues to publish videos episodically, mainly on the encrypted messaging app Telegram.
19. As part of the campaign against jihadist content launched in 2015 by numerous video sharing platforms and most social media platforms, the links to this video, like those that will be mentioned within the rest of this chapter, are no longer accessible.
20. This is a line that every Muslim must utter prior to reciting a Quranic sura. It is also the opening of the "al-Fatiha" sura.
21. American military detention center created by George W. Bush to imprison and torture captured Islamist militants and fighters, notably during operations in Afghanistan and Iraq. Its location in Cuba on a military base means that it eludes the American judicial system. It is a symbol of persecution and humiliation for jihadists.
22. Jean-Louis Comolli compares these videos to porn movies: "It isn't simply a matter of seeing but of seeing in detail. The details, the close-up shots, all signal an urge to see everything, up close and personal, without shame, unimpeded." See Comolli, Daech, *Le cinéma et la mort* (2016), 16.

23. On social media, much doubt was expressed as to the authenticity of this video. Bloggers and graphic artists affirm that the immolation was entirely or partially staged using CGI.

24. See: Molin Friis, "'Behead, burn, crucify, crush'" (2018), 243–67.

25. This took place in Syria near Raqqa, after he ejected from his plane after engine failure on 24 December 2014.

26. As in all execution scenes, the victim doesn't make a sound, the soundtrack featuring only the sound of whatever technique is being used to kill.

27. See Ortalli, *La peinture infamante du XIIe au XVe siècle* (1994).

14

WHEN AN IRANIAN BLOCKBUSTER STAGES THE VIDEO PRODUCTION OF THE ISLAMIC STATE

Agnès Devictor

Damascus Time, with its considerable special effects and breathless pacing, tells the story of an Iranian pilot—Ali Rostami—who comes to Syria to drop food supplies into the territories conquered by the Islamic State (IS)*. Mission accomplished, he flies to Damascus airport where he meets his father, Yunis Rostami, himself a pilot and a senior manager of this military air base, who is looking for a pilot to fly back some Syrian civilians holed up at the Palmyra airport ever since the city came under IS control. Poised to return home to Iran, Ali Rostami changes his mind and chooses to stay and join this mission along with his father, leaving his wife about to deliver a baby in Tehran. Once in Palmyra, he manages to take off with a plane full of civilians but also prisoners, including a Syrian sheikh and his family who have pledged allegiance to the IS. They somehow free themselves and, after various twists and turns, require the plane to return to Palmyra. As soon as it lands, another IS group, made up of international fighters—and led by Abu Bakr al-Tchitchani, "the Chechen"—murders the Sheikh over some disagreement and takes the crew hostage to execute them in a macabre staging filmed by "Talha the Belgian" among the Roman ruins of the city. Ali and Yunis are not executed. Once again, the plane is loaded with prisoners (Afghans, Pakistanis, Iraqis, Lebanese, and Iranians), detained in a cage. Captain Rostami is assigned a female co-pilot, Umm Salma, who compels him to turn the plane into a suicide vehicle without telling the crew. Managing to save the lives of the prisoners in time (by hooking their cage to parachutes), then blowing up the plane to preclude the planned suicide attack, Ali Rostami sacrifices himself as a martyr.

This film is written and directed by Ebrahim Hatamikia, a director of war films who began his career as a camera operator with the Islamic Revolutionary Guard Corps (IRGC)* during the Iran–Iraq war (1980–1988) and remained a faithful supporter of the regime's most conservative wing. Produced in 2017 by the strongly official Owj Center created by the IRGC,[1] *Damascus Time—* the first mainstream film on the Iranian intervention in Syria—is the product of an internal political and social context. In spring 2017, the presidential election resulted in another term for Hassan Rohani, signatory to the 2015 Vienna Agreement on Iranian nuclear weapons control,[2] denounced by the conservatives. Tensions rose further with the election of Donald Trump, who threatened to withdraw from the agreement and step up sanctions against Iran, weakening the Iranian president and lending even more credibility to the conservatives and the IRGC. In June of that same year, attacks claimed by IS struck Iran for the first time and seemed to be drawing Iran into a war that until then had been remote. Between August and September, an unprecedented national mobilization all over the country celebrated the remains of an Iranian soldier, Mohsen Hojjaji, beheaded by IS,[3] giving a new visibility to the Iranian intervention in Syria. Presented with grand pomp at the Fajr Film Festival in Tehran in February 2018, *Damascus Time* earned broad distribution in Iran, thanks to powerful political and media backing.[4] It reasserts the purpose of Iran's presence in Syria following the official line in force since 2012: the Iranians are providing military advice to the Syrian high command, with training and aid for civilians. This film, which adheres to this line, defines moreover the actors in the conflict (allies and enemies), and broadly describes the Syrian population and territory in a war devoid of any historicity.[5] Even though the subject does not appear paramount in the action-packed plot, the presentation of the international IS recruits as "PR staff" more than combatants is undeniably pertinent to Hatamikia as war film director. I will thus begin by illustrating how in the second part of the film, the filmmaker stages the way IS frenetically elaborates and exploits its videos: in this film, IS is much more defined by its production of violent videos than by its fights (we never see IS fighting its official adversaries). I will then analyze how Hatamikia appropriates the enemy's images within a framework of citations and borrowings that serve his own production.

Make Movies Not War

Hatamikia devotes three mutually distinct sequences to the manufacture and dissemination of images by IS.[6] The first focuses on the one that creates the most media buzz: the execution video. This idea enters at a turning point in the plot, when the flight crew is captured by the international members of IS; Hatamikia therefore shows that the whole point of this abduction is to make a film. Driven in a bus, the prisoners each receive an orange jumpsuit and a morphine injection.[7] Walking in single file through the ruins of the grand Palmyra amphitheater, they are then lined up across the stage, facing outward. The filming, orchestrated from the back of a pick-up truck transformed into a super-production command post, starts with the shout "Action!" (in English), as on Hollywood film sets (Figure 14.1). The executioners, dressed in all black and balaclavas, each come forward and take one of the knives arranged in a star shape on a platter (Figure 14.2). Each then takes position behind a prisoner (rendered docile thanks to the morphine injection), who first kneels, then is laid out for the execution itself (Figure 14.3). Talha-the-Belgian has them retake the scene once, then asks an adolescent armed with a pistol and experienced in its use to urge their partisans the world over to take up arms, making a solemn declaration. The filmmaker guides the drone that records this scene, fine-tuned to the millimeter (Figure 14.4), while another camera assistant is shooting from the pit of the amphitheater. Hatamikia depicts the enemy not as a warrior, which would have involved the Iranians appearing as combatants, but as a demiurgic creator. Like an orchestra conductor who knows his score, Talha attests to a proficiency undoubtedly acquired over a long period of time in his perfectly mastered filming of this execution.

14.1. Talha shouts "Action!" © Owj Media Center.

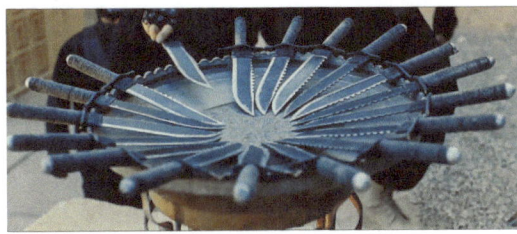

14.2. The knives. © Owj Media Center. The film can be openly accessed for free at the Persian language training site, iNoor Institut Noor. My stills came from this site.

14.3. The prisoners are set in place. © Owj Media Center.

14.4. The adolescent filmed by a drone makes his declaration. © Owj Media Center.

Another sequence, peculiar and very brief, refers to the effects of an IS video seen in Iran. Hatamikia films Ali Rostami, who has returned to the plane, called to by Talha-the-Belgian, who says to him in English, in a jubilant tone: "We're going to turn you into a hero. An Iranian superstar!" This sequence is a direct allusion to the decapitation video of the soldier Hojjaji, filmed by IS, and the massive effect its broadcast had in Iran.[8] That video came out in August 2017, thus at the end of the production process of this film, meaning this short sequence must have been added at the very last minute. Hatamikia is thereby pointing to a violence of war that circulates easily and quickly via images. This allusion to the "Hojjaji event," understood by only Iranians, additionally reinforces the filmmaker's connivance with the national audience. The third and final mention of IS's audiovisual arsenal deals with the making of multiple recordings that the combat group will be using. Before the prisoner cages and the other IS members get back on the plane, Talha the Belgian sets up small cameras in the cabin in preparation for shooting the entire operation, inside and outside the plane, which will be broadcast live "to the world." Then he films Abu Bakr the Chechen making a declaration from inside the plane (Figure 14.5). The rest is seen live by the characters (Rostami the pilot, Umm Salma the suicide-copilot, Talha the filmmaker) and the spectator, either on the tablet placed in the cockpit, or on Talha's computer (Figure 14.6). Added are the images recorded on the runway by a drone (Figure 14.7), and again observed from different points of view (Figure 14.8). After a series of further developments, Ali Rostami will succeed in thwarting the plan of Abu Bakr and Umm Salma who, we find out thanks to another video, was once a singer in a nihilistic heavy metal band. This sequence, lasting over twelve minutes, is made up of a multitude of actions, all recorded and viewed on different platforms. Hatamikia thus defines IS production as a panoptical system giving rise to a totalizing visibility of their operations addressed to the world, while at the same time monitoring every member of the group by the same means. He makes frequent use of *mise-en-abyme* images within images, a cherished technique in Iranian cinema that Hatamikia himself has often deployed.

14.5. Abu Bakr the Chechen makes his statement © Owj Media Center.

14.6. The scene from Talha's computer © Owj Media Center.

14.7. Abu Bakr on the landing strip. © Owj Media Center.

14.8. The scene from the cockpit. © Owj Media Center.

Appropriation of the Enemy's Images

If Hatamikia depicts IS as a public relation firm, he also appropriates the combat group's visual universe to serve his own staging. Throughout this part of the film, the Iranian director deploys citations that border on remakes. He quotes videos, images, or objects that have become stereotypes and immediately call to mind the torture practiced by IS, like the row of prisoners in orange jumpsuits (before the execution), the knives (for slitting throats, or a saber for decapitating), and the cage (for death by fire).[9] The execution sequence, one of the film's more spectacular scenes, is even directly inspired by a video shot by IS in Palmyra and posted online on 4 July 2015, in which adolescents executed twenty-five Syrian soldiers in the grand amphitheater of Palmyra[10] (Figure 14.9). Hatamikia's staging is not identical, however, despite the setting: it is not adolescents who carry out the execution—even if a teenage boy does come to make a declaration, revolver in hand—and the prisoners do not die in the same manner. Hatamikia does not turn it into a public execution, unlike IS, but just a macabre *mise-en-scène* staged only to be filmed. The filmmaker's imagination is unquestionably nourished by the IS-made scenario; however, the way he films it relies on a visual escalation, even stronger than in the IS videos. He further aestheticizes violence in this film: the single file of prisoners in orange jumpsuits is set off sharply against the black of the executioners' uniforms; the overlaid symphonic cello music is enhanced by a choir that adds melodramatic depth; and the shot is expanded with an overhead view that takes in the grandiose setting of ancient Palmyra (Figure 14.10). Hatamikia builds his own lyricism out of the IS imaginary as it translates into its videos. He trivializes the barbarity and films it as one stage of his scenario, attenuating the violence by sparing the two protagonists, and thereby producing a sense of relief and rendering the scene less shocking for the audience.

14.9. IS video of the execution of twenty-five Syrian soldiers in Palmyra (posted online on 07/04/2015).

Among the visual motives he borrows, Hatamikia resorts to that of caged prisoners, which serves to valorize only one of the two protagonists (Yunis Rostami) at the expense of this character's fellow sufferers, who are nevertheless allies of Iran. For instance, during the final hijacking scene, the cages—filled with prisoners—are loaded onto the plane. Abu Bakr states that they are Afghans, Pakistanis, Iraqis, Lebanese, and Iranians. Though Yunis Rostami (the only Iranian) is among them, the other prisoners are deprived of any on-screen existence, as is often the case in action films to highlight a protagonist. But in the production context of this film, the choice to not grant screen time to the forces allied with Iran, to preclude the audience locking eyes with them, hearing their voices, and seeing them as individuals, is based on a strategy of erasure, or rendering invisible. The camera films them only as a group in a cage. At the end of the final credits, the use of the shorthand term "the Defenders,"[11] indicates that these prisoners belong to armed groups linked to the IRGC (implicitly, the Afghans and Pakistanis). In this sequence, then, they are reduced by Hatamikia to mere accessories to foreground the visual motif of the cage borrowed from IS. This directorial choice further depoliticizes his representation of war.

14.10. Aerial shot of the Palmyra amphitheater. © Owj Media Center.

Even more problematic from an ethical standpoint is the sympathetic parody sketched by the Iranian director. In this part of the film, the three major enemies are ambivalently defined: while they are professionals in the tasks they undertake, they are also intended as caricatures. Abu Bakr the Chechen appears for the first time riding a thoroughbred stallion, saber raised, like a storybook character (Figure 14.11). Umm Salma embodies an evil power: eyes heavily made-up, English-speaking—a convert in search of meaning. She is the icon of Western decadence, and swaps her outfit as "Queen of Hate" in a heavy metal band for that of a suicide attacker for IS.[12] Talha the Belgian represents the image of the mercenary, one of many Europeans who joined up to serve in the IS communications division in exchange for a salary. All three are granted a comic moment that aims to humanize them and to create a familiar closeness with the audience: the terrifying Umm Salma suddenly offers Ali Rostami some snacks (Figure 14.12), Abu Bakr cracks jokes with the two Iranians, and Talha makes funny faces like a comic book character.

14.11. Abu Bakr the Chechen. © Owj Media Center.

14.12. Umm Salma offers Rostami some snacks. © Owj Media Center.

Conclusion: In the Camp of Sensationalism

With *Damascus Time*, Hatamikia radically broke with the way he once filmed war. *The Scout* [*Didehban*, 1989][13]—which had its claim to fame at the end of the Iran–Iraq war, even raising him to the rank of auteur in Iranian cinema circles—shunned the sensationalizing of violence of any kind. Captain Rostami displays the same reluctance as the scout to embark upon a one-way mission, with the same doubts and moments of weakness. But back then, Hatamikia was inventing a form that, by its silences, the length of the shots, and the pacing of the edit, left the audience some room to roam, destabilizing them when it came to expecting a simplistic decision to make the ultimate sacrifice. Here, however, he shirks that approach in favor of maximum spectacular effectiveness, according to criteria he shares with IS and which, in theory, come from the sworn enemy of both: the Hollywood movie industry. This film also stands apart from what constitutes the official visual production surrounding the Holy Shrine Defender*.[14] It contains only two references to Sayyida Zaynab*, first orally by the father and son when the knife is at their throat in the Palmyra amphitheater and they pray for her intercession, and again at the end of the film where, even though we can make out the three cages suspended from parachutes with the prisoners saved by Rostami, it is the Zaynab Mausoleum that stands out (Figure 14.13).

14.13. The Zaynab Mausoleum. © Owj Media Center.

The visual culture gradually constructed in Iran since the 1979 Revolution that refers to one of Shiism's founding events, the Battle of Karbala*, to narrate a war or a challenge that the country must overcome,[15] is conspicuously absent from *Damascus Time*. This film breaks with a singular national cinematographic genre that has been elaborated by filmmakers closest to the regime, and that depicts the Iran–Iraq war and the Holy Shrine Defense[16] according to narratives and forms derived from this same religious and national visual culture. Although Hatamikia had already yielded somewhat to the temptations of sensationalism in his previous films, *Damascus Time* manifests—for him and his powerful producer the IRGC—the explicit choice to represent the Holy Shrine Defense, diametrically opposed to this aesthetic, and to side with a globalized visual culture that includes Hollywood and IS, both enemies of Iran.

NOTES

1. Alipour, Z., "IRGC funding for cinema stirs debate in Iran," Al Monitor, 03/15/2018.
2. Signed on 14 July 2015 by the United States, Russia, China, France, the United Kingdom, Germany, the European Union, and Iran, this framework agreement aimed at monitoring Iran's nuclear program and lifting economic sanctions that were affecting Iran. On 8 May 2018, Donald Trump announced the U.S.'s withdrawal from this agreement and the strengthening of economic sanctions against the Islamic Republic of Iran.
3. See Chapter 11: "The Circulation of Images from the Front."
4. The film *Damascus Time* [*Be vaqt-e sham,* Ebrahim Hatamikia, 2018] which is said to have cost 2 million euros (a sizable budget for an Iranian film), is reported to have earned 2.3 million euros thanks to media hype and political backing for distribution. A seven-week screening attracted some 1.4 million movie-goers. The film was sold to Japan, Poland, Lebanon, and South Korea. Agence France Presse (AFP), 05/16/2018.
5. An opening intertitle attempts to situate the film: "In February 2011, with the start of the civil war, Syria was in deep crisis. Abu Bakr al-Baghdadi, head of the Islamic State, aspired to establish a government in Syria and Iraq. Cities were falling one after the other [. . .] A humanitarian catastrophe loomed. The only way to get supplies was by air. Iranian pilots were the first to provide relief." There is no date to set the film in time, as if there were no political or military developments that coincided with this conflict.
6. Or nineteen minutes of a film lasting one hour and forty-eight minutes.
7. The use of the orange jumpsuit has become code since Guantanamo, to designate a humiliated war prisoner. The Islamic State, like a range of other fighter groups, use this uniform for their prisoners.
8. See Chapter 11: "The Circulation of Images from the Front."
9. See Chapter 13: "Terrorizing and Killing with Images."
10. In Sasan Fallahfar's documentary, The Battle of Palmyra [Nabord-e Palmira, 2016], the filmmaker samples an excerpt from this IS video that features prisoners on stage and children walking in the pit. The execution is not shown, but this borrowing demonstrates that this video was seen in Iran.
11. The official term to designate fighters in Syria and Iraq under IRGC authority is "Holy Shrine Defender."
12. Let me emphasize here that of everyone I spoke with during the interviews I conducted in Iran (between 2017 and 2019) with fighters under Iranian command in Syria, Umm Salma represents the archetypal figure of the Western convert who joins the IS.

13. Written before the war was over, the script tells the story of a scout who accepts a mission that is probably a no-return assignment. It involves reestablishing communication, broken off by the Iraqi enemy, between a battalion of armed Iranian volunteers holding advanced positions at the front, and the rest of the troops. Only he can guide the Iranian artillery. With minimal visual effects, Hatamikia convincingly depicts the fear experienced by an ordinary soldier, his doubts, and even his discouragement throughout his time on the battlefield.
14. Devictor, 2019.
15. Chelkowski and Dabashi, *Staging a Revolution* (2000).
16. See Chapter 11: "The Circulation of Images from the Front."

CONCLUSION
GAUGING THE DEPTH OF IMAGES AND SOUNDS

THE PRECARIOUS NOTION OF ARCHIVE

Cécile Boëx and Agnès Devictor

The chapters of this book have sketched out a cartography of uses and practices of video during the revolution and war in Syria, highlighting the quite varied ways that people relate to the medium, be they civilians, activists, or fighters belonging to official armed forces or more ad hoc combat groups. Accompanying the evolution of the conflict over time has made it possible to examine different moments, intensities, and dimensions of protest and combat. Depending on how elaborate they are and which situations they are documenting, these audiovisual productions give a particularly stark account of the asymmetrical power dynamics between protesters and the regime, but also within the same camp. Visibility is on the side of the "weak," of those with no choice but to use the pictures they take by posting them to the Internet to make known their words and actions, while the ruling authorities opt for strategies of secrecy, deletion, retention, restricted dissemination, or distortion. Since 2011 the transformation of images, just like the scaling of the affiliations and political agendas of those who produce them, has shed light on the ways the revolt was gradually marginalized, in favor of an internationalization of the conflict that has ended up obscuring the genesis and very existence of that revolt. The analyses collected here have dealt with different representations of engagement, combat, and violence, all caught in the moment on camera with a sensitive eye and using the audiovisual devices at hand to capture a range of lived experience, affects, subjectivities, and emotions. This sensitivity, just like the fragility and fragmentary character of the videos these authors worked on, involves unique methodological issues that we wish to address in our conclusion. This will involve a brief return to our guesswork when faced with the volatility of the revolutionary and wartime context, not to mention the challenges of the digital world, which will inevitably raise the question of the instability of the very notion of archive—a problem that has emerged in some chapters.

Methodologies: Dealing with Uncertainty

The digital landscape and the shape-shifting context of conflict further exacerbate the paradox of profusion and lack. From the outset of this work, we have pointed to the proliferation of digital images with which we were able to work, while at the same time emphasizing that the specificity of our research has less to do with comprehending this audiovisual mass than with identifying the modes of accessibility to images, with their eclectic assortment and volatility. In fact, our image searches were often subjected to algorithms whose logic remains impenetrable. As for the analysis of images stored on cell phones or computers belonging to activists, combatants, or civilians, this implies our being able to meet up with them, which in turn presupposes an accessibility to and experience in the field—some parts of which are hazardous. Furthermore, we called attention to the dearth of background information concerning the videos and stills posted on the Internet (often via circuitous paths), which often fails to indicate either date or location and, even more often, the names of the people filmed or those doing the filming and/or posting online. Each contribution, according to its author's specific modalities, took a patient labor of contextualization. Our analyses attempt to reduce the opacity surrounding the images by allowing clusters of interpretation to emerge from accumulated viewings and data, by comparing a same event, situation, person filmed, person filming, shooting style, etc. and allowing them to mutually resonate, without ever attempting to establish total legibility. We did not process the videos and still photos of our research set like data whose authenticity had to be verified by digital tools (TinEye, Google Reverse Image Search, FotoForensics or YouTube Data Viewer, to cite only these), but as puzzles to be solved, a few clues to which we have elucidated. Many questions remain unanswered. We still do not always know who did the filming, or for whom and for what purpose. We are aware of the fragmentary aspect of our analyses.

The work of contextualizing, describing, and interpreting also proceeds from each of our individual ways of seeing things, each gaze struck by the intensity of the images of revolt and war, where it was always a matter of life and death, and where those who were filming did so at enormous risk to their personal safety. How could we not become custodians of such images, not feel moved by them? And how to measure up to the astounding narratives of courage, violence, and powerlessness like those told by Hatem A. and F. H. that emerge from our interviews? Images are not simply data; they are made of flesh and blood. The diversity of our approaches shows how much our methods are situational, empirical, and transitory, having to adapt to formats, lacuna, and tools, as well as constantly being updated, through which the images transit and vanish. We felt it essential to approach this audiovisual material by stressing how embodied it is, to show how it hinges on lived experience but also on memories of events, allowing for their reminiscence. When encounters with the picture-takers was not possible, immersion in the materiality of the videos—in their formal details, textures, framings, movements, and sounds—made it possible to restore the image-making acts, underpinned by intentions and projections. We surveyed these images the way one surveys a territory, with their share of exhilarating, destabilizing, or repulsive encounters.

Timelines and Trajectories of the Archive

The research work brought together in this book was carried out while the conflict was still underway, at a temporal distance from the events. Our analyses therefore take place within an extremely volatile timeframe, typical of a revolutionary or wartime context. Likewise, the instability of the digital environment puts us, despite ourselves, on an emergency footing. Numerous videos analyzed in this work are no longer accessible, while others have disappeared altogether. Similarly, most online downloading software is no longer capable of recognizing certain videos shot with cell phones posted in 2011. What will be left in a few years' time of those still available online? Will platforms like YouTube still be accessible? Under what conditions? And what about the storage hardware for digital images—cell phones, memory cards, USB drives, hard disks—that grow obsolete so quickly? The current profusion of images is almost defined by the imminence of their loss. Our texts here are also acts, however modest, of safeguarding before an inescapable disappearance. In the same vein, the importance of digital devices in the audiovisual traces left by the conflict in Syria raises the question of archives, which are in the process, or soon to be, of coming together. Every revolt, and every conflict, produces specific archives depending on existing techniques and devices. In Syria, most of the traces of the revolt and the war produced by the actors are intangible. In fact, they open up further battlegrounds.

A case in point, for the foreign combat groups, notably Lebanese Hezbollah and the division of Afghan Fatemiyoun* under Iranian command, the issue of archiving combat images from their action in Syria reveals tensions between the compiling of an official memory—which tends to leave out the simple fighters or to monopolize their images in order to make specific points about their role in this war—and those rare autonomous memorial gestures when fighters seek to arrange for their own memorials, so as not to be forgotten or have their memory subsumed into some outside agenda. The set of problems posed by the archive was already germinating at the moment of combat, with the issue of who controlled the image taking, and how such images were being conserved—an issue that digitalization has made even harder to manage. On the Syrian side, the regime was attempting to claim a monopoly of the archive and of memory[1] by erasing the revolt and its actors, deeming them traitors for glorifying only "their" dead. The civilians, activists, or fighters opposed to the regime had no memorial except the thousands of tribute videos made by family and friends, whether in Syria or in exile, who disseminated them via YouTube.[2] For Syrians engaged in the revolution, the archive felt implicitly like admitting defeat, at a time when they were being dispossessed of the events and people's perception of them. The archive issue emerged in 2013 when jihadist groups were on the rise and the revolt and armed struggle were sliding toward an international conflict.[3] This came with a reframing of media coverage and the politics of the fighting that situated the war as a struggle against terrorism. Furthermore, the archiving of videos of jihadist groups by individuals, researchers, and institutions is relatively systematic and accessible, which says something about the dominant perception of this conflict. From the revolution's perspective, archiving translates the powerlessness of images as a means of making sense of the present. This passage into the archive is also linked to uprootedness and exile since these initiatives are undertaken from the only place possible: outside of Syria.

Nevertheless, at the same time, they represent by default a space where activism can continue. It was during this same period, 2013–2014, that two major digital audiovisual archive sites came into being. The first, The Creative Memory of the Syrian Revolution,[4] based in Beirut, gathers and preserves artistic, cultural, and intellectual production stemming from the revolution, in the form of texts, photographs, and videos. The second, Syrian Archive,[5] based in Berlin, strives to collect and verify videos and photos to make them available to journalists and human rights groups, so that they might serve as evidence in judicial cases. Meanwhile, there were signs of spontaneous archiving practices that consisted either of posting a new video on the anniversary of a particular event with the word "archive" in the caption or, more elaborately, creating a YouTube channel whose purpose would be to archive and remember the revolt and the conflict.[6] This backed-up content is quite diverse and stems from personal choices that often feature the most widely circulated videos. They concern all Syrian cities, and the earliest moments of the revolt are especially present. These archiving practices were taking the shape of a scattered and fragile memory that is also highly sensorial.

How an archive emerged from the audiovisual and digital production stemming from the revolt and conflict in Syria thus had to entail different practices of collection, back-up, filing, description, and transmission, often with very limited means.[7] The archive signifies a political and memorial act that struggles against erasure and looks toward the expectation of justice or acknowledgment, displacing and stretching the initial temporality of the images to project them into the future. In this context, the issue of archiving, with its multitude of trajectories, plays an integral part in the conflict, which is prolonged and relocated via the archive through these same acts of safeguarding, memorial storytelling, or hopes of eventual reparation. The time of the event and the time of the archive have thus never been so proximate, which does not come without a certain blurring effect that makes it hard to account for the (necessarily long) transformation processes underway, compressed and disposed of in the intense succession of events, key dates, emblematic figures, and objects or already formatted narratives. The rush to archive must not fossilize the events and actors, but rather restore the thickness of these years of revolt and combat, which profoundly transformed society and individuals in Syria and beyond.

NOTES

1. For example, through the "non-governmental" organization Wathiqat Watan [Document of a nation], based in Damascus and created in 2018 by Bouthaina Shaaban (communications advisor to Bashar al-Assad) and other personalities close to the Syrian regime. Comprising a site in Arabic and in English, its purpose is to compile "an archive of documented testimonials that form a reference data base for Syria and the Arab world, intended for all researchers and those interested in oral history." Cf. http://wathiqat-watan.org/, accessed 11 June 2024.
2. See Boëx, "Figures remixées des martyrs" (2018).
3. Many jihadist videos, for example, are available at the Internet Archive site (https://archive.org), as well as at the Jihadology site (https://jihadology.net/), subject to registration.
4. Accessible in Arabic, English, and French, the site also offers a chronology that covers the period from 2011 to 2016, as well as an interactive map that situates part of the archived documents. Cf. https://creativememory.org.
5. Cf. https://syrianarchive.org/en.
6. See, for example, the YouTube channel "Archive of the Syrian Revolution," [translated from the Arabic] created on 4 July 2018, with 4,618 views by 11 June 2024. Cf. https://www.youtube.com/channel/UCl-u_kAFsX9D2F3-5xj9tJw/videos?view=0&sort=da&flow=grid.
7. These practices are currently under study at the Agence Nationale pour la Recherche SHAKK-Conflits, Déplacements, Incertitudes (2017–2025). In partnership with Alain Carou and Julie Guillaumot, heads of the video department at the Bibliothèque nationale de France, this research program created a collection of videos that emerged from the conflict and the revolution, made available by researchers and activists. The online videos cited in this book are preserved in this program's archival collection .

GLOSSARY

Ahrar al-Sham (Islamic Movement of the Free Men of the Levant)
The battalions of Ahrar al-Sham *(Harakat ahrar al-Sham al-islamiya)* were officially created in January 2012 by the jihadist militants released shortly before from the Saidnaya Prison, near Damascus. This movement did not join the Free Syrian Army*, which then constituted the dominant trend in the armed struggle that emerged from the revolution. Unlike the latter, Ahrar al-Sham defined itself as an ideological faction with its own Islamist political agenda—distinct from transnational jihadism—claiming independence from al-Qaeda* and acting exclusively within a national framework. Backed by Qatar and Turkey, the movement remained, until July 2017, the principal Syrian rebel unit with manpower numbering between 10,000 and 20,000 men. In early 2018, the group merged with Harakat Nour al-Din al-Zenki to form the Syrian Liberation Front *(Jabhat Tahrir Suriya)*.

Al-Bayada Martyrs' Brigade *(Katibat shuhada' al-Bayada)*
Founded in May 2012, Katibat shuhada' al-Bayada was made up of young men from the al-Bayada neighborhood of Homs, which is also the home of its most famous commander, 'Abd al-Basit al-Sarut. Though claiming no ideological affiliation, this brigade did display the colors of the Syrian revolution until its disappearance in 2015, despite a brief phase among the founding ranks of the Faylaq Homs*, an Islamist formation active for some time in the northern part of the Homs governorate.

al-Furqan Brigades *(Alwiya' al-furqan)*
Brigades affiliated with the Free Syrian Army* bringing together some 2,000 men in 2014 and led by Muhammad Majid al-Khatib. They fought mainly in the regions of Aleppo, Idlib, Daraa, Quneitra, and greater Damascus.

al-Qaeda
Literally "the base" in English, al-Qaeda is an armed Islamist organization founded in 1987 by Sheikh Abdullah Yusuf 'Azzam and his student Osama Bin Laden, in the context of the struggle against Soviet occupation in Afghanistan. After the Taliban took Kabul in 1996, Bin Laden organized the training of Arab combatants (mujahidin), thereby developing the organization's networks. The al-Qaeda camps trained thousands of militant Islamists the world over. Upon their return, the "Afghans" (returnee fighters from Afghanistan) took part in various conflicts, such as in Algeria, Chechnya, Egypt, Indonesia, Somalia, Yemen, Kosovo, and Bosnia-Herzegovina. After the 11 September 2001 attacks, al-Qaeda became the best known and most dangerous jihadist group. To destroy it, the United States, backed by other countries, invaded Afghanistan. Al-Qaeda lost its training camps, and with its members on

the run, created branches in Iraq, in the Maghreb in 2007 (AQMI), as well as in Yemen and in Saudi Arabia in 2009 (AQAP). Al-Qaeda also deployed in Syria in 2012 via the Nusra Front*. Despite its rivalry with the Islamic State*, it remains the benchmark of global jihadism*.

Brigade for the Liberation of Qalamoun (*Liwa' tahrir al-Qalamoun*)
This fighting group was part of the brigade of the Descendants of the Prophet (*Ahfad al-rassul*) founded in 2012 and affiliated with the Free Syrian Army*, which rallied between forty and fifty rebel factions in 2013 and brought together between 7,000 and 9,000 men. In 2014, the Descendants of the Prophet Brigade was dissolved, and its fighters joined other groups.

Caliphate (*Khilafa*)
After the death of the Prophet Muhammad in 632, the question arose as to who would succeed as leader of the community of the faithful. The caliph (literally, "the successor"), as chief executive, is also the head of the faithful. The first caliphs, called the "rightly guided" (ar-Rashidun) in Islam, are Abu Bakr as-Siddiq (573–634), Omar ibn al-Khattab (584–644), Othman ibn Affan (574–656) and Ali ibn Abi Talib (656–661). The grand dynasties that followed conserved this politico-religious institution before being abolished by Mustafa Kemal in 1924 with the dismantling of the Ottoman Empire. The desire to restore the Caliphate runs through different Islamic trends. It is particularly present in jihadist movements*. On 29 June 2014 at the Grand Mosque of Mosul in Iraq, the head of the Islamic State* organization, Abu Bakr al-Baghdadi, proclaimed the restoration of the Caliphate, which is not recognized by any other religious authority.

Farouq Brigades (*Kata'ib al-Farouq*)
Originally a simple battalion within the Khalid ibn al-Walid Brigade, trained by deserters from the Syrian army based in the governorate of Homs during the summer of 2011, the Farouq Brigades (of nationalist roots) gradually became the principal armed opposition force at the turn of 2011–2012. They distinguished themselves especially in the fighting at Baba Amr in February 2012.

Fatemiyoun Division (*lashkar-e fatemiyoun*)
This Division consisted almost exclusively of exiled Shiite Afghans living in Iran and Syria and, starting in 2013, Afghans of the Shiite Hazara ethnic group coming from Afghanistan. Its name comes from Fatima al-Zahraa, daughter of the Prophet who married Ali, with whom she had two sons, Hasan and Hoseyn, and two daughters, Zaynab and Om Kalthum. The Fatemiyoun proclaim their Shiite identity, which is thought to justify their commitment to the protection of the Mausoleum of Zaynab*. In 2012, this first group joined the Iraqi Shiite brigade Abu Fadl al-Abbas, until

in late 2013 when they came together as an independent brigade, the Fatemiyoun *(tip-e Fatemiyoun)*. Deployed mainly in Damascus, Aleppo, and in the governorate of Daraa, this brigade became a division in 2015 by increasing its recruits. According to different sources in 2016, their number varied between 3,000 and 14,000.

Free Syrian Army (FSA)
Founded in July 2011 by deserters from the Syrian Army and civilian volunteers, the Free Syrian Army (FSA) was, until 2013, the principal armed force emerging from the revolt to oppose the Bashar al-Assad regime. It included multiple trends (secular, nationalist, and Islamist). In actuality, the FSA exerted little control over the numerous local armed groups created to defend a neighborhood or village. Made up of some 40,000 men in 2012, it consisted of a multitude of brigades and battalions of varying longevity and enrolment. This motley and scattered resistance army, which emerged in reaction to the regime's fierce repression, was devoid of a specific ideology. Even though these factions were nationalist and pursuing a common goal of bringing down the regime, their sensibilities (Islamist or secular) were diverse and evolved over time. This ideological indeterminacy fostered a certain volatility of affiliations: numerous brigades quickly came apart or merged with others. The FSA benefited from the backing of Western countries, though it was more diplomatic than financial. The Russian air strikes in support of the regime starting in 2015 precipitated its collapse. The FSA groups gradually lost their bastions. Some rejoined the Syrian National Army, a new coalition directly linked to Turkey, which in turn sent them to fight against the Kurds in 2018 and 2019. In 2020, the last FSA fighters were cornered in Idlib. In Daraa, despite the "reconciliation" agreement under the aegis of Russia, an insurrection led by former FSA fighters has persisted.

Hijra
A term which in Arabic literally means "emigration" and refers to the exile of the Prophet Muhammad from Mecca to Medina in 622, hijra is the founding event that marks the beginning of the Muslim lunar calendar (16 July 622). In Salafist circles, which are fundamentalist Sunni movements that advocate a return to the more primal Islam of pious predecessors *(al-salaf al-salih)* who were the Prophet and his companions, hijra designates the emigration of a Muslim living in a non-Muslim country to a Muslim country. Upon the proclamation of the Caliphate* by Islamic State* (IS) in June 2014, it became a central feature of IS propaganda, put forward as an obligation for Muslims, just like jihad*. The urging to hijra is built on a grand apocalyptic narrative founded on hadiths indicating the imminence of the battle at the end times *(al-Malhama al-Kubra)*. Proof of this imminence is notably based on geographic coincidences: the land of Sham* and Dabiq, a village located to the north of Aleppo, where according to Muslim eschatological tradition a major battle between Muslims and *"al-rum"* (literally, the Romans) is supposed to take place. It is by virtue of its

symbolic importance (rather than strategic) that IS conquered this village in August 2014, after the Free Syrian Army had controlled it since 2012. The main online IS magazine that appeared between 2014 and 2016 in Arabic, English, French, and German was also called *Dabiq*. This apocalyptic narrative aimed to legitimize al-Baghdadi's Caliphate and convince its members and future recruits that they belonged to the vanguard of the chosen ones.

Holy Shrine Defenders *(modafehan-e haram)*
Modafehan-e haram represent Shiite combatants from different countries united under the authority of the IRGC*. The use of this term dates back to April 2013 in Iran after the destruction in Syria of the Shiite sanctuary of Hujr ibn ʿAdi (located in ʿAdra near Damascus) and the announcement on 30 April 2013 of an attack on the Sayyida Zaynab* sanctuary in Damascus. Starting in September 2012, the Iraqi Shiite brigade Abu al-Fadl al-ʿAbbas was created to defend this sanctuary.

Homs Legion *(Faylaq Homs)*
Islamist-inspired military unit established in June 2014 in the northern countryside of the Homs governorate on bases belonging to eight local revolutionary forces, a part of which were coming from the formerly besieged neighborhoods of Homs. The al-Bayada Martyrs' Brigade*, headed by ʿAbd al-Basit al-Sarut, was at one point a member of this armed faction.

Islamic Revolutionary Guard Corps (IRGC) *(sepâh-e pasdaran-e enqelab-e eslami)*
Created in 1979 by the Iranian government as a security force in charge of internal repression, this corps has been dedicated, alongside the regular army, to the defense of national borders ever since the Iran–Iraq war (1980–1988). It has become a major military, political, and economic force in the Islamic Republic of Iran.

Islamic State *(Tandhim al-Dawla al-Islamiya)*
The early days of the Islamic State Organization (IS) go back to Iraq in 2004 with the creation of the Islamic State in Iraq (ISI), the Iraqi branch of al-Qaeda*. Its whole purpose was to eject the American forces present since 2003 and create a zone of Sunni power in response to the monopolization of political power by the Shiites. In 2010, Abu Bakr al-Baghdadi assumed leadership of this organization. Taking advantage of the violence in Syria, the group gained momentum and in 2013 became the Islamic State in Iraq and the Levant (ISIL), henceforward known under the (pejorative) acronym of "Daesh." The rivalry with al-Qaeda intensified due to Abu Bakr al-Baghdadi's contesting the authority of al-Qaeda leader Ayman al-Zawahiri over Syria, and his hope to absorb the Nusra Front*. The break was complete when, on 29 June 2014, ISIL announced the restoration of the Caliphate* in the territories under its control, took the name "Islamic State," and proclaimed its leader, al-Bagh-

dadi, "caliph." In 2015, IS controlled about 40 percent of Iraq (170,000 km²) and 33 percent of Syria (60,000 km²), but the organization lost its last territories in Iraq in December 2017, and in Syria in 2019. Since the death of al-Baghdadi during an American raid in northwest Syria in October 2019, it is Abu Ibrahim al-Hashimi al-Qurayshi, former prison mate of his predecessor, who is currently leading IS.

Jihad

In Arabic, *jihad* means "effort," "struggle," or "resistance." Muslim tradition distinguishes two categories of jihad: the great jihad, which implies the effort each believer exerts upon him or herself to overcome their passions and elevate themselves spiritually, and the minor jihad, the one involving worldly endeavors, such as work and war. In the Islamist lexicon, it designates combat for God and the fight against the infidels, but its use is much broader. In the context of the Syrian conflict, the term is used by most of the combatant actors, such as those of the Free Syrian Army* (majority Sunni) and militias affiliated to the regime (notably Shiites and Christians), to highlight the religious meaning of their engagement. The concept of jihad is also at the core of movements coming out of the jihadist trend that appeared in the 1980s during the war in Afghanistan with the emergence of Abdullah Azzam (considered the founding father of jihadism), which then gave rise to various currents and groups such as al-Qaeda* or the Islamic State Organization* (IS). These groups advocate armed struggle to liberate Muslim countries from foreign occupation, but also to remove regimes they consider godless.

Karbala (Battle of)

The Battle of Karbala (October 680 CE) was the result of an ambush set by the Umayyad power for Imam Hussein (grandson of the Prophet and son of Ali), his family, and his companions, who had left to join their partisans at Kufa and who refused to swear allegiance to the new Umayyad caliph Yazid. After days of siege, the occupants of the camp were exterminated by Yazid's numerically superior military forces. Imam Hussein was beheaded. The women, including his sister Zaynab, and the children, were brought as captives to Damascus. Every year during the month of Moharram, Shiites commemorate this tragedy—one of the founding events of Shiism.

Kurdistan Workers' Party, PKK *(Partiyan Karkeren Kurdistan)*

Founded in Turkey in 1978, the PKK has been carrying out a guerilla war since 1984. Headed since its creation by Abdullah Öcalan, it is listed as a terrorist organization by many Western countries.

Kurdish Democratic Union Party, PYD *(Partiya Yekîtîya Demokrat)*

Founded in 2003, this Kurdish political party is the Syrian branch of the PKK*. Until 2017, it was led by Salih Muslim.

Local Coordinating Committees *(Lijan al-Tansiq al-Mahaliya)*
Put together by actors in the peace movement based on their informal contacts and trusted acquaintances, these committees emerged during the earliest days of the revolt in March 2011 to organize demonstrations at the neighborhood level and report them on the Internet. The first was created in the city of Darayya, in the suburbs of Damascus. These committees would later coordinate at the level of cities and regions to ensure logistics, security, filmed documentation, and media coverage of the demonstrations. They were also active in helping displaced people and in setting up makeshift clinics. In June 2011, there were more than seventy of them throughout the territory and 131 by 2012. Some were also behind experiments in civic self-governing in the liberated zones, through the formation of local councils *(majalis mahaliyya)* whose point was to ensure the continuity of municipal authority in the absence of services from the State.

Martyrs of Islam Brigade *(Liwa' Shuhada' al-Islam)*
A fighting unit created in March 2013 from the merger of eight groups of the Free Syrian Army* (FSA) active in Darayya, in the southern suburbs of Damascus. With 1,800 fighters, it was the largest of this city besieged from 2012 to 2016. Backed by the United States, the group received BGM–71 TOW anti-tank missiles. This brigade was unique for its total dependence on the local civic council *(majlis mahali)* of Darayya. It was also part of the fifty brigades that made up the Southern Front, a joint command center founded on 14 February 2014 and active until July 2018 in the governorates of Daraa, Quneitra, and Damascus, counting some 20,000 men. When the city was retaken on 25 August 2016 as part of an agreement negotiated with the regime, most of the fighters in this brigade were evacuated to the governorate of Idlib, in northern Syria. In May 2018, it merged with ten other groups of the FSA to form the National Liberation Front in the governorates of Idlib and Hama.

Muslim Brothers *(Jama'at al-Ikhwan al-Muslimun)*
A transnational Sunni Islamic organization founded in Egypt in 1928 by Hassan al-Banna. The Muslim Brothers' objective is the establishment of Islamic republics in place of the secular regimes in majority Muslim countries such as Egypt, Libya, Syria, or Tunisia. They call for a return to Quranic precepts, rejecting Western influences. This agenda got them suppressed and/or banned, as happened in Syria in 1980. After the 2011 Egyptian revolution, the Muslim Brothers came to power with the first free democratic legislative elections. In May 2012, Muhammad Morsi, the Muslim Brothers candidate, became the first democratically elected civilian candidate in Egypt, before he was overthrown in a coup that brought General al-Sisi to power.

Nashid (plural, *nashids*)
A hymn that, in the jihadist context, is sung a cappella as musical instruments are proscribed, and constitutes a major form of expression in jihadist culture. Blending

religious and warrior expression, the *nashid* is both discursive and emotional. In Arabic, the term channels not only religious connotations but is also used to designate, for instance, the national anthem *(al-nashid al-watani)*.

Nusra Front *(Jabhat al-Nusra li ahl al-Sham)*
The "Front of Support to the Population of the Levant" was founded when Abu Muhammad al-Julani, a Syrian jihadist having fought in Iraq, declared jihad* in Syria on 23 January 2012. The Front consisted of members of Islamic State in Iraq (ISI), but al-Julani, sticking to a Syrian agenda, turned down the offer made by its leader, Abu Bakr al-Baghdadi, to merge and form the Islamic State in Iraq and the Levant (ISIL). Thus, from 2013 to 2016, the Nusra Front was affiliated with al-Qaeda* and was particularly present in northwestern Syria. On 3 January 2014, alongside rebel forces, the group went to war against ISIL and later rejected the Islamic State's proclamation restoring the Caliphate. In January 2016, the Nusra Front made a merger offer to Ahrar al-Sham* which they declined, not wanting any connection with al-Qaeda. What followed were skirmishes between the two groups in the governorate of Idlib. On 22 August 2016, the Nusra Front finally broke with al-Qaeda and renamed itself the Front for the Liberation of al-Sham *(Jabhat Fath al-Sham)*. This entity was dissolved on 28 January 2017, the date of the merger of four rebel Islamist groups to form the Organization for the Liberation of the Levant* *(Hay'at Tahrir al-Sham)*.

Organization for the Liberation of the Levant *(Hay'at Tahrir al-Sham)*
This new combat group, an offshoot of the Nusra Front, renamed the Sham Fath Front since its break with al-Qaeda in 2016, was formed on 28 January 2017 by its merger with five other Syrian Islamist groups: Harakat Nur al-Din al-Zinki, the Ansar al-Din Front, the Liwa' al-Haqq*, the al-Sunna Army, and the Free Men Army. In addition, many members of Ahrar al-Sham* defected to join this new unit, such as Hashim al-Sheikh who led it until October 2017. Active mainly in the governorate of Idlib, it numbered around 30,000 men in 2018.

People's Protection Units YPG *(Yekineyen Parastina Gel)*
Created by the PYD*, these armed forces mainly include the inhabitants of the Rojava* region and were made official in 2011. On their website, these units mention an earlier underground formation dating back to 2004. In 2020, they are composed of several tens of thousands of fighting men and women.

Quds Force (sepâh-e quds, lit. "the Jerusalem force")
A special unit of the IRGC* in charge of exterior operations, officially created after the Iran–Iraq war in 1990. It was led by General Qasim Sulaimani from 1997 until his death in Baghdad on 3 January 2020, and then by Esmail Qaani.

Qusayr

Agricultural plain located fifteen kilometers from the border, between the Lebanese town of Hermel and Homs. In early 2012, this is where Islamist brigades and the Free Syrian Army* retreated after being driven out of Homs. In June 2013 the troops of Bashar al-Assad, backed by Hezbollah fighters coming especially from the town of Hermel, retook control of this region.

Rojava

This term is the contraction of the Kurdish expression *"Rojavaya Kurdistanē"* which means "Western Kurdistan." This region is located in northern Syria and is made up of three cantons that border on Turkey and part of Iraq.

Sayyida Zaynab

Granddaughter of the Prophet, daughter of Ali and Fatima al-Zahra'. Following the Battle of Karbala*, she was taken captive to Damascus where her sanctuary now stands in the southern suburbs. This mausoleum is a pilgrimage site for Shiites.

Shabbiha

This term, derived from colloquial language in Syria, originally designated thugs acting within mafia networks (protection rackets, contraband, drug trafficking, gambling) connected to the al-Assad clan, developed in the wake of the Lebanese civil war (1975–1990). Since 2011, these gangs have been mobilized as paramilitary forces and partly restructured inside the Committees for People's Defense *(Lijan Sha'biya)* and National Defense Forces *(Quwwat al-Difa' al-Watani)* created in 2012 to support the Syrian army. These henchmen of the regime, often in civilian dress, play a key role in the repression and violence committed against the population: aggression against demonstrators, abductions, sexual violence, pillaging, mass killings, torture, etc. The majority of *shabbihas* belong to the Alawi community, and their acts have contributed to the polarization of sectarian relations.

Sham

Meaning "Levant" in Arabic, it is the historic place-name designating the region of the Middle East that includes Syria, Lebanon, Jordan, and Palestine *(Bilad al-Sham)*. In Syria, it also designates, in Arabic dialect, the city of Damascus, capital of the Umayyad caliphate until 750 CE. In the context of the Syrian conflict, this name is often used by jihadist* groups. In the Quran, after Mecca and Medina, it is the land of *Sham* that is the most sacred. The word is particularly mobilized in Islamic State discourse which cites numerous *hadiths* and is used by theologians who refer to it, associating *Shām* with their eschatological vision. For instance, issue no. 3 of the review *Dabiq*, Ramadan 1435 (Hejira) cites Ibn Taymiya (1328), a central reference for IS: "In the end times, Islam shall be most apparent in Shām [. . .] The best people of the earth in the end times will be those who stay the longest in the place where Ibrahim made the hijra*, that is, *Sham*." [Compilation of Fatawa *(Majmu' al-Fatawa)* Vol. 27, p. 41].

Syrian Democratic Forces (SDF)
Created in 2015 with backing from the United States, this coalition brings together local Kurdish battalions coming from various ethnic, tribal, or religious communities united in the fight against the Islamic State. The YPGs* and the YPJs* account for most of its members.

Syrian Martyrs Brigades, or Coalition of Battalions and Brigades of the Martyrs of Syria *(Tajammu' kata'ib wa-alwiyat shuhada' Surya)*
Founded in December 2011 in northern Syria in the Jabal al-Zawiya, they assembled, as of March 2012, around 45,000 fighters led by Jamal Ma'ruf, a former construction worker. Affiliated with the Free Syrian Army*, this fighting coalition was active mainly in the governorates of Idlib, Aleppo, and Hama. In late 2013 and early 2014, its fighters participated in the battles of Qalamun and Maaloula.

Syrian National Council, SNC *(al-Majlis al-Watani al-Suri)*
A political transition authority created on 15 September 2011 and officially announced on 2 October 2011 in Istanbul, it aimed to represent opponents inside and outside Syria, and to establish the foundations of a civil, plural, and democratic State. Composed of 140 members at the outset, later expanding to 230, the Syrian National Council (SNC) brings together organizations and personalities of diverse backgrounds: the Local Coordinating Committees* (until November 2012), the Muslim Brothers* (banned in Syria since 1980), secular opposition parties, Kurdish parties, the Assyrian Democratic Organization, tribal representatives, independents, and technocrats. On 29 November 2011, the Free Syrian Army* recognized the SNC's authority. However, the Council soon failed in its representation of the opposition since it had lost its credibility inside Syria (none of its members had gone to Syria prior to summer 2012), while internal dissension was growing.

Takfir
Takfir originally refers to the movement called al-Takfir wa-l-Hijra, founded in 1971 in Egypt. Its partisans, who refer to themselves under the name Jama'at al-Muslimun (Association of Muslims), radically oppose their fellow believers who do not share the same hardline approach to religious practice. These more lenient Muslims are labeled as "apostates" *(kafirun)* and become a legitimate target of attacks. The use of the term *takfir*, which designates the act of anathematizing the other, was later broadened to include different movements covering a range of doctrines and practices. It has become an instrument wielded more generally by individuals or groups for

the purpose of discrediting their adversaries. Those who get labeled with the epithet *takfiri* can also include those who commit illegitimate violence in the name of Islam, which they are accused of distorting by practicing spurious excommunications and resorting to violence.

Voice of Truth Brigade *(Liwa' Sawt al-Haqq)*
Also called *Liwa' al-haqq*, this was an Islamist brigade founded in 2013. In 2017, it was one of the six groups that merged to form the Organization for the Liberation of the Levant *(Hay'at Tahrir al-Sham*)*, an offshoot of the Nusra Front* dissolved in 2017.

Women's Protection Units, YPJ *(Yekîneyên Parastina Jin)*
Gender-exclusive equivalent of the YPGs, created in 2013.

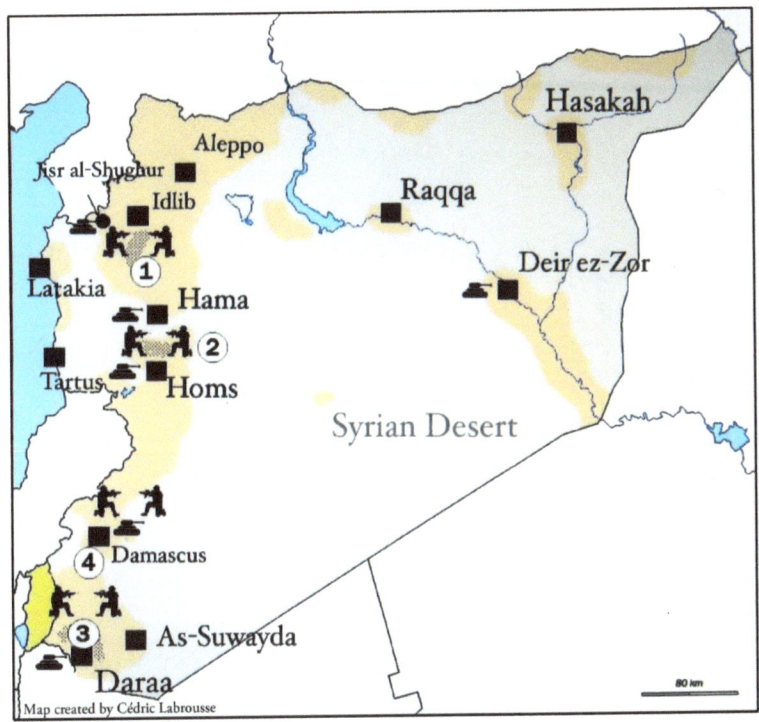

MAP 1. Start of Contestation and Organization of the Armed Struggle (March 2011-January 2012)

■ Provincial center

Start of contestation

■ Principal zones affected by demonstrations starting on 15 March 2011

 Mass repression from March 2011 to March 2012 (siege of Daraa, siege of Hama, siege of Homs).

Militarization of the revolt

 First major desertions from army ranks (May 2011 to January 2012: (1) Jabal al-Zawiya (2) Rastan (3) Daraa (4) Darayya.

 First combat between rebels and loyalists (June 2011 to January 2012).

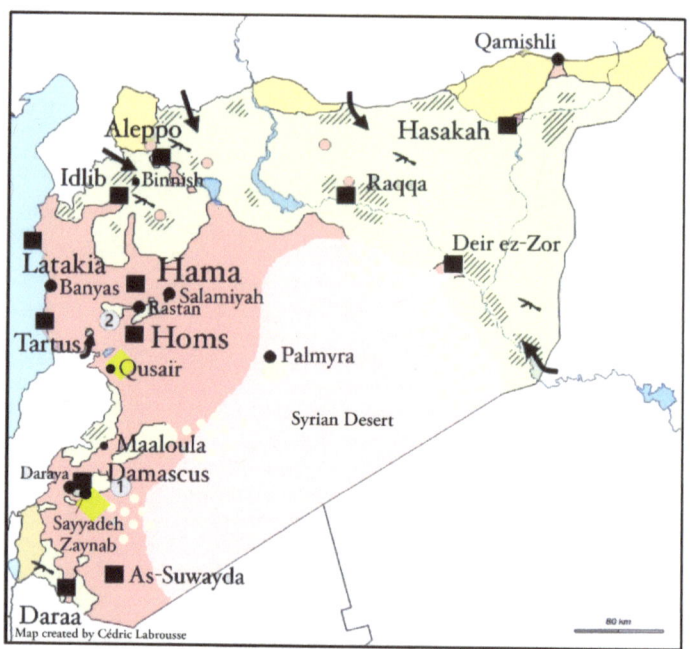

**Map 2. Involvement of Regional and International Actors
(Late August 2013)**

■ **Provincial center**

●●● Cities and villages

(1) Region of Houla
(2) Ghouta of Damascus

A conflict takes hold over time

☐ Zones controlled by the
rebellion (late August 2013)

☐ Zones controlled by
the regime (late August 2013)

☐ Zones controlled by
the YPGs (late August 2013)

▨ Jihadist footholds (Nusra Front
and Islamic State in Iraq and
the Levant. Late August 2013)

**Involvement of regional and
International actors**

◆ Zones of operation of Shiite militias (linked to Iran
and Hezbollah)

✦ Military, political, and
ideological backing to certain
rebel forces (Qatar, Turkey,
Saudi Arabia)

➤ Entry points of international jihadists

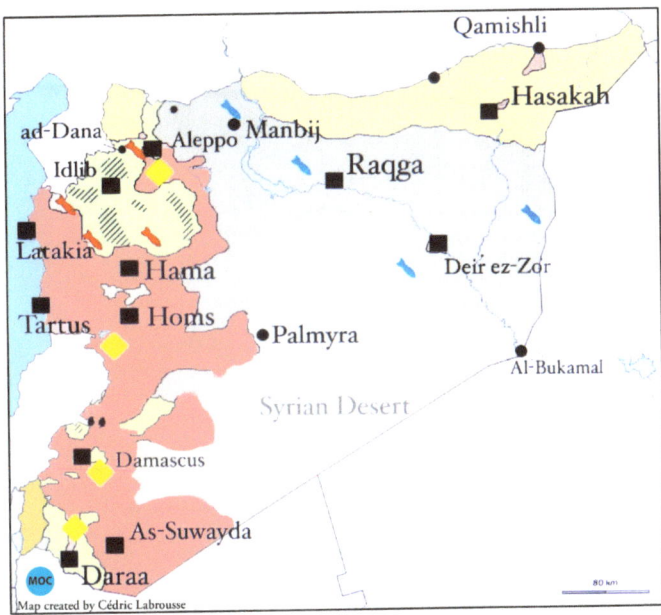

**Map 3. Internationalization of the Conflict
(Late August 2015)**

■ **Provincial center**

●●● Cities and villages

Increasing polarization

☐ Zones controlled by
the rebellion (late
December 2015)

☐ Zones controlled by the regime
and its allies (late December 2015)

☐ Zones controlled by Syrian
Democratic Forces
(late December 2015)

☐ Zones controlled by the Islamic
State (late December 2015)

▨ Nusra Front footholds.

Internationalization of the conflict

⬧ Intervention by the international coalition against the
Islamic State group

⬧ Russian intervention (starting
September 2015)

◆ Shiite militias' zones of
operation

🔵 MOC (Military Operation
Center) for coordination and
support of the Free Syrian
Army in southern Syria, established by several countries
including the United States,
Jordan, and Saudia Arabia

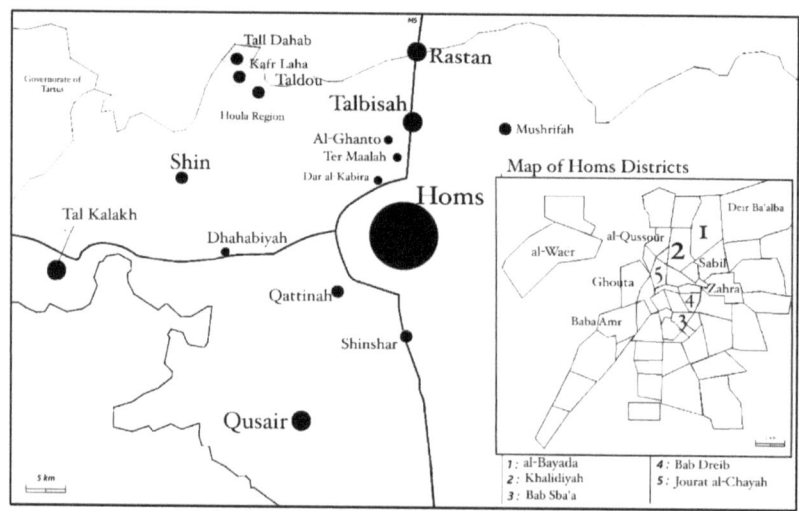

Map 4. The Region of Homs

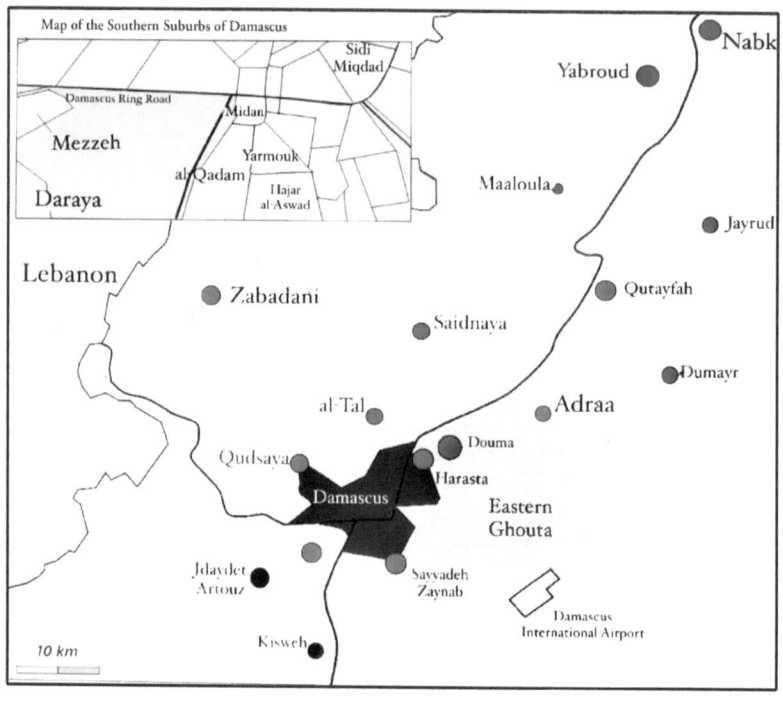

Map 5. The Damascus Region

BIBLIOGRAPHY

Abboud, Samer N. *Syria*. Polity Press, 2015.

Abiyaghi, Marie-Noël, and Erminia C. Calabrese. "Penser le militantisme en contexte de guerre, de répression, et d'exil. Pérégrinations militantes entre le Liban et la Syrie." *Revue internationale de politique comparée* 25, no. 1 (2018): 13–19.

Allard, Laurence, Laurent Creton, and Roger Odin, eds. *Téléphone mobile et création*. Armand Colin/Recherches, 2014.

Andén-Papadopoulos, Kari. "Media Witnessing and the Crowdsourced Video Revolution," *Visual Communication* 12, no. 22/24 (2013): 341–357.

Andén-Papadopoulos, Kari, and Mervi Pantii. "The Media Work of Syrian Diaspora Activists: Brokering Between the Protest and Mainstream Media." *International Journal of Communication* 7 (2013): 2185–2206.

Anzalone, Christopher. "The Multiple Faces of Jabhat al-Nusra/Jabhat Fath al-Sham in Syria's Civil War." *Insight Turkey* 18, no. 2 (2016): 41–50.

Artières, Philippe. *La banderole. Histoire d'un objet politique*. Autrement, 2013.

Aubin-Boltanski, Emma, and Oussama Khalbous. "Qualifier l'engagement Des Syriennes Dans La révolution. Les Retournements Du Mot   (Femmes Libres)." *Lexique vivant de la révolution et de la guerre en Syrie* (2020). https://doi.org/10.21428/3633fae9.e30065a4.

Audoin-Rouzeau, Stéphane. *Une initiation: Rwanda (1994–2016)*. Seuil, 2017.

_____. *Combattre*. Seuil, 2008.

Baczko, Adam, Gilles Dorronsoro, and Arthur Quesnay. *Syrie. Anatomie d'une guerre civile*. CNRS Éditions, 2016.

Bazan, Stéphane, and Christophe Varin. "Le Web à l'épreuve de la 'cyber guerre' en Syrie." *Études* 417 (2012): 595–606.

Bégin, Richard. "L'image au corps." *Vertigo* 1, no. 48 (2015): 6–16.

Bennafla, Karine. "La région de la Bekaa: les mutations d'un espace frontière entre Syrie et Liban." *Revue de l'économie méridionale* 5, no.1–2 (2005): 211–218.

Bertin-Maghit, Jean-Pierre. *Lettres filmées d'Algérie. Des soldats à la caméra (1954–1962)*. Nouveau Monde Éditions, 2015.

_____. "Analyse des films de soldats réalisés pendant la guerre d'Algérie (1954-1962): une méthode historienne." *Les lettres de la SPF*, no. 28 (2012).

Beurrier, Joëlle. "La Grande Guerre, matrice des médias modernes." *Le Temps des médias* 1, no. 4 (2005): 162–175.

Bichara, Azmeh. *Suriya. Darb al-alam nahu al-hurriya* [Syria. A Hard Path toward Freedom]. *Arab Center for Research & Policy Studies* 5, no.1–2 (2013).

Blondeau, Olivier. *Devenir Média. L'activisme sur Internet, entre défection et expérimentation*. Éditions Amsterdam, 2007.

Boëx, Cécile. "Figures remixées des martyrs de la révolte en Syrie sur YouTube. Réinterprétations politiques et mémoire vernaculaire de la mort des gens ordinaires." *Archives des sciences sociales des religions*, no. 181 (2018): 95–118.

———. "La création cinématographique en Syrie à la lumière du mouvement de révolte. Nouvelles pratiques, nouveaux récits." *Revue des mondes musulmans et de la Méditerranée*, no. 133 (2013): 145–156.

———. "La grammaire iconographique de la révolte en Syrie: usages, techniques et supports." *Cultures & Conflits*, no. 91/92 (2013): 65–80.

———. "Montrer, dire et lutter par l'image. Les usages de la vidéo dans la révolution en Syrie." *Vacarme*, no. 61 (2012): 118–131.

Boltanski, Luc, Élisabeth Claverie, Nicolas Offenstadt, and Stéphane Van Damme. *Affaires, scandales et grandes causes. De Socrate à Pinochet*. Stock, 2007.

Bozarslan, Hamit. *Histoire de la violence au Moyen-Orient*. La Découverte, 2008.

Branche, Raphaëlle. *La torture et l'armée pendant la guerre d'Algérie (1954–1962)*. Gallimard, 2001.

Brunet, François. "La critique des images de guerre aux États-Unis. À propos de Believing is Seeing d'Errol Morris." *Écrire l'Histoire*, no. 9 (2012): 57–67.

Burgat, François, and Bruno Paoli, eds. *Pas de Printemps pour la Syrie. Les clés pour comprendre les acteurs et les défis de la crise (2011–2013)*. La Découverte, 2013.

Calabrese, Erminia C. "Ruptures et continuités dans le militantisme: parcours des combattants du Hezbollah libanais en Syrie." *Revue internationale de politique comparée* 25, no. 1 (2018): 39–51.

———. "'La cause c'est nous': militants du Hezbollah au Liban face à la guerre en Syrie." *Confluences Méditerranée* 98, no. 3 (2016): 103–114.

———. "Al-Ghâlibûn: le Hezbollah et la mise en récit de la 'société de la résistance' au Liban." *Revue des mondes musulmans et de la Méditerranée*, no. 134 (2013): 171–181.

Cardon, Dominique, and Fabien Granjon. *Médiactivistes*. Les Presses de Sciences Po, 2013.

Castells, Manuel. *Communication et pouvoir*. Maison des Sciences de l'Homme, 2013.

Centlivres, Pierre. "Vie, mort et survie des Bouddhas de Bamiyan (Afghanistan)." *Livraisons de l'histoire de l'architecture*, no. 7 (2009): 13–26.

Chaib, Kinda. "Le Hezbollah libanais à travers ses images: la représentation du martyr." In *Les mondes chiites et l'Iran*, edited by S. Mervin, 113–131. Éditions Karthala, 2007.

Chelkowski, Peter, and Hamid Dabashi. *Staging a Revolution: The Art of Persuasion in the Islamic Republic of Iran*. Booth-Clibborn Editions, 2000.

Christensen, Christian. "Uploading Dissonance: YouTube and the US Occupation of Iraq." *Media, War & Conflict* 1, no. 2 (2008): 155–175.

Cimino, Matthieu, ed. *Syria: Borders, Boundaries, and the State.* Palgrave Macmillan, 2020.

Coleman, Biella. "Les temps d'Indymedia." *Multitudes 2*, no. 21 (2005): 41–48.

Comolli, Jean-Louis. *Daech, le cinéma et la mort.* Verdier, 2016.

De Angelis, Enrico. "The Controversial Archive: Negotiating Horror Images in Syria" in *The Arab Archive: Mediated Memories, and Digital Flows*, edited by Donatella Della Ratta, Key Dickinson, and Sune Augbolle, 69–88. Institute of Network Cultures, 2020.

Delage, Christian. *La vérité par l'image.* Denoël, 2006.

Della Ratta, Donatella. *Shooting a Revolution.* Pluto Press, 2018.

_____. "Violence and Visibility in Contemporary Syria: An Ethnography of the 'Expanded Places.'" *CyberOrient 9*, no. 1 (2015): 7–31.

Della Ratta, Donatella, Kay Dickinson, and Sune Haugbølle, eds. *The Arab Archive: Mediated Memories and Digital Flows.* Institute of Network Cultures, 2020.

Devictor, Agnès. "De la 'Défense sacrée' (1980–1988) à la 'Défense des Lieux saints' (2012–2017): Imaginaires de guerre et pensée de l'image en Iran." *Revue d'études des mondes musulmans et de la Méditerranée 1*, no. 145. Presses universitaires de Provence (2019): 115–144.

_____. *Images, combattants et martyrs, la guerre Iran-Irak vue par le cinéma.* Karthala-IISMM-IFRI, 2015.

_____. "Massoud, le Commandant à la caméra." *Que peut une image? Les Carnets du Bal,* no.4, 29–47. Le Bal Éditions Textuel/Centre National des Arts Plastiques, 2013.

_____. "Du cadavre au martyr ou la représentation de la mort dans la presse iranienne lors de la guerre Iran-Irak." *Questions de communication*, no. 20 (Fall 2011): 19–48.

_____. *Politique du cinéma iranien. De l'âyatollâh Khomeyni au président Khâtami.* CNRS Éditions, 2004.

Didi-Huberman, Georges. *Images malgré tout.* Les éditions de Minuit, 2004.

El Difraoui, Abdelasiem. *Le djihadisme.* Presses Universitaires de France, 2016.

_____. *Al-Qaida par l'image: la prophétie du martyre.* Presses Universitaires de France, 2013.

al-Dik, Majd. *À l'Est de Damas, au bout du monde. Témoignage d'un révolutionnaire syrien.* Éditions Don Quichotte, 2016.

Downing, John. "Film and Video." In *Radical Media: Rebellious Communication and Social Movements,* edited by John Downing, 192–200. Sage Publications Inc., 2001.

Ellul, Jacques. *Propagandes.* Armand Colin, 1962.

Ferro, Marc. *Cinéma et Histoire.* Denoël et Gonthier, 1977.

Fleury-Villate, Béatrice, ed. *Les Médias et la guerre du Golfe.* Presses universitaires de Nancy, 1992.

Frosh, Paul, and Hami Pinchevski, eds. *Media Witnessing: Testimony in the Age of Mass Communication.* Palgrave Macmillan, 2009.

Ghalioun, Burhan, and Farouk Mardam Bey. "Un printemps syrien." *Confluences Méditerranée,* no. 44 (2003): 7–10.

al-Ghazzi, Omar. "'Citizen Journalism' in the Syrian Uprising: Problematizing Western Narratives in a Local Context." *Communication Theory* 24, no. 4 (2014): 435–454.

Gilbert, Victoria. "Sister Citizen: Women in Syrian Rebel Governance." *Politics & Gender* 17, no. 4 (2020): 552–79.

Gorgas, Jordi T. "Les Kurdes de Syrie, de la 'dissimulation' à la 'visibilité?'" *Revue des mondes musulmans et de la Méditerranée,* no. 115–116 (2006): 117–133.

Gunthert, André. "Pour une analyse narrative des images sociales." *Revue française des méthodes visuelles,* no. 1 (2017).

al-Haj Saleh, Yassin. "Tahdiq fi wajhi-l-fazi' [Gaze at the horror]." *Al Jumhuriya,* online, 2015.

Hallin, Daniel. "Images de guerre à la télévision américaine. Le Vietnam et le Golfe persique." *Hermès, La Revue* 1, no. 13–14 (1994): 121–132.

Harb, Zahera. *Channels of Resistance in Lebanon: Liberation Propaganda, Hezbollah and the Media.* I.B. Tauris, 2011.

Haugbølle, Sune. "Holding Out for the Day after Tomorrow. Futurity, Memory and Transitional Justice Evidence in Syria." In *Resolving International Conflict: Dynamics of Escalation, Continuation and Transformation,* edited by Isabel Bramsen, Poul Poder, and Ole Waever, 229–244. Routledge, 2019.

Hegghammer, Thomas, ed. *Jihadi Culture: The Art and Social Practices of Militant Islamists.* Cambridge University Press, 2017.

Heydemann, Steven. "Upgrading Authoritarianism in the Arab world," Analysis Paper 13. Saban Center for Middle East Policy at the Brookings Institution, 2007.

Hinnebusch, Raymond. "Syria: from Authoritarian Upgrading to Revolution?" *International Affairs* 88, no. 1 (2012): 95–113.

Holliday, Joseph. "Syria's Armed Opposition." Middle East Security Report no. 3, Institute for the Study of War, March 2012, online. https://www.understandingwar.org/sites/default/files/Syrias_Armed_Opposition.pdf.

El-Houri, Walid. *The Meaning of Resistance: Hezbollah's Media Strategies and the Articulation of a People.* PhD diss. University of Amsterdam, 2012.

Huët, Romain. "Quand les 'malheureux' deviennent des 'enragés': ethnographie de moudjahidines syriens (2012–2014)." *Cultures & Conflits* 1, no. 97 (2015): 31–75.

Humphrey, Michael, ed. *The Politics of Atrocity and Reconciliation: From Terror to Trauma.* Routledge, Routledge Studies in Social and Political Thought, 2014.

International Crisis Group. "Tentative jihad: Syria's Fundamentalism." Middle East Report no. 131, October 2012.

Ismail, Salwa. *The Rule of Violence: Subjectivity, Memory and Government in Syria.* Cambridge University Press, 2018.

al-Junaidy, Bassel. "The Tale of 'the Friends of Saidnaya': The Strongest Three Men in Syria." *Al Jumhuriya*, translated by Rana Issa, 2013.

Kahf, Mohja. "Two Nonviolence Campaigns Initiated by Women in Syria." In *Women Rising: In and Beyond the Arab Spring,* edited by Rita Stephan, and Mounira Charrad, 58–67. NYUP, 2020.

Kannout, Lama. *In the Core or on the Margin: Syrian Women's Political Participation.* Syrian Feminist Lobby, 2017.

Kelly, John, and Bruce Elting. "A Portrait of the Persian Blogosphere." In *Politics and Culture in Contemporary Iran: Challenging the Status Quo,* edited by Abbas Milani, and Larry Diamond, 141–163. Lynne Rienner Publishers, 2015.

Kleinberger, Alain. "Ruptures narratives, catharsis ou convention: représentation de la mort dans les films de guerre américains (1942–1945)." In *Les Mises en scène de la guerre au XXe siècle, Théâtre et cinéma,* edited by Lescot David, and Laurent Véray, 185–205. Éditions Nouveau Monde, 2011.

Lafont, Alexandre. "La photographie privée de combattants de la Grande Guerre: perspectives de recherche autour de la camaraderie." *Matériaux pour l'histoire de notre temps* 3, no. 91 (2008): 42–50.

Lamloum, Olfa. "Le Hezbollah au miroir de ses médias." In *Le Hezbollah, état des lieux,* edited by Sabrina Mervin, 21–45. Actes Sud, 2008.

Latte-Abdallah, Stéphanie. "Vers un féminisme politique hors frontières au Proche-Orient. Regard sur les mobilisations en Jordanie (Années 1950-années 2000)." *Vingtième Siècle. Revue d'Histoire* 3, no. 103 (2009): 177–195.

Layerle, Sébastien. *Caméras en lutte en Mai 68. Par ailleurs, le cinéma est une arme.* Nouveau Monde Éditions, 2008.

Lebow, Alisa. "Shooting with Intent: Framing Conflict." In *Killer images. Documentary Film, Memory and the Performance of Violence,* edited by Ten Brinck, Joram K., and Joshua Oppenheimer, 41–62, Columbia University Press, 2012.

Lim, Merlyna. "Framing Bouazizi. 'White lies,' Hybrid Network and Collective/Connective Action in the 2010–2011 Tunisian Uprising." *Journalism* 14, no. 7 (2013): 921–941.

Lindeperg, Sylvie. *La voie des images. Quatre histoires de tournage au printemps-été 1944.* Verdier, 2013.

_____. *Les écrans de l'ombre: la Seconde Guerre mondiale dans le cinéma français (1994–1969).* CNRS Éditions, 1997.

Lindeperg, Sylvie, and Ania Szczepanska. *À qui appartiennent les images?*. Maison des sciences de l'Homme, 2017.

Lindeperg, Sylvie, and Annette Wieworka. *Le Moment Eichmann*. Albin Michel, 2016.

Lund, Aron. "Syrian Jihadism." *UI Brief*, no. 13, 2012.

Maarouf, Joumana. *Lettres de Syrie*. Éditions Buchet/Chastel, 2014.

Meis, Mareike. "Mobile Death Videos in Protest Movements: Cases from Iran and Syria on Television: Balancing Privacy and Voyeurism." *Thanatos* 2, no. 2 (2013).

Mermier, Franck, ed. *Écrits libres de Syrie. De la révolution à la guerre*. Classiques Garnier, 2018.

Mirzoeff, Nicholas. *Watching Babylon: The War in Iraq and Global Visual Culture*. Routledge, 2005.

Mitchell, William J.T. *Cloning Terror: Ou la guerre des images du 11 septembre au présent*. Les prairies ordinaires, 2011.

Molin Friis, Simone. "'Behead, burn, crucify, crush': Theorizing the Islamic State's public displays of violence." *European Journal of International Relations* 24, no. 2 (2018): 243–267.

Monsutti, Alessandro. *Homo itinerans, la planète des Afghans*. PUF, 2018.

Munif, Yasser. *The Syrian Revolution: Between the Politics of Life and the Geopolitics of Death*. Pluto Press, 2020.

Mustata, Dana. "'The Revolution Has Been Televised . . .' Television as Historical Agent in the Romanian Revolution." *Journal of Modern European History* 10, no. 1 (2012): 76–97.

Naef, Silvia. *Y a-t-il une question de l'image en Islam*. Téraèdre, 2015.

Neveu, Erik. "Trajectoires de soixante-huitards ordinaires." In *Mai-Juin 68*, edited by Dominique Damamme, Boris Gobille, Frédérique Matonti, and Bernard Pudal. Éditions de l'atelier, 2008.

Ortalli, Gherardo. *La peinture infamante du XIIe au XVe siècle*. Gérard Monfort, 1994 .

Oxley, Noémie. "'The Real Nasty Side of War': An Iconology of Amateur Productions Shot by American Soldiers in Iraq." PhD diss. EHESS/Goldsmiths College, 2016.

Pastinelli, Madeleine. "Pour en finir avec l'ethnographie du virtuel! Des enjeux méthodologiques de l'enquête de terrain en ligne." *Anthropologie et Sociétés* 35, no. 1–2 (2011): 35–52.

Perron, Tangui. *Cinéma du front populaire et guerre d'Espagne*. Association Histoire et mémoire ouvrière en Seine-Saint-Denis, 1999.

Perthes, Volker. *Syria under Bashar al-Asad: Modernisation and the Limits of Change*. Oxford University Press, 2004.

Picard, Elizabeth. *Liban-Syrie, intimes étrangers. Un siècle d'interactions sociopolitiques*. Sindbad/Actes Sud, 2016.

Pierret, Thomas. "La révolution syrienne, morphologie d'une militarisation." *Les Cahiers de l'Orient* 3, no. 107 (2012): 75–82.

Pinto, Paulo G. "The Shattered Nation: The Sectarianization of the Syrian conflict." In *Sectarianization: Mapping the New Politics of the Middle East,* edited by Nader Hashemi, and Dany Postel, 123–142. Hust & Company, 2017.

Poujeau, Anna. *Des monastères en partage. Sainteté et pouvoir chez les chrétiens de Syrie.* Société d'ethnologie, 2014.

Qaddur, 'Umar. "I'tisâm Manzilî!" *Collectif al-Awān,* 2013.

Rekik, Dhouha. *La fabrique audiovisuelle de l'État Islamique. La vidéo comme arme de guerre, outil de légitimation et de recrutement.* iReMMO/L'Harmattan, 2018.

Riboni, Lune U. "Chercher, trouver, conserver: enjeux et méthodes de la constitution d'un corpus de vidéos en ligne." In *Pérenniser l'éphémère. Archivage et médias sociaux,* edited by Caroline Derauw, Véronique Fillieux, Urore François, and Anne Roekens, 45–56. Academia/L'Harmattan, 2018.

Riceputi, Fabrice. "Au-delà du mur, enquête sur deux photos de la torture en Algérie," posted on 05/18/2020, (accessed on 11/28/2020). https://textures-dutemps.hypotheses.org/4027. Academic website.

Saber, Dima, and Paul Long. "'I will not leave, my freedom is more precious than my blood.' From Affect to Precarity: Crowdsourced Citizen Archives as Memories of the Syrian War." *Archives and Records* 38, no. 1 (2017): 80–99.

Saleh, Layla. "'The Factory of the Revolution': Women's Activism in the Syrian Uprisings." In *Women Rising: In and Beyond the Arab Spring,* edited by Rania Stephan, and Mounira Charrad, 354–362. NYUP, 2020.

Salloukh, Bassel F. "The Sectarianization of Geopolitics in the Middle East." In *Sectarianization: Mapping the New Politics of the Middle East,* edited by Nader Hashemi, and Danny Postel, 35–52. Hust & Company, 2017.

Seurat, Michel. *L'État de Barbarie.* Seuil, 1989.

Snowdon, Peter. *The People Are Not an Image: Vernacular Video After the Arab Spring.* Verso Books, 2020.

Staffell, Simon, and Akil N. Awan, eds. *Jihadism Transformed: Al-Qaeda and Islamic State's Global Battle of Ideas.* Oxford Scholarship Online, 2017.

Stora, Benjamin. "Le cinéma américain pendant la guerre du Vietnam le mythe de 'l'avalanche.'" *Vingtième Siècle, revue d'histoire,* no. 49 (1996): 149–155.

Tarnowski, Stefan. "What have we been watching? What have we been watching?" Bidayyat, 2017. https://bidayyat.org/opinions_article.php?id=167&fbclid=IwAR2SCErcIjvGYfRa_owvA90QoffT6VKaZaFR5Xna0-0yzGXXwIG3PdW6Mgs.

Traïni, Christophe. "Dramaturgie des émotions, traces de sensibilités. Observer et comprendre des manifestations anti-corridas." *Ethnographies.org,* no. 21 (2010). www.ethnographiques.org/2010/Traini.

Üngör, Ugur Ü. "On the Multiple Uses of Video Footage among Contemporary Perpetrators." *Journal of Perpetrator Research* 2, no. 2 (2019): 207–215.

Véray, Laurent. *Avènement d'une culture visuelle de guerre. Le cinéma en France de 1914 à 1928.* Nouvelles Éditions Place/Ministère des Armées, 2019.

Virilio, Paul. *Guerre et cinéma, Logistique de la perception.* Cahiers du cinéma, 1991.

Wall, Melissa, and Sahar El Zahed. "Embedding Content from Syrian Citizen Journalists: The Rise of the Collaborative News Clip." *Journalism* 16, no. 2 (2014): 163–180.

Wedeen, Lisa. *Ambiguities of Domination: Politics, Rhetoric, and Symbols in Contemporary Syria.* University of Chicago Press, 1999.

Weizman, Eyal. "L'image en conflit. La violence au seuil de sa détectabilité." In *Penser l'image III. Comment lire les images?,* edited by Emmanuel Alloa, 231–56. Les Presses du réel, 2017.

Wessels, Joshka. *Documenting Syria: Film-making, Video Activism and Revolution.* I.B. Tauris, 2019.

_____. "Video Activists from Aleppo and Raqqa as 'Modern-Day Kinoks'? An Audiovisual Narrative of the Syrian Revolution." *Middle East Journal of Culture and Communication* 10, no. 2–3 (2017): 159–174.

White, Hayden. "Historiography and Historiophoty." *The American Historical Review* 93, no. 5 (1988): 1193–99.

Yassin, Rosa. "Les femmes dans les coulisses. La présence effective et continue des Syriennes dans la révolution," online, December 23, 2011.

Yassin-Kassab, Robin, and Leila Al-Shami. *Burning Country: Syrians in Revolution and War.* Pluto Press, 2016.

Yazbek, Samar. *19 femmes: Les Syriennes racontent.* Stock, 2019.

_____. *Les portes du néant.* Stock, 2016.

_____. *Feux croisés. Journal de la révolution syrienne.* Éditions Buchet/Chastel, 2012.

Zabunyan, Dork. *L'insistance des luttes: images, soulévements, contre-révolutions.* De l'Incidence Éditeur, 2016.

Zelizer, Barbie. "On 'Having Been There': 'Eyewitnessing' as a Journalistic Key Word." *Critical Studies in Media Communication* 24, no. 5 (2007): 408–428.

www.ingramcontent.com/pod-product-compliance
Ingram Content Group UK Ltd.
Pitfield, Milton Keynes, MK11 3LW, UK
UKHW052207121125
3565IPUK00004B/7/J